Graphic Migrations

In the series *Asian American History and Culture*,
edited by Cathy Schlund-Vials, Shelley Sang-Hee Lee, and Rick Bonus.
Founding editor, Sucheng Chan; editors emeriti, David Palumbo-Liu,
Michael Omi, K. Scott Wong, and Linda Trinh Võ.

Also in this series:

Heidi Kim, *Illegal Immigrants/Model Minorities: The Cold War of Chinese American Narrative* (forthcoming)
Chia Youyee Vang with Pao Yang, Retired Captain, U.S. Secret War in Laos, *Prisoner of Wars: A Hmong Fighter Pilot's Story of Escaping Death and Confronting Life* (forthcoming)
Timothy K. August, *The Refugee Aesthetic: Reimagining Southeast Asian America* (forthcoming)
L. Joyce Zapanta Mariano, *Giving Back: Filipino Diaspora and the Politics of Giving* (forthcoming)
Manan Desai, *The United States of India: Anticolonial Literature and Transnational Refraction*
Cathy J. Schlund-Vials, Guy Beauregard, and Hsiu-chuan Lee, eds., *The Subject(s) of Human Rights: Crises, Violations, and Asian/American Critique*
Malini Johar Schueller, *Campaigns of Knowledge: U.S. Pedagogies of Colonialism and Occupation in the Philippines and Japan*
Crystal Mun-hye Baik, *Reencounters: On the Korean War and Diasporic Memory Critique*
Michael Omi, Dana Y. Nakano, and Jeffrey T. Yamashita, eds., *Japanese American Millennials: Rethinking Generation, Community, and Diversity*
Masumi Izumi, *The Rise and Fall of America's Concentration Camp Law: Civil Liberties Debates from the Internment to McCarthyism and the Radical 1960s*
Shirley Jennifer Lim, *Anna May Wong: Performing the Modern*
Edward Tang, *From Confinement to Containment: Japanese/American Arts during the Early Cold War*
Patricia P. Chu, *Where I Have Never Been: Migration, Melancholia, and Memory in Asian American Narratives of Return*
Cynthia Wu, *Sticky Rice: A Politics of Intraracial Desire*
Marguerite Nguyen, *America's Vietnam: The Longue Durée of U.S. Literature and Empire*
Vanita Reddy, *Fashioning Diaspora: Beauty, Femininity, and South Asian American Culture*
Audrey Wu Clark, *The Asian American Avant-Garde: Universalist Aspirations in Modernist Literature and Art*
Eric Tang, *Unsettled: Cambodian Refugees in the New York City Hyperghetto*
Jeffrey Santa Ana, *Racial Feelings: Asian America in a Capitalist Culture of Emotion*
Jiemin Bao, *Creating a Buddhist Community: A Thai Temple in Silicon Valley*

A list of additional titles in this series appears at the back of this book.

Praise for Kavita Daiya's *Graphic Migrations*

"Kavita Daiya has written a panoramic study of post-Partition studies. The remnants of the mid-twentieth-century Partition may be the debris of long colonial histories, but these very remnants return to haunt the suffering memories of migrants and minorities who are frequently disfigured as enemies 'within' or displaced as enemies 'without.' Daiya argues that post-Partition remnants are dangerously weaponized by ethno-nationalists, who weaponize traditions of the sacred in order to demean the democratic ambitions of secular pluralism. Daiya's wide scholarly purview ranges across literature, cinema, graphic novels, and the creative arts, as she assembles a rich archive of contemporary reflection and critical relevance."—**Homi K. Bhabha,** Anne F. Rothenberg Professor of the Humanities, Harvard University

"Kavita Daiya's reading of decolonization is centered on the vast and heterogeneous cultural production generated by Partition's aftermath in South Asia and its diaspora. *Graphic Migrations* opens up new and exciting vistas for Partition studies. It also enhances our contemporary understanding of statelessness, 'subaltern' secularism, gender, and precarity by viewing this historical catastrophe within a brilliantly conceptualized global framework of connections and resonances."—**Rajeswari Sunder Rajan,** Global Distinguished Professor of English, New York University

"*Graphic Migrations* represents an important and unique contribution to the field of Partition studies specifically, and to the fields of postcolonial studies, memory studies, and diaspora studies more generally. Daiya advances important debates concerning religion, secularity, and subalternity, with insights into the crisis of secularism and how the Partition prompts a rethinking of the refugee. The book's archive is at once expansive and eclectic, encompassing visual culture, film, novels, media, and digital memory projects. This is a beautifully written, finely argued, and original study."—**Asha Nadkarni,** Associate Professor of English, University of Massachusetts Amherst

"This is a sophisticated and provocative set of reflections on migration stories as sites for alternative understandings of the secular at a time when the term itself is under scrutiny. Bringing together a fascinating variety of texts with connections to South Asia and its Partition histories, Daiya offers deft and sophisticated readings which speak to the emergence of what she calls 'the subaltern secular,' a resource for hope in our difficult century. *Graphic Migrations* is an important contribution to both South Asian literature and migration studies."
—**Priyamvada Gopal,** Professor in Postcolonial Studies, University of Cambridge

"Daiya constructs a dazzling mosaic of Partition images—drawn from the intimate literary, graphic, and visual representations of gendered statelessness, precarity, and survival—to produce a new motto for the decade: the subaltern secular. Weaving critical theory, oral history, digital humanities, and more traditional literary and filmic texts, along with graphic novels and emerging digital forms, *Graphic Migrations* is a journey into a new historiography of an old, previously underexplored trauma."—**Henry Schwarz**, Professor Emeritus, Georgetown University

KAVITA DAIYA

Graphic Migrations

Precarity and Gender in India and the Diaspora

TEMPLE UNIVERSITY PRESS
Philadelphia • *Rome* • *Tokyo*

TEMPLE UNIVERSITY PRESS
Philadelphia, Pennsylvania 19122
tupress.temple.edu

Copyright © 2020 by Temple University—Of The Commonwealth System
of Higher Education
All rights reserved
Published 2020

Library of Congress Cataloging-in-Publication Data

Names: Daiya, Kavita, 1970– author.
Title: Graphic migrations : precarity and gender in India and the diaspora / Kavita Daiya.
Other titles: Asian American history and culture.
Description: Philadelphia : Temple University Press, 2020. | Series: Asian American history and culture | Includes bibliographical references and index. | Summary: "Examines the literary and cultural archive of migration stories surrounding the 1947 Partition of India following Indian independence. Considers the representation of refugees, secularism, and gendered citizenship and how these narratives about migration and community influence and challenge dominant ideas about secularism and citizenship in India and the diaspora"— Provided by publisher.
Identifiers: LCCN 2020010615 (print) | LCCN 2020010616 (ebook) | ISBN 9781439920244 (cloth) | ISBN 9781439920251 (paperback) | ISBN 9781439920268 (pdf)
Subjects: LCSH: South Asians—Migrations. | South Asian diaspora in literature. | Partition, Territorial, in literature. | Forced migration—India. | Collective memory—India. | Secularism—India. | Gender identity—India. | Refugees in art. | India—History—Partition, 1947—Influence.
Classification: LCC DS480.842 .D35 2020 (print) | LCC DS480.842 (ebook) | DDC 305.9/06910954—dc23
LC record available at https://lccn.loc.gov/2020010615
LC ebook record available at https://lccn.loc.gov/2020010616

for
riya, maya, sunny
and
my parents

Contents

Acknowledgments ix

Introduction: Theorizing Subaltern Secularism
in the Crisis of Modern Migration 1
- The Remains of Partition: Art, Storytelling, and Public Culture 4
- Secularism in Crisis 9
- Restorying Migration: The Popular Representation
  of Refugees' Stories 17
- Ecologies of Displacement: Migrants, Refugees, Citizens 23
- #rememberingpartition: Unpacking the Archive 27

1 "Partition Is Still Happening": Transmedia
and Graphic Secularism 37
- Drawing Embodied Secularism: Religion and Pedagogical
  Nationalism in Print Culture 39
- Gender, Displacement, and Ecologies of Loss in
  Vishwajyoti Ghosh's Graphic Anthology *This Side,
  That Side: Restorying Partition* 49
- Photojournalism and Bearing Witness in Margaret
  Bourke-White's Photography 79

2 The Ethics and Aesthetics of Witnessing: Refugees, Literary
Modernism, and the American Diaspora 86
- Disability, Patriarchal Violence, and Witnessing
  in Bapsi Sidhwa's *Cracking India* 90
- Migration, Reproductive Femininity, and Citizenship in
  Shauna Singh Baldwin's *What the Body Remembers* 95

- Citizenship and Expulsions in Arundhati Roy's *The Ministry of Utmost Happiness* — 100
- Media, Violence, and Reparations in the Conflict Zone — 107

3 **Melodrama, Community, and Diasporas in Popular Hindi and Accented Cinema** — 111
- Asian Americans and Secular Crisis in Rakeysh Omprakash Mehra's *Delhi-6* — 115
- Surviving Gendered Citizenship and Death in Shyam Benegal's *Mammo* — 125
- Indo-Pak Intimacy and Border Crossings in Meghna Gulzar's *Raazi* and Kabir Khan's *Bajrangi Bhaijaan* — 129
- Pakistan, Political Violence, and Failed Intimacies in Sabiha Sumar's *Khamosh Pani* — 138
- Conclusion: Performing the Secular, Inventing Peace — 144

4 **Transnational Asia, Testimony, and New Media** — 147
- Border-Crossing Advertising: Google and Secular Intimacies in the Commercial "Reunion" (2013) — 149
- Intergenerational Memories: Rebuilding Life and Reckoning with Loss in Mumbai, Pune, Hong Kong, and Washington, D.C. — 160
- New Art and Digital Archive Memory Projects: Testimony and Peace — 169

Conclusion: Rethinking Mid-Twentieth-Century Asia and the Present — 179

Notes — 183
Bibliography — 205
Index — 219

Acknowledgments

This book's journey began with the stories I initially started gathering on digital video in 2008, as part of my digital humanities project 1947Partition.org. It could not have been written without those stories of Partition migrants and their descendants from three continents, who have shared their memories and reflections of a mass migration that remained, until recently, in the shadows of public discussions of independence. So, to my uncle Gul Mansukhani, and to friends including Sagar and Reena Banka, Surendra and Vijay Gambhir, Shanta Hirani, Sushila Kamlani, Maya Lalwani, Chitra Panjabi, Chandrabhushan and Varsha Panjabi, Surendra Shah, Ho-chin Yang, and many others, I owe a heartfelt thanks for their generosity and warmth, their trust in me, and their willingness to share their memories.

I thank the Andrew W. Mellon Foundation, whose two fellowships with the Penn Humanities Forum supported the development of this manuscript. From 2012 to 2013, under Kevin Platt's direction of the theme "Peripheries," I researched refugees' construction as peripheral subjects in postcolonial India. From 2014 to 2015, Chi-ming Yang's direction of the theme "Colors" vividly inspired this book's investigation of print culture, media, and graphic narratives of citizenship and migration. Throughout, Jim English and Chi-ming Yang asked tough questions and shared perceptive insights with good humor, wit, and genuine friendship, and this book bears the imprint of their incredible generosity, vision, and solidarity. I am grateful to my colleagues from my time as a Fellow at the Penn Humanities Forum, especially Meredith Bak, Dhanveer Brar, Faisal Choudhary, Wazmah Osman, Sheshalatha Reddy, and Jennifer Harford Vargas; many of the insights in this book have roots in their engagement and feedback.

I thank the National Endowment for the Humanities (NEH) for its endowed chair in the humanities at Albright College (2015–2016), which gave me critical institutional support. There, interdisciplinary conversations on "Migration and Culture" with wonderful colleagues shaped this analysis. I thank Mindy Cohen, Beth Kiester, Jennifer Koosed, Rachel Liberatore, Samira Mehta, Shreeyash Palshikar, Rob Seesengood, and Marian Wolbers for their generous dialogue and friendship.

Many other institutions have helped me bring this project to fruition. Several awards and travel grants from the Sigur Center of Asian Studies and the Columbian College of Arts and Sciences at George Washington University (GW) enabled the completion of my research at the National Film Archives of India. Deans Ben Vinson III and Paul Wahlbeck at GWU provided critical research time and support. Invitations to share this work with different audiences at the Center for 21st Century Studies at the University of Wisconsin–Milwaukee, Lehigh University, Amherst College, Brandeis University, the Godrej India Culture Lab, the U.S. State Department's Foreign Services Institute, Georgetown University, Hyderabad's English and Foreign Languages University, the University of Hyderabad, GW's Sigur Center for Asian Studies, and the conferences of the Modern Language Association, the National Women's Studies Association, the Annual South Asia Conference at Madison, the Association of Asian American Studies, the American Studies Association, and the Oral History Association have indelibly sharpened and animated my argument. Funding from the NEH and the University of Pennsylvania allowed me to organize an interdisciplinary symposium, "Partition Stories: Media, Memory, and Politics in South Asia," in April 2016 to grow the public dialogue I hope to inspire about refugee stories. I thank my editors and publishers for permission to republish early versions of some of the analyses here: "Refugees, Gender, and Secularism in South Asian Literature and Cinema," in *Representations of War, Migration, and Refugeehood: Interdisciplinary Perspectives*, edited by Daniel H. Rellstab and Christiane Schlote (New York: Routledge, 2014), pages 263–280 (used by permission of Taylor and Francis); "Visual Culture and Violence: Inventing Intimacy and Citizenship in Recent South Asian Cinema," in *South Asian History and Culture* volume 2, issue 4 (2011), pages 589–604 (© Taylor and Francis); "Why Partition Survivors in the US Believe It's Vital to Keep Talking about the Trauma of 1947," in *Scroll.in*, August 23, 2016 (first appeared in the digital newspaper *Scroll.in*.).

A special and heartfelt thanks to the wise and wonderful Sarah Munroe, my editor, Cathy J. Schlund-Vials, the series editor at Temple University Press, and my anonymous readers, for their terrific, incisive, and generous feedback. Their voices strengthened, in vivid and distinctive ways, the story I tell here. From the start, Aaron Javsicas has graciously shepherded this project, and I am grateful for his stewardship. In the midst of a pandemic, I also owe my sincere thanks to Shaun Vigil, Gary Kramer, Kate Nichols, Ashley Petrucci, and Heather Wilcox at the press for their expertise, patience and kind support. I hope I have done justice to this collective generosity and incredible dialogue.

A vast community of new and old friends and colleagues in the academy and beyond, has offered friendship and conversation that nourished me. As I developed this book, the engagement and insight from conversations with Amber Abbas, Lopamudra Basu, Deepika Bahri, Homi Bhabha, Jim English, Asha Nadkarni, Mika Natif, Pramod Nayar, Judith Plotz, Sreyoshi Sarkar, Henry Schwarz, Rajini Srikanth, Jennifer Hartford Vargas, and Chi-ming Yang, have critically shaped the story I tell here. I am especially grateful for the friendship, hospitality, mentorship, and solidarity of Judith and Paul Plotz over the last two decades. Judith's love, wit, and wisdom are much cherished. It has been a privilege to serve as associate editor with Pradyumna Chauhan, who has been an inspiring mentor and visionary editor at *South Asian Review* for me, from 2012 to 2018. Over the years, I have appreciated the solidarity and friendship of Sareeta Amrute, Ulka Anjaria, Amit Baishya, Guneeta Singh Bhalla, Nilufer Bharucha, Debjani Bhattacharyya, Urvashi Butalia, Vikram Chandra, Melanie Abrams Chandra, Vijay Chauhan, Nirmala Menon, Chitra Panjabi, Crystal Parikh, Sangeeta Ray, Amritjit Singh, and Zohreh Sullivan. At GW, I thank an exceptional community of colleagues in the English department; the Women's, Gender, and Sexuality Studies Program; and beyond, from whom I have learned much: Eric Arnesen, Nemata Blyden, Geoffrey Carter, Elizabeth Chacko, Erin Chapman, Patricia Chu, Cynthia Deitch, Arie Dubnov, Evangeline Downie, Holly Dugan, Mary Ellsberg, Shirley Graham, Jennifer Green-Lewis, Chad Heap, Benjamin Hopkins, Jennifer James, Dane Kennedy, Caroline Laguerre-Brown, Antonio Lopez, Melani McAlister, James Miller, Dan Moshenberg, Deepa Ollapally, Rachel Riedner, Yongwu Rong, Kristen McKnight Sethi, Lisa Page, Kelly Pemberton, Katrin Schultheiss, Eiko Strader, and Jung Yun. I deeply appreciate the early conversations with Parmesh Shahani in 2009–2010 in Mumbai and in 2017 at Godrej India Culture Lab, which bookend this story in important ways. A special thanks to Diane Taurro (Godrej India Culture Lab) and Arpita Das-Ribeiro (Yoda Press) for their generous support in obtaining some of the images reproduced. I am lucky to have had these steady friends and generous interlocutors; their feedback and friendship animate the story I tell in this book. Of these people, I miss James (Jim) Miller dearly; many conversations remain unfinished.

A shout-out and heartfelt thanks to Kristen Gleason Block, Rizina Chatterjee, Katherine D'Amora, Sheetal Gupta, Berryl Hirani, Shipra Mishra, Dara Morales, Vivian Murray, Madhu Narula, Alero Ogedegbe, Riti Patel, Shilpa Rao, Diana Robertson, Smita Sanghvi, Aneesha Saran, and Priya

Taori, whose wit, wisdom, and genuine friendship have sustained me in ways that I cannot possibly enumerate.

I am so grateful for the support, good humor, and friendship of Connie Kibler in the English Department and Niacka Carty in the Women's, Gender, and Sexuality Studies Program. Working with them is a joy. It has been a pleasure to discuss these ideas with my students in the English Department and the Women's, Gender, and Sexuality Studies Program at GW and at Albright College: Ashley Atilano, Georgia Bobley, Ashley Canning, Turni Chakrabarti, Rachel Davidson, Stephanie Force, Sarah-Anne Gresham, Breya Johnson, Trey Johnston, Farisa Khalid, Elizabeth Moser, Michelle Nguyen, Tawnya Ravy, Sukshma Vedere, Vicki Woods, and others. Dialogue with these students in my Bollywood Cinema courses influenced my analysis in Chapter 3: Emory Aboulhassani, Samsara Counts, Aksa Khan, Zeeshan Irani, Rishab Jain, Kaajal Joshi, Anna Kaji, Prabhlean Kaur, Katherine Leone, Mahhum Naqvi, Logan Othmer, Kavery Nimana Poonacha, Natalia Simmons-Thomas, Priyanka Walimbe, Zoya Wazir, Renea Williams, Anna Woodward, Phoebe Workman, and others. I have enjoyed working with GW's many dynamic student groups, including the South Asian Students Association, the Feminist Student Union, the Asian American Students Association, GW-Women of Color, and the Women's, Gender, and Sexuality Studies Students' Association. Nichole Smith's and Sarah-Anne Gresham's timely research assistance and Turni Chakrabarti's and Patrick Henry's swift editorial and organizational assistance with permissions and several revisions of this manuscript have been truly invaluable.

Finally, and most importantly, I am thankful for my family and my extended family in Mumbai, Hyderabad, Chicago, Toronto, Pune, Haddonfield, Arlington, Atlanta, Boston, San Diego, Jersey City, Orlando, and San Francisco, who have been my anchor through the writing of this book. The shade of my parents Devyani and Dilip Daiya's love has sustained and nourished me in ways I cannot enumerate. Their courage, selfless generosity, and joy for life anchor me and have kept my work steadily on course. It is a privilege to be their daughter, and I am so lucky to have their luminous inspiration. My husband, Sunny, has been a true life partner, whose critical solidarity and steadfast love animate me and my work in amazing ways. From hearing out my ideas, to encouraging me on dark days, to taking over the tasks of everyday life on so many days and nights so that I could write, he has been there for me and held me close. I am grateful for our life together, every single day. My shining, brave, and strong daughters Riya and Maya light up my life. Riya's wise poems, beautiful art, witty sense of humor, and warm hugs inspire me in magical ways. Maya's fierce kisses, abundant cuddles, unicorn drawings, and creative knock-knock jokes fill my heart with magical joy. To all of these people, it is time to say thank you, for your love and your faith.

Graphic Migrations

Introduction

*Theorizing Subaltern Secularism
in the Crisis of Modern Migration*

> As the postcolonial and post-Cold War model of global authority takes shape . . . we need to . . . consider how a deliberate engagement with the twentieth century's histories of suffering might furnish resources for the peaceful accommodation of otherness in relation to fundamental commonality.
>
> —Paul Gilroy, *Postcolonial Melancholia*[1]

> [T]he pervasive losses of the twentieth century need to be engaged from the perspective of what remains. . . . This attention to remains generates a politics of mourning that might be active rather than reactive, prescient rather than nostalgic, abundant rather than lacking, social rather than solipsistic, militant rather than reactionary.
>
> —David Eng and David Kazanjian,
> "Introduction: Mourning Remains"[2]

During a taxi ride to the University of Pennsylvania's Van Pelt library on a freezing day a few years ago, my elderly driver, Naveed Samuel, noted my accent and asked me with an old-fashioned politeness, "Where are you from, Miss?" This usual and too familiar ethnic exchange, typical of immigrants with un-American accents in the United States, led to my revealing that I was from India and asking him where he was from. Immediately, he switched languages and replied in Urdu, "I am not from India—I am from Pakistan." Acknowledging this, I then inquired about what part of Pakistan he hailed from. "I am from Karachi. But my parents were from India: my father was from Allahabad, and my mother was from Palanpur," he replied. "Did they go to Pakistan during the Partition?" I asked him. "Yes, they went there in 1947," he said, "because of the Partition." He then grew quiet; nothing more was shared about the Partition or his parents'

Figure I.1: Dividing a library. (David Douglas Duncan, *Life Magazine*, 18 August 1947). Harry Ransom Center. The University of Texas at Austin.

displacement. I do not know why I then added, "My grandfather was from Karachi." And then we fell silent: both, in some ways, divided and linked through the history of Partition's mass displacements, through this shared history of migration, of places lost to our respective families in the melee of the fragmented formation of nations.

I share this small story because it reminds me that the 1947 Partition of India is not only an event that I have been studying and writing about for the last twenty years in the libraries I have inhabited around the world; it is also an unfinished past that scattered millions across the subcontinent and also, eventually, to other shores: North America, East Africa, Hong Kong, and the United Kingdom. When the British announced their plans to decolonize and divide India in August 1947, to create the new nations of India and Pakistan on the basis of religion, what followed the drawing of borderlines (over a hasty seven weeks) by the Boundary Commission chaired by the English lawyer Cyril Radcliffe is by now well documented, including in W. H. Auden's famous 1966 poem "Partition." Using incomplete and likely inaccurate census data, Radcliffe's plan distributed cities and villages like cards in a deck. A wave of ethnic violence and mass migration followed. As Hindus and Sikhs attacked Muslims and Muslims attacked Hindus and Sikhs, by unofficial counts, two million died, and between twelve and sixteen million migrated across the new borders by June 1948. This event was, as noted Pakistani American author Bapsi Sidhwa observes, "the largest and most terrible exchange of population known to history."³ In this conflict, women and children especially were subjected to sexual violence, abduction, mutilation, and murder.⁴ Post-47, new political-institutional formations as well as public discourse instantiated religion as a central category that shaped the identity of citizens across South Asia. Along with the subcontinent's own particular web of social stratification, this shift ensured that the place of the secular within the national community would remain a vexed affair. The complex relationship between religion and secular citizenship in South Asia has historically shaped how Partition refugees have been treated in postcolonial nation-states; it has also laid the groundwork for, among other things, the hegemonic production of cultural communities as religious communities in Hindu-majority India and Muslim-majority Pakistan.

This book begins with an exploration of two issues that dominate public discourses about nationalism across many spaces in the world today—namely, migration and the role of religion in public life. As we mark the seventy-third anniversary of the 1947 Partition in 2020, this book takes up David Eng's and David Kazanjian's invitation and turns to what remains after Partition—what Urvashi Butalia calls "the business of living with the consequences of that history."⁵ This spirit—of seeing what remains and what has been created after Partition—animates my inquiry into migration stories across diverse media archives, exploring how they have shaped secularism and citizenship in India and in its diaspora. In doing so, I argue that Partition's history of violent displacement continues to be a constitutive, everyday dimension of many South Asian lives around the world. In the literal sense, this assertion is true: since 1947, India and Pakistan have fought four wars, Bangladesh was created from East Pakistan after a bloody war in 1971, and the region of Kashmir remains a critical flashpoint for potential nuclear conflict between India and Pakistan. In this context of conflict and crisis, tracking the afterlife of the Partition migrations through the public cultural archives of literature, film, photography, and print culture can help us recognize what else remains (or has been created) after 1947. In the analysis that follows, I draw upon a range of texts and objects that are primarily, although not exclusively, from India and constitute a public cultural archive about migration and citizenship. I show how this archive has created a minor, critical discourse about "restorying" (to use Vishwajyoti Ghosh's term) the post-47 animosities of Partition. This archive, my book suggests, offers new political visions of secularism and geopolitical peace in the subcontinent.⁶ *Graphic Migrations* thus analyzes the cultural discourse about migration and refugees' experience from the 1947 Partition, as represented across a range of media, to ask: what is the relationship between the intergenerational narration as well as recuperation of Partition's migration stories and the contemporary political crisis of secularism unfolding in India and its diaspora?

I turn to the migration stories embedded in this book's cultural archive as performances that, to appropriate Yến Lê Espiritu's words, "conjure up social, public, and collective remembering."[7] Following Espiritu, I see this book as a "bringing together of seemingly different and disconnected events, communities, histories, and spaces in order to illuminate what would otherwise not be visible about the contours, contents, and afterlives of war and empire," past and ongoing, in transnational South Asia.[8] In *Nothing Ever Dies*, Viet Thanh Nguyen describes what he calls "an ethics of memory" in the texts and objects that address the U.S. war in Vietnam; this ethics, for Nguyen, is "a just memory that strives to remember both one's own and others."[9] This commitment to a just memory resonates: my desire is not only to write the gendered refugee's memory into the story of the nation in South Asia and in South Asian America but also to argue that it is through this labor of remembering and storying the legacies of division and displacement, at once aesthetic and political, that we can reinvent a just community in the public sphere. This goal is urgent, especially because Partition's particular combination of the religious territorialization of political division, the "expulsions" (to use Saskia Sassen's term) of millions, and the production of normative citizenship on the basis of religion and ethnicity have become too familiar and banal on the stage of world history in the contemporary moment. Witness the mass expulsions of Rohingya Muslims, Syrians, or Tamil Sri Lankans by war and state violence in the twenty-first century, accompanied by the new, often institutionalized modes of discrimination against Muslims in democratic societies, including the United States.[10] The story I tell here, then, about what remains and what has been created after the 1947 Partition migrations is one that reflects more broadly on how geopolitical conflict, religion, and displacement have unfolded in world history and across many national contexts in the ensuing decades. A comparative and transnational approach to decolonization, division, and displacement in the mid-twentieth century has grown increasingly visible in contemporary public culture as well as scholarship. From a host of interdisciplinary and multimedia standpoints, recent cultural production as well as scholarly conversation have endeavored to recast apparently disparate national histories as part of a transnational history of modern migration. In the following section, I explain how this book resonates with this new comparative dialogue and intervenes in it, by way of its focus on migration stories and the cultural imagination of gendered secular citizenship.

The Remains of Partition: Art, Storytelling, and Public Culture

The cultural restorying of the Partition migrations, in ways that situate 1947 in a transnational conversation about world history, has attracted new energy in the last decade. For instance, a 2013 exhibition of videos, prints, photographs, paintings, sculptures, and installations titled *Lines of Control* at Cornell University's Herbert F. Johnson Museum of Art was part of an ongoing initiative started in 2005 by the London-based nonprofit arts organization Green Cardamom. Curated by Iftikhar Dadi, Hammad Nasar, and Ellen Avril, the exhibition explored partition as a productive space in a transnational context. The works were startling, playful, and profoundly moving, as they addressed the issues that emerge (and, indeed, remain) when land and communities are divided to create new nations. While a majority of the artists focused on India, Pakistan, and Bangladesh, the exhibition also included work by artists and scholars who expansively addressed partition in other geographies, including North and South Korea, Ireland and Northern Ireland, Israel and Palestine, and Sudan and South Sudan.[11] The exhibition thus exemplified postcolonial critique, insofar as "postcolonialism has always been about the ongoing life of residues, living remains, [and] lingering legacies."[12] Relatedly, Arie Dubnov and Laura Robson have curated a similar comparative historical exploration of decolonization and partitions. They observe, "Partition is not a long-standing or natural solution to the problem of pluralism; it is a consequence of a particular alignment of global interests, dating from the inter-war period, that privileged ethnic nationalisms and ethnically purified nation-states as the building blocks of a modern world order."[13] Inherent in these geopolitical conditions of the mid-twentieth century, then, were the tendencies toward ethnic homogeneity and ethnonationalism that, in the 1980s and 1990s, would generate genocidal violence and mass expulsions across Asia and Africa. If, as Deepika Bahri notes, "the work of the artist remains the exercise of memory and recollection,"[14] then the *Lines of Control* exhibition foregrounded two dimensions of postcolonial modernity central to *Graphic Migrations*. One is that geopolitical partition—whether called that or not—has dominated the post-1947 political histories of belonging and citizenship in many geographies across the world. Spanning such spaces as India, Korea, Vietnam, China, Germany, and others, the act of political division to create different nation-states has split many societies hitherto undivided. The other is that artistic praxis can create new spaces for us to apprehend and illuminate that which remains, recollects, and is created after partition. Talal Asad suggests, "The past is a legitimate object of critique from the standpoint of the present just as the present is an object of critique from the standpoint of the past."[15] This dual approach informs my approach to the past of the Partition migrations, as I turn to them to understand their specific shape and texture as well as to understand present-day India and South Asian America.

Questions that preoccupy this inquiry include the following: How did the violent Partition migrations, given that they were shaped by religious or ethnic difference, shape postcolonial discourses about secularism in independent India and beyond? In our cultural archives—of fiction, memoir, oral histories, and visual culture—what is the relation between stories about displacement and rhetorics about ethno-nationalism? What is the role of gendered refugees in new postcolonial national cultures, and what is their relation to the secular? What new insights into the legacies of the Partition migrations emerge through the South Asian diaspora? This book tracks the changing fates of the secular and secular citizenship in South Asian and South Asian American art and media after Partition's ethnic migrations. Further, it argues that this archive of art and media makes visible the tensions that coalesce around religion and citizenship, even as it identifies an insurgent practice, a "subaltern secular," that displaces many of the ethno-nationalist verities of post-Partition South Asia and South Asian America. Doing so also entails "provincializing Europe" as well as America;[16] it requires displacing Europe and America as the primary subjects of world history, attending instead to the political divisions and related migrations that accompanied mid-twentieth-century decolonization and pre–Cold War politics across the world. *Graphic Migrations* dwells on these divisions, displacements, and secular intimacies of post-47 Asia and explores their impact on the Asian American experience. Resonant with the new energies of Critical Refugee Studies and Asian American approaches to Cold War studies, as exemplified in such works as Yến Lê Espiritu's *Body Counts: The Vietnam War and Militarized Refugees*, Lisa Yoneyama's *Cold War Ruins: Transpacific Critique of American Justice and Japanese War Crimes*, Lisa Lowe's *The Intimacies of Four Continents*, Cathy Schlund-Vials's *War, Genocide, and Justice: Cambodian American Memory Work*, Josephine Nock-Hee Park's *Cold War Friendships: Korea, Vietnam, and Asian American Literature*, and Viet Thanh Nguyen's *Nothing Ever Dies: Vietnam and the Memory of War*—which, in different ways, note the intricate historical relations between Asia and North America constituted through violence and displacement—I insist that we cannot separate the story of modern decolonization in South Asia from the intimate, immigrant histories of contemporary Asian American life.

Since the late 1990s, new attention to this gendered history and memory of the Partition has generated the field of Partition Studies, as historians and cultural studies scholars—especially feminist scholars—have revisited Partition from a range of perspectives. While literary and film critics have analyzed the prolific works that bear witness to the complex violence of Partition, feminist historians have criticized the patriarchal construction of women as objects of families and communities at this time—a construct that undermines their access to equal rights as political subjects as well as citizens. It also underlies the subsequent forced repatriation of women who had been abducted and raped in 1947 and since resettled with new families in India and Pakistan.[17] A substantial body of work also now exists on the regional histories of particular linguistic communities—Sindhis, Bengalis, and Punjabis—that were the largest populations affected by Partition.[18] Finally, much critical attention in this field, including in my own work, hitherto has been devoted to ethnic violence, memory, and trauma.[19]

Extending the arena of these scholarly conversations in Partition Studies but shifting focus to the dimension of displacement, this book's purpose is to examine the migration stories of 1947 and their legacies for the cultural imagination of secularism and gendered citizenship. In this aim, it traverses the subcontinent and its diasporas; while anchored in literary cultures, it is engaged with the subcontinental and diasporic public cultural exploration of the remains of decolonization through other media, objects, and practices. Accordingly, it considers literary fiction in dialogue with cinema, photography, oral histories, advertising, experimental art installations, and new digital media archives of migrant testimonies, such as the 1947 Partition Archive. The Partition migrations' increased relevance in South Asian public spheres across media forms is evident in the transnational, new media oral history projects that have emerged in the last decade. It is also evident in the proliferation of literary and cinematic production as well as in the phenomenal success of the 2013 Partition-themed commercial "Reunion," which Google created for its South Asian markets; I evaluate this neoliberal aesthetic mapping of Partition's trauma and globalization later. It is clear, then, that the remembering of 1947 is complex and newly resonant across South Asia. As I show through the feminist and queer perspectives and representations considered here, it is also profoundly gendered: just as ethnic/religious difference functions as a central category defining citizenship, heteronormative conceptions of gender, sexuality, and belonging critically mark the experiences of displacement and citizenship in the cultural archive under consideration in this book. Among my arguments is that this remembering of Partition is, at least in part, an ethico-political response to the current crisis of secularism unfolding in India, where minority citizens continue to experience increasingly violent disenfranchisement, loss of citizenship, gendered violence, and daily discrimination (I elaborate on the signs of this crisis later in this Introduction). Thus, in the memory work ongoing across texts, media, and institutions, intellectual vigilance must attend not only to memorializing Partition but also to *how* we institutionally memorialize it toward bipartisan political ends.

This question of how memory projects address the standpoint of the present and articulate modes of recuperation and redress has been central to much Asian American scholarship. Viet Thanh Nguyen argues, "Given the scale of so many historical traumas, it can only be the case that for many survivors, witnesses, and inheritors, the past can only be worked through together, in collectivity and community, in struggle and solidarity. This effort of a mass approach to memory should involve a confrontation with the present as much as the past, for it is today's material inequalities that help to shape mnemonic inequities."[20] My book uncovers how migration stories and their graphic address of national citizenship in this multimedia archive imagine collectivity, negotiate community, and forge transnational as well as secular solidarities. As it chronicles the representation of Partition migrations across various media—literature, film, new media, and print culture—*Graphic Migrations* offers a new story about how the 1947 migrations, decolonization, and the refugee experience have shaped discourses about gendered citizenship and secularism in India and, more broadly, in South Asian America.

I draw upon the work of Ranajit Guha and the Subaltern Studies Collective, which, nearly four decades ago, called for seeing the Indian peasant less as an object and more as an agent of national history. In this book, I argue that we must recognize the migrant—and, indeed, the refugee—as an agent of national history. In other words, the refugee is constitutive of the nation. I realize that this claim is radical; by convention, refugees are often discursively constructed as outsiders, as objects of pity, as peripheral subjects, and as burdens on the places and nations in which they arrive. Yet I am arguing, as have other scholars, for the urgent necessity of displacing this dominant rhetoric as well as this political view. Yasmin Saikia eloquently observes, "To assert its power, official history in South Asia since the colonial times and even now depends on people forgetting much of the lived past. We cannot afford this kind of history any longer. The different, possible narratives preserved in people's memories must be explored and acknowledged if we in South Asia are to confront what decolonization really means."[21] *Graphic Migrations* explores narratives of Partition migrants' memories and engages these with the cultural representation of decolonization and displacement in literature, film, print culture, advertising, and photography. By weaving together a range of representations of migration across media, I labor to uncover how migrants and refugees, through their embodied signification and their ethical practices, have become political critics as well as literal and figurative producers of secular imagined communities in postcolonial South Asia.

In the following sections, I discuss *subaltern secular* and *migrant*, the key epistemic categories that organize my analysis and constitute its conceptual scaffolding. In the ensuing chapters, I orient them toward feminist aesthetic, ethical, and ecological critiques of state, citizenship, and geopolitical conflict. Whether South Asian or Syrian, migration narratives are a powerful starting point from which we can rethink recent debates about how and

when religion and secularism appear in public life and shape community—
witness the work of Saba Mahmood, Talal Asad, Judith Butler, and others
in the last decade. The South Asian negotiation of migration, religion, and
conflict in public culture offers an alternative to the model of secularism
in European Enlightenment modernity, where it has largely signaled the
desacralization of cultures. I use the terms *ethnic* and *religious* interchange-
ably when referring to the political modernity of colonial identities, such as
Hindu and Muslim; my goal is to interrupt discourses that reproduce the
false binary of religion versus modernity, such that particular non-Western
religious communities and identities get marked as atavistic, communal,
not modern, and recidivistic others to the project of post-Enlightenment
modernity.[22] Further, engaging Subaltern Studies with anthropologist Talal
Asad's concept of a historically mobile "secular" (as distinct from the static
ideology of secularism), I describe what I call the *subaltern secular*—the set
of embodied acts, practices, performances, and representations in public
culture that emerges from/about migrants and minorities in the nation-
state. Following this discussion, I present the stakes that organize the story
of how migration animates the lived secular and problematizes the postcolonial state, even as it inaugurates new vernacular aesthetic modes of building imagined communities. The next section explains the contours of the
current crisis of political secularism in India and its transnational links
to post-9/11 America, Islamophobia, and the Indian American diaspora.
This contemporary crisis shapes minority rights and citizenship in the subcontinent and the diaspora; it also signals the stakes and relevance of this
project to rethink Partition and the postcolonial nation-state's production
of statelessness.

Secularism in Crisis

Scholars following developments in India through mainstream news media
and public sphere accounts will be familiar with the changing face of ethno-
nationalist public discourse since the 1990s, as Indians across classes and
communities have debated the meaning and relevance of secularism,
national culture, and equal citizenship in India. There is a new sense of
anxiety, as recent political developments as well as embodied violence experienced by members of minority communities have created fear and concern across urban and rural India. In this atmosphere of anxiety and fear,
geopolitical relations in the region are complex and ambivalent. Tensions
over the political reorganization of and suppression of dissent in Jammu
and Kashmir are high. Yet, in a heartening pro-peace development, a new
bilateral agreement between India and Pakistan has led to the opening of
the Kartarpur Corridor, allowing Indian citizens to cross the border to visit

one of the holiest Sikh shrines in Kartarpur for the very first time; visitors get a special permit for the day and thus bypass the formidable process of getting a visa. The corridor was inaugurated by Indian prime minister (PM) Narendra Modi and Pakistani PM Imran Khan on November 9, 2019. Thus far, leading political figures, such as former Indian PM Manmohan Singh, as well as ordinary citizens have crossed the border to visit the shrine.[23] This opportunity to facilitate cross-border travel, although undergirded by the privileged status accorded to religious pilgrimage, represents a positive political step between the two nation-states. At the time of this writing, it is unclear what the future holds for Kashmir, India, and South Asia; for anyone following Indian politics, it should be increasingly evident that, since 2014, secularism in India has been in crisis.

Of course, the long history of India's move to the right over the course of the twentieth century has made secularism a contested discourse. Shabnum Tejani has well documented the evolution of an ideology of secularism in India through the anti-colonial nationalist movement, from 1890 to 1950.[24] My concern is with the increasingly under siege space for secularism post-1990, in a country whose political institutions had constitutionally enshrined the idea of the Indian nation as a secular and inclusive community. In *Walled States, Waning Sovereignty*, Wendy Brown notes, "As it is weakened and rivaled by other forces, what remains of nation-state sovereignty becomes openly and aggressively rather than passively theological. So also do popular desires for restored sovereign might and protection carry a strongly religious aura."[25] Brown's theorization of the sovereign theological and walled nation-state illuminates the changing nationalisms we are witnessing across Asia, Europe, and North America. In 2007, Rajeswari Sunder Rajan and Anuradha Dingwaney Needham edited a collection of essays that analyze the Indian crisis of secularism from a range of disciplinary perspectives.[26] These essays, as Rajan and Needham note, are committed to "revisioning secularism and its modalities: secularism possesses too much energy for it to be only dismissed as useless or obsolete."[27] They address the spread of violent extremism and polarization across India, its historical roots and cultural antecedents, and its particular imbrication with other forms of difference, such as caste and gender. Since that reckoning, this crisis of secularism in the face of hegemonic ethno-nationalism has persisted—and, I suggest, intensified.[28] Public and private discourses in India have increasingly diminished the spaces in which interethnic or interreligious relations are unmarred by othering and conflict. Significantly, a parallel mode of polarization emerged in the United States after the attacks of September 11, 2001, that racialized religious identities and instigated the growing visibility of minority immigrant identities oriented around religion in the South Asian American diaspora. Hate crimes and other forms of discrimination against Arab Americans, Sikh Americans, Muslim Americans, and anyone appearing Brown dramatically changed the experience of a hitherto invisible model minority group, which became a threatening "other" after 9/11. This shift unleashed new modes of racialization and community formation for South Asian Americans. While I have commented on this racialization of US citizenship elsewhere, scholars including Lopamudra Basu have recently documented its impact through Asian American culture, as in Ayad Akhtar's plays.[29] From the emergence of religion-based identities in the diaspora, such as "Hindu American"; the proliferation of minority student organizations on US campuses that center on religion; and the increasing memberships and political clout of affluent religious sectarian communities (courted by local politicians from New Jersey, to Illinois, to Georgia), we are witnessing a reinvention of South Asian American identity that fissures along religious lines, nurtured in community centers that are increasingly based inside spaces of worship, be they Hindu temples, Sikh gurdwaras, or Muslim mosques.[30]

What is the genealogy of this disappearing secular and its effect on lives in post-47 South Asia and Asian America? How can we understand its changing historical manifestation in the spaces of culture, lived experience, and storytelling? In what sense might we call the secular a minority discourse and a subaltern practice, despite its constitutional enshrinement? Priya Kumar notes the complexities and contradictions of the political understanding of "secularism" as it appears in India's constitutional commitment: "If it has been asked to grapple with the thorny question of multireligious and multiethnic coexistence and to serve as a means of unifying the nation, then it has also been deployed to provide state protection to minority religious communities. Thus, it has been asked to negotiate between uniform rights and liberal citizenship on the one hand, and special rights for minority religious groups, on the other."[31] In the Indian context, questions about religion and secularism have been intimately tied to the notion of justice since independence. As Lloyd and Susanne Rudolph observe, rather than being based on the division between the state and religion, the "Indian constitution declares India to be a secular (and socialist and democratic) state," one that is "neutral and impartial toward all religions."[32] Thus, the constitution recognizes all religions as equal and as constitutive of equal but separate communities: "In the language of Article 25 of the Constitution, as interpreted by the Supreme Court, every person shall have the protection of the law to profess, practice and propagate his/her religion."[33] Yet there is a difference between formal constitutional political secularism and the historical realities of secularism as they play out in state politics as well as in the lived experience of Indian citizens. Anshuman Mondal ably parses this difference: as he points out, while the Indian state constitutionally adopts "a position of secular neutrality" standing above and beyond all religious or faith-based communities, in practice, it has functioned to protect minority communities and interests through such mechanisms as separate electorates as well as "reserved quotas for government appointments, resource distribution and the recognition of special legal provisions for Muslims with respect to personal law."[34]

Mahmood invites us to historicize such formations of secularism in postcolonial societies in the Global South as they relate to minority rights and equal citizenship. By analyzing secularism's relation to the modern nation-state as well as civil society in Egypt, Mahmood illuminates how the "two dimensions of political secularism—its regulatory impulse and its promise of freedom—are thoroughly intertwined, each necessary to the enactment of the other." Thus, she reminds us that, for many such communities and societies, secularism "also entails the reordering and remaking of religious life" in ways that might be "themselves foreign to the life of the religions and peoples it organizes." Given this situation, Mahmood cautions us to be alert to the possibilities and perils of secularism in postcolonial societies: "This dimension of political secularism—shot through as it is with paradoxes and instabilities—needs to be understood for the life worlds it creates, the forms of exclusion and violence it entails, the kinds of hierarchies it generates, and those it seeks to undermine."[35] In this book, I hope to remain attentive to this duality that characterizes political secularism; I want to explore the imaginative possibilities and the historical limits of the invention and performance of the lived secular and its impact on minority rights as well as citizenship in South Asian cultural contexts. In other words, I locate what Robert J. Young describes as the secular practices that "still figure in significant ways in an alternative configuration with the religious."[36] Thus, while I acknowledge Mahmood's argument that political state secularism can be productive of the very interreligious or interethnic conflict that it claims to be an alternative to, I want to create space, through my analysis of a unique cultural archive, for uncovering new formations and performances of the "secular"— in migrant and refugee experiences— that interrogate not only ethno-nationalism but also the political institutions of state modernity from a minor perspective. In the process, I suggest, these cultural texts about migration, memory, and citizenship are counternarratives that invent alternative ways of imagining community within and beyond the nation.

The complexity of the relations among the state, religious identities, and citizens' rights and the creation of a peaceful civil society are well addressed in the prolific body of work by Mushirul Hasan. Acknowledging the historical reality of the political life of Islam and documenting the heterogeneity of what constitutes it, Hasan argues that beyond the simplistic and reductive polarization of the secularism versus communalism debate, we need to examine how religion is lived in syncretic modes in a global and secular civil society, even as we carefully attend to the relation between the state and religion. Indeed, Hasan asserts, "in a society where religion plays a dominant role in virtually every walk of life it is my business and the business of every historian to bring secularism into our discussions, and to affirm its validity as a principle guiding the nation."[37] Hasan invokes here the responsibility of the scholar to offer a political critique of ethno-nationalism and to contest its claims on the nation as an imagined community. Similarly, Asad notes the link between secularism and the liberal state, arguing that "secularism and liberal democracy were centrally involved in linking religion to the nation, attaining civil rights for citizens (especially social and political equality), and thus forming the liberal democratic state as a power state."[38] In India, Deepa Ollapally reminds us that, although the Indian Supreme Court has consistently upheld political secularism, "the Indian state's political secularism had become increasingly strained, particularly since the 1980s."[39] Interestingly, after September 11, 2001, the question of religion and its role in the public sphere also emerged at the forefront in public debates about citizenship and belonging in European American contexts.[40] Yet this question has long held much resonance in postcolonial societies, where decolonization was often marked by religious/ethnic violence that displaced large numbers of people, turning them into ethnically marked refugees (internal and external) stranded in a system of nation-states.

Disentangling these various connotations of secularism for the Indian context is the first step. In his anthropology of secularism, Asad suggestively argues that instead of subscribing to discourses that posit religion and secularism as inherently opposed and static ideologies, we are better served by exploring the "secular" as constituted through a set of embodied practices, as an articulation always in flux.[41] He proffers that the secular is "a concept that brings together certain behaviours, knowledges, and sensibilities in modern life."[42] Arguing that "the sacred and the secular depend on each other,"[43] Asad offers "a counter to the triumphalist history of the secular" that shows how the secular "is neither continuous with the religious that supposedly preceded it (that is, it is not the latest phase of a sacred origin) nor a simple break from it (that is, it is not the opposite, an essence that excludes the sacred)."[44] In her analysis of secularism, Tejani similarly argues for a rethinking of the simplistic divisions between secularism and communalism that have long shaped discourses about the role of religion in public and political life in India. Working back from our present moment of crisis, the chapters of this book open up a series of inquiries into the secular as it becomes legible in the stories of migration and the refugee experience from the 1947 Partition of India—a modern division of territory based on religion. Questions under consideration include the following: Did the violent Partition migrations of 1947 generate the cultural demise of the secular? Does the experience of forced migration, statelessness, and loss turn the refugee away from the secular? Beyond the official discourses of state secularism, what can our cultural archive of the Partition migrations illuminate about modern statelessness, citizenship, and lived secularism?

Displacing conventional approaches that treat secularism as an elite cosmopolitanism or a Western political ideology, and building on the work of Edward Said, Judith Butler, and Talal Asad, I deploy the term *secular* in a performative sense: it refers to the set of embodied acts, practices, and representations through which one articulates an ethical relationship with subjects who occupy that space of difference. In an interview in which he was questioned about his brave conception of secular criticism and the secular intellectual, Said explained that, for him, "the dense fabric of secular life can't be herded under the rubric of national identity or can't be made entirely to respond to this phony idea of a paranoid frontier separating 'us' from 'them'—which is a repetition of the old sort of Orientalist model."[45] This productive dissonance between secular life and the borders of national identity could not be more evident than in the novels of Bapsi Sidhwa, Arundhati Roy, and Shauna Singh Baldwin or in the Indian and Pakistani films *Mammo* and *Khamosh Pani* that this book examines. The cultural works I consider represent the fraught, incomplete, and dense fabric of secular life as it is invented, contested, and under erasure. In *The Idea of Human Rights*, Charles Beitz illuminates why we need to understand human rights not as an abstract political idea but as "an emergent political practice."[46] Similarly, I suggest that the secular emerges as a political *and* ethical practice, following the violent, religion-based mass migrations of decolonization in South Asia. In *The Intimate Enemy: Loss and Recovery of Self under Colonialism*, Ashis Nandy observes that within India and the West, we can find the capacious ability to live with cultural ambiguity and instability, a mode that rejects the simplistic and false opposition of mythic spiritualism or a radical Westernized rationality.[47] This generative instability for me is linked to the emergent secular—a resistant embodied performance, a practice, and an ethical mode of living that, with this book, I try to identify in the spaces of public culture and everyday life. For me, this mode of living is a form of planetary cohabitation that instantiates a political critique of decolonization and ethno-nationalism.

In *Graphic Migrations*, then, I inquire into the discursive grammar of "the secular" as it appears in Indian and South Asian American culture, even as I unravel the relationship between migration and the secular after the 1947 Partition. Engaging Asad's conception of "the secular" as a presence and a practice constantly made and remade through representations, actions, bodies, and objects in everyday life, I track how literary and film texts as well as print and digital cultures invent and address the relationship between violent migrations and this historically mobile "secular" (distinct from the static ideology of "secularism") in the sensual, political formation of individual subjectivity and collective community. In the process, I alight on particular aesthetic representations of gendered migrants and citizens as I map hegemonic as well as critical discourses about belonging, nationalism, and religion in India and its North American diaspora.

One might ask why I turn to migration stories to tell the story about Indian secularism or South Asian secular practices. To be sure, many scholars, including Rajeswari Sunder Rajan, Manav Ratti, and Priya Kumar, have well analyzed the literary representation of Indian secularism more broadly.[48] Further, within the field of South Asian literature and culture, as Neha Vora has also observed, the study of Indian migration has traditionally involved a focus on the circuits that took Indians to the West.[49] However, I turn to migration stories about and after 1947 to interrupt the present circumstance of hegemonic and violent ethno-nationalism in South Asia and South Asian America. I argue that the historical experience of Partition's mass migration—its cultural representation and its political legacies—offers us new "fugitive knowledges" of how the secular and religion are imbricated, then and now; it illuminates how, from the midst of violent, religion-based dispossession, those who are abjected and exiled can forge the "secular" as a political practice and as an ethical, nonviolent response toward geopolitical peace in the subcontinent. Indeed, Butler suggests that "the very possibility of ethical relation depends on a certain condition of dispossession from national modes of belonging, a dispossession that characterizes our relationality from the start, and so the possibility of any ethical relation."[50] The radical marginality (if not invisibility) of millions of dispossessed Partition refugees in our hegemonic histories and discourses of the Indian nation-state marks their minority perspectives, at times, as subaltern, in relation to the nation-state. The texts in my cultural archive locate the emergence of a minor, ethical secular in this subalternity. Engaging the scholarship of the Subaltern Studies Collective, in this book, I identify and name this minor secularism—one emerging in the spaces of minorities' lived experience—the "subaltern secular." This secular does not entail the rejection of religion; indeed, it is a mode of pluralism, planetary cohabitation, and relationality that is premised on the recognition that, "very often, religion functions as a matrix of subject formation, an embedded framework for valuations, a mode of belonging, and embodied social practice."[51]

How gender, race, class, caste, nationality, ecology, and disability shape the cultural imagination of Partition's refugees, citizens, and subaltern secularisms is part of the story I tell in this book.

As such, gender is central in my intersectional analysis of the public cultural representation of post-47 migration and secularism. Recent feminist scholarship across the disciplines on South Asia and South Asian America by Kumkum Sangari, Sudesh Vaid, Rajeswari Sunder Rajan, Asha Nadkarni, Jigna Desai, and Gita Rajan (among others) has illuminated the history of South Asian women's identities, roles, and rights in the context of colonialism and postcolonial independence.[52] In Partition Studies, Ritu Menon and Kamla Bhasin uncover the violence experienced by abducted women during the Partition, tracing the complicity of the patriarchal state and ethnic community in rendering female agency and access to equal citizenship subaltern.[53] In this book, I complement this feminist historiography by examining how notions of heteronormative masculinity and femininity have marked subjectivity, citizenship, and statelessness during and after decolonization. In this multimedia archive of migration stories, most of the artists and cultural producers considered are women and feminists. They represent displacement and citizenship, as well as its failures, and provide a keen eye on how heteronormative gender norms have shaped historical experience and subject formation under decolonization and patriarchal postcoloniality. They illuminate subaltern intimacies and minority solidarities; their stories about gender, embodiment, violence, family, and kinship offer a powerful critique of heteronormative ethno-nationalism, often suggesting a more inclusive and secular vision as an alternative. On the one hand, my analysis uncovers how dominant texts—from Hindi cinema to media and print culture—reproduce or rearticulate heteronormative ideas about gendered citizenship and the national family. On the other, it argues that some literary works as well as art films disrupt these sedimented normative ideas about gender, sexuality, and belonging, offering in the process a feminist critique of how hegemonic nationalism and geopolitical conflict generate statelessness. Linking both is my analysis of how encoding gendered embodiment and bodily performance becomes central, across media, to the cultural project of imagining belonging and witnessing histories of loss on the peripheries of the nation. Schlund-Vials has analyzed how some Cambodian American cultural texts do memory work that challenges the state-sanctioned forgetting of genocide. They "memorialize the passing of family members, homelands, and childhoods to instantiate juridical claims of profound communal injury in need of recognition and justice" as well as to "monumentalize survivor remembrance and recuperate refugee selfhood."[54] In the next section, I consider how collective storytelling events in the South Asian American diaspora about the Partition migrations can constitute one form of diasporic memory work—bearing witness to the refugee experience under decolonization and instantiating a transnational, ethical secular.

Restorying Migration: The Popular Representation of Refugees' Stories

> The chronicler is the history-teller. . . . In the storyteller the chronicler is preserved in changed form, secularized, as it were.
> —WALTER BENJAMIN, *"The Storyteller"*[55]

In April 2016, a unique community event in Philadelphia aimed at generating a new public dialogue on the 1947 Partition migrations revolved around storytelling. In a tiny, intrepid gallery called Twelve Gates Arts that was devoted to South Asia–related artwork, I was part of a collaboration to organize an event called "Voices of Partition," presenting witness voices from India and Pakistan. In the birthplace of America, Indian and Pakistani Americans gathered to share memories of the birth of India and Pakistan. Cohosted by the artists and historians behind the online digital video project the 1947 Partition Archive as part of their global series 'Voices of Partition,' it was an unexpected success: a flood of RSVPs meant that the gallery had to double its seats; people were standing and sitting on the floor in the aisles, just squeezing into the space to listen. Three local South Asian American senior citizens—Hindu and Muslim—shared their memories of migrating as children across the new and bloody borders of India and Pakistan in 1947. Dr. Sagar Banka and Dr. Reena Banka had ties to Lyallpur and Lahore (Pakistan), while Mrs. Khurshid Bukhari was originally from Patiala (India). They described the fragmented, episodic memories of how they heard about ethnic violence in August 1947, how their parents decided to leave their homes, and how they slowly rebuilt their lives in new countries, in the shadow of homes and friends lost. Many commonalities emerged across their stories: all said that their parents thought that they were moving temporarily—just until things calmed down. None imagined the closed borders and wars that the two countries share today.

As the gentle and eloquent speakers narrated their experiences and shared old black-and-white photos, a new and palpable emotional community was forged between them and their multigenerational audience. The witnesses shared their memories of that troubled time, inevitably colored by their childhood. Mrs. Bukhari's harrowing tale of a narrow escape from Amritsar, to which her Patiala-based family had fled after increasing violence, ended with her reminiscing about a certain kachori stall in Patiala. She said, "Oh, I would love to eat those kachoris again." Someone from the audience warmly replied, "I'm from Patiala, and that kachori wala is still there!" During the question-and-answer session that followed the presentation, others in the audience who had also migrated in 1947 started sharing their stories, their journeys. A twenty-one-year-old South Asian American young man noted that when he discovered that his grandfather had migrated to Pakistan during Partition, it had transformed his sense of his identity: "I guess we were refugees. *Refugees.*"

What emerged in this diasporic gathering of those who once were refugees was an eagerness to remember that experience, without rancor toward the other religious community: for example, Dr. Sagar Banka affirmed that beyond religion, the Punjabi language often bound him in closer friendships with Pakistani Punjabis in the United States than with Indians from different parts of India. The shared familiar itineraries of beloved cities (Lahore, Dehradun, Patiala) and schools spun new interreligious, international emotional bonds in this contingent community, surrounded by the red and gold paintings of the Lahore-based artist Komail Aijazuddin. To draw upon Espiritu's words in a different context, this dialogue vividly illuminated "the living effects of what seems to be over and done with." Straddling public worlds and private memories, it became a way to "reclaim the 'something else' that resides at *the intersection between private loss and public commemoration* [my italics]."⁵⁶

Established in 2011, Twelve Gates Arts's goal is, in its founder Aisha Khan's words, to "create and promote projects that cross geographic and cultural boundaries. The 'gates' refer to the fortified gates that walled many ancient cities such as Delhi, Lahore, Jerusalem, and Rhodes—inside which lay the heart of each city's art and culture."⁵⁷ Cathy Caruth argues, "In a catastrophic age, that is, trauma itself may provide the very link between cultures: not as a simple understanding of the pasts of others, but rather, within the traumas of contemporary history, as our ability to listen through the departures we have all taken from ourselves."⁵⁸ This Voices of Partition event opened the gates of our political borders and divided cultures, starting an unfinished conversation about the shared losses of Indian, Pakistani, and Bangladeshi Americans. This dialogue enacted what Schlund-Vials describes, in a different context, as the "renegotiation of history through survivor memory."⁵⁹ It allowed people, through the sharing of remembrances past, to not only see that Indians and Pakistanis have much more in common than our politicians would like us to acknowledge but also to forge new relations of peace that might have consequences in the subcontinent. In this sense, then, the Voices of Partition conversation that day emerged from what Nguyen calls the idea of "just memory," where the remembrance of one's refugee past also invokes the contemporary suffering of other refugees today.⁶⁰ These storytelling practices, as art historian Svetlana Boym notes in her work on immigrant experiences, "do not reconstruct the narrative of one's roots"; rather, they tell "the story of exile."⁶¹ The event showed how telling stories about migration, loss, and trauma can create exilic intimacy. This intimacy, in Boym's words, "does not cover up the common loss and pain of displacement but allows one to survive it, to go beyond it."⁶² Of course, the project to recall and recognize refugee dispossession also raises the question of what counts as justice and redress. As Yoneyama argues in a different context, "Any idea of a successful transitional justice must then embrace a critical awareness of Cold War legacies in the region [Asia], thus ultimately challenging the dialectics of redressable and unredressable as integral to the (in)justices sustained by post–World War II neocoloniality and the structures of American dominance."⁶³ This problem of identifying what injustices and traumas are redressable or unredressable under the conditions of post–World War II neocoloniality, and how they are so, is embedded in many of the literary, film, and aesthetic works considered in the forthcoming chapters. Among my arguments is that many of the cultural texts in this archive perform the secular as a way to redress the violence of the modern state's neocoloniality; they critique the failure of the state and state secularism to protect their displaced subjects while performing, from the periphery, a subaltern secularism.

Refugee stories have not always been welcomed and heard as these were in 2016 in Philadelphia. While the Holocaust scholar Shoshana Felman suggests that "testimony is the literary—or discursive—mode par excellence of our times, and that our era can precisely be defined as the age of testimony,"⁶⁴ in the South Asian context, until the emergence of scholarly work done over the last two decades by Indian feminists and publishers such as Butalia, Menon, and Bhasin, testimonies about the 1947 Partition were largely ignored. To be sure, the facts and figures existed in extensive social scientific studies, especially of the Punjab and Bengal experience.⁶⁵ But the curious elision of Partition refugees' testimonies in part stems from the long history of political censorship of refugees' voices immediately after 1947 in India. For instance, in my first book, *Violent Belongings: Partition, Gender, and National Culture in Postcolonial India* ([2008] 2011), I show how in the early national period, articles in urban English-language newspapers in India repeatedly express the fear that refugees' traumatic stories would incite further ethnic violence against local Muslim citizens. In London, the August 15, 1947, issue of the *Times* printed the following news item: "District Aflame: The trouble in the east Punjab started about a month ago in the Hoshiarpur district, where refugees from Rawalpindi spread tales of suffering and requested co-religionists to avenge them. A peaceful district was thus set aflame." On August 26, 1947, an article in the *Lahore Times* argued,

"The chief danger at the moment is that the tens of thousands of Muslim refugees who are trekking westwards with tales that are grim enough in reality, but become more lurid with every telling, will cause a wave of reprisals in West Punjab." In one news report, a Sikh man waiting in the long queues for passage via ship from Karachi to Bombay in 1947 is quoted as saying, "Our community is on good terms with the others. We have no fear of our neighbors but fear that feelings may be stirred up against us by the refugees from Punjab" (*Times*, August 30, 1947). Similarly, an editorial from the *Times* in August 1947 asserts: "As the refugees toil across the frontier in each direction ... [s]tories brought by Sikh and Hindu survivors from the Western Punjab caused the slaughter of Muslims in Paharganj and other wards of old Delhi by neighbors with whom they have dwelt in amity for centuries" (*Times*, September 13, 1947). In the *Illustrated Weekly of India*, an editorial from September 14, 1947, laments:

> The aftermath of the horror in the Punjab is sporadic outbreaks of violence in many parts of the country. Much of this trouble is undoubtedly due to the stories carried by refugees which are one-sided, often distorted and lose nothing in the telling. Refugees deserve everyone's sympathy and aid in their plight, but however pitiable their cases may be, they cannot be allowed to become a source of vengeance propaganda or the organizers of further killings.

In these accounts, refugees' narratives are variously described as "propaganda," "one-sided," "distorted," "communalism," and sources of "vengeance." Through rhetoric negation, their stories become seen as stories that cause "slaughter." Such fear and anxiety generated widespread censorship of refugees' narratives in the Indian public sphere, even as this refugee experience has remained collectively unmemorialized and unmourned for more than seventy years by the nation-states involved—Indian, British, and Pakistani. (This failure to memorialize the Partition is rendered especially tragic by the fact that even the traumatic and shameful Komagata Maru experience of 355 British Asian migrant subjects denied entry into Canada in 1914 has been memorialized by the Indian and Canadian governments.) The above anxious journalistic and political representations of refugees evince the simultaneous universalization and demonization of refugeeness that, as Liisa Malkki shows, mark public discourse about refugees even today: they are at once "a focal object of intervention and knowledge," a threat to the national community and its private citizens, and a polluting danger in their liminality to "the categorical order of things."[66] Yet, Malkki writes, if we "radically historicize our visions of culture and identity," then we might come to recognize how the migrant's displacement "can generate a different and sometimes subversive reshuffling of nationalist verities."[67] Sassen argues that it is time we recognize that contemporary "migrations are acts of settlement and of habitation."[68] Insofar as recent scholarship in Postcolonial Studies and Asian American Studies historicizes geopolitical migration by pointing to neocolonial and imperial wars and politics, and insofar as it points to the dissonance between state borders and the shared human realities across those borders, it resonates with the inspiration for, and the stakes of, this book. Through its aesthetic archive of migration stories across literature, film, and media, *Graphic Migrations* interrogates the ethno-nationalist verities of present-day India and South Asian America. In returning to the 1947 Partition migrations, I identify an insurgent archive that incites political empathy to forge new relations toward international peace. Across media, much cultural production considered here is marked by what Rajini Srikanth describes as empathy: "Without giving up our right to furious rage and deep sorrow, we can also find within us the emotions and perspectives that could lead to reconciliations and new friendships. . . . We cannot be selective about who we identify and accept as our neighbor, because we are constituted by all our neighbors as they are constituted by us."[69]

In any analysis, the language used to name those displaced is key if we are to understand the aesthetics and politics of representing displacement and of historicizing migrants' belonging and unbelonging in the nation. In the Indian context, Partition refugees' positionality is complex: in the years immediately following Partition, depending on whether the refugee was Hindu or Sikh as well as such factors as gender, location, class, and caste, that individual has often simultaneously been constructed in public discourse as an Indian citizen in need of assistance from the Indian state. Nonetheless, the Indian state has seen fit to suppress refugees' voices and narratives of pain and suffering through its censorship of news media, fearing that they would incite more ethnic hatred in civil society. Underlying this national anxiety is the often unspoken assumption that, given that British India was partitioned in 1947 on ethnic grounds, the Hindus and Sikhs displaced as a result would espouse anti-Muslim prejudice, and the Muslims displaced would espouse anti-Hindu and anti-Sikh feelings. Indeed, L. K. Advani, one of the foremost leaders of the Hindu nationalist Bharatiya Janata Party (BJP), was once a Partition refugee, as are some contemporary supporters and workers of that party. However, the voices and texts in this archive complicate such assumptions. For instance, some of the most influential personalities in the Hindi film industry—including G. P. Sippy, B. R. Chopra, and Yash Chopra—were Partition refugees, and their cinematic oeuvre bears the imprint of this displacement, even as it creatively contributes to the cultural imagination of the secular in India.[70]

By exploring how the secular appears in cultural narratives about migration and normative citizenship across media, I aim to track the convergences and divergences of these stories about ethnic violence and displacement with the dominant discourse about refugee experience that shaped the reception—and, I would argue, erasure—of refugees' perspectives in South Asia. Giorgio Agamben suggests that, increasingly, "states of exception" have become the norm in most Western democracies and that the refugee "is nothing less than the limit concept that radically calls into question the fundamental categories of the nation-state, from the birth-nation to the man-citizen link."[71] What categories and politics might be renewed by refugee stories from South Asia and South Asian America? Such scholars as Yến Lê Espiritu, Lisa Yoneyama, Rajini Srikanth, Viet Thanh Nguyen, Mimi Thi Nguyen, Cathy Schlund-Vials, Victor Bascara, Asha Nadkarni, Josephine Nock-Hee Park, and others have generated important new dialogues in the fields of Critical Refugee Studies and Asian American Studies. This path-breaking scholarship has reinvigorated attention to displacement and memory in the context of the American empire and located the experience of raced minority citizenship in the United States as constituted by its transnational history of war and geopolitical conflict in Asia.[72] Simultaneously, even as the world's population of refugees grows every year, affluent nations from Australia, to Germany, to the United States ambivalently struggle with accepting refugees from Asia and Africa. As the World Health Organization (WHO) reports, 258 million international migrants and 763 million internal migrants live in the world today, with 86 percent of the world's forcibly displaced population hosted by developing countries.[73] Like Malkki, Mimi Thi Nguyen has noted how the refugee is a complex figure: "A historical event, a legal classification, an existential condition of suspension or surrender . . . and a focal point for rescue or rehabilitation, the refugee figure is mired in complicated and ever-emerging matrices and crises of referentiality."[74] I draw upon the energy of new Asian American scholarship on refugees, citizenship, and justice in transnational Asia to examine the changing representation of South Asian migrants and refugees in and after 1947 as a point of departure from which we might reconsider the nation-state, citizenship cultures, and secularism in South Asia and South Asian America. My desire here then, in part, is to write the specific and diverse experience of Partition refugees into the story of independent, secular India as well as that of South Asian America. I do so to recast this peripheral story not as an anomaly but as a constitutive part of contemporary, transnational South Asian life. More broadly, the stakes of this project also emerge from my Arendtian investment in reframing the contemporary, global crisis of growing statelessness produced by war, authoritarianism, and conflict that extends around the world, from Syria to Iraq, Guatemala, Honduras, Yemen, and the United States. If, when, and how we represent the precarity generated by modern migration in our media and our public culture matters—and the next section gestures to the broader public relevance of rethinking how dominant media represent gendered migrants and refugees, by turning to the political philosopher Hannah Arendt's theorization of statelessness and her critique of the modern system of nation-states.

Ecologies of Displacement: Migrants, Refugees, Citizens

Much European and American journalistic discourse about migrants and refugees draws upon the rhetoric of naturalization to represent them as threats to the nations and regions in which they arrive. A typical headline on a *New York Times* (*NYT*) article about Syrian refugees at the height of the 2015 violent displacement is ominous in tone: "A Mass Migration Crisis, and It May Yet Get Worse."[75] In the last few years, when refugees have been in the news, they are often the subjects of such dire headlines, embodying crisis. This article notes that the current numbers of refugees and migrants resemble those from World War II. Failed wars or interventions by the United States, France, and Great Britain in Syria, Iraq, and Afghanistan have generated millions of refugees, but the headlines of most mainstream news media omit this detail. For instance, initial *NYT* headlines in 2015 read, "A Flood of Refugees" and "Influx of Refugees"; later, one reads, "A River of Refugees." Toward the end of 2015, a *NYT* report notes that these refugees "arrived in an unceasing stream."[76] So, the Syrian refugee threat moved from flood to river before being downgraded to a stream. This ecological media discourse about refugees persists; a November 2016 *NYT* headline warns, "Erdogan Threatens to Let Migrant Flood into Europe Resume."[77] A PBS television news story from October 2018 is titled "As Europe Battles over Border Policy, Migrants Flood to Spain."[78]

These striking ecological metaphors equating refugees with "nature" and "natural" calamities dehumanize them, stripping them of historical subjectivity; discursively, these figures of speech erase from view the historical reasons (and, in many cases, European and American involvement in conflicts) that have rendered millions of Syrians, Iraqis, and Afghanis *stateless*. For me, this media discourse immediately recalls nearly identical headlines in 1947 in English-language newspapers, with their negative representations of refugees of decolonization in South Asia. I turn to the transnational archive of literature and culture here, then, as a site through which we might contextualize and interrogate the simplistic, dehistoricizing, and dehumanizing address of migrants and refugees in decolonized South Asia and around the world. The multimedia texts and objects I consider illuminate the experience of statelessness in the context of national and world history and the violent experience of citizenship under postcoloniality. This attention to the historical production of displacement and statelessness is important. As Sassen observes, "Nation-states in Europe contributed to the production of the refugee through their aspiration to administrative sovereignty. . . . [W]ith its endless series of wars and revolutions, Europe (throughout the nineteenth century and in the aftermath of two world wars) created," as the imperial United States now contributes to, the mass displacements of the late twentieth and twenty-first centuries.[79]

I draw upon Arendt's seminal work as a starting point to consider two terms central to my story: *migrant* and *refugee*. Perhaps no one else captures the intimate dispossessions of modern statelessness and bordermaking as well as Arendt. As early as the mid-twentieth century, rooted in her own experience of exile as a German Jew fleeing the Nazis, Arendt distilled the unique situation of minorities who became refugees with the rise of the system of nation-states. In Part II of *The Origins of Totalitarianism*, titled "Imperialism," she lays out her analysis of the constitutive links between the Holocaust and the more than two hundred years of European colonization of the world that preceded it. Her analysis of the twentieth century is resonant, even prophetic, for our time. She shows how the strengthening of the European system of nation-states and the increasing control of their political borders in the late nineteenth century resulted in the restricted movements of people, such that the conditions of Europe's minorities grew increasingly precarious, unless they were protected by special rights and/or the state. The twentieth century has seen growing numbers of minorities expelled because of language, religion, and so forth from the new nations that were created and consolidated after World War II. As if predicting the future, writing in 1968, Arendt observes, "Much more stubborn in fact and much more far-reaching in consequence [than the problem of minorities] has been statelessness, the newest mass phenomenon in contemporary history, and the existence of an ever-growing new people comprised of stateless persons, the most symptomatic group in contemporary politics."[80]

Arendt observes that once minorities lose the protection of the state and become stateless, this loss of nationality also leads to the loss of all rights. Although human rights have been regarded as inalienable, one becomes rightless when one becomes stateless. Thus, she points out, "the internment camp—prior to the second World War the exception rather than the rule for the stateless—has become the routine solution for the problem of domicile of the 'displaced persons.'"[81] In an earlier essay, Arendt had already crystallized this sharp observation about the condition of modern refugees: "A refugee used to be a person driven to seek refuge because of some act committed or some political opinion held. . . . Now, refugees are those of us who have been so unfortunate as to arrive in a new country without means and have to be helped by refugee communities."[82] Herein, she also notes, "Apparently, nobody wants to know that contemporary history has created a new kind of human beings: the kind that are put in concentration camps by their foes, and in internment camps by their friends."[83]

Rooted in her own experience of exile, Arendt's writing challenges two things: the treatment of stateless people and the new languages of governmentality used to refer to human beings who have lost access to human rights and legal protection. In doing so, she essentially asserts in *The Origins of Totalitarianism* that the responses of the European nation-states to the plight of the stateless are no better than the abjection that people are fleeing: "The postwar term 'displaced persons' was invented during the war for the express purpose of liquidating statelessness once and for all by ignoring its existence. Non-recognition of statelessness always means repatriation, i.e. deportation to a country of origin, which either does not recognize the prospective repatriate as a citizen, or, on the contrary, urgently wants him back for punishment."[84] In differentiating among the "recognized" stateless, the "de facto stateless," and the "de jure stateless," Arendt says, the world's governments are essentially refusing to deal with the issue of statelessness—that is, with the refugee question.

This refusal has profound consequences for the right to asylum, Arendt notes. While the right to asylum actually dates to the earliest beginnings of regulated political life, modern nation-states have effectively abolished this ancient right: the Rights of Man, supposedly inalienable, become unenforceable "whenever people appeared who were no longer citizens of any sovereign state."[85] Arendt illuminates the radical modernity of this political condition in the twentieth century: "The first loss which the rightless suffered was the loss of their homes, and this meant the loss of the entire social texture into which they were born and in which they established for themselves a distinct place in the world. This calamity is far from unprecedented; in the long memory of history, forced migrations of individuals or whole groups of people for political or economic reasons look like everyday occurrences."[86] But, as Arendt explains, "what is unprecedented is not the loss of a home but the impossibility of finding a new one. Suddenly, there was no place on earth where migrants could go without the severest restrictions, no country where they would be assimilated, no territory where they could found a new community of their own. This, moreover, had next to nothing to do with any material problem of overpopulation; *it was a problem not of space but of political organization* [my italics]."[87] This radical insight is central to her critique of the modern nation-state's response to statelessness.

Arendt's work on European minorities is profoundly relevant to considering the treatment of minorities and migrants in Asia in the same time period she is writing about: the 1940s. One of Arendt's most brilliant insights in *The Origins of Totalitarianism* is her insistence that what has been unique about twentieth-century modernity, above all, has been the invention of statelessness. By *statelessness*, she means the condition of being a minority, losing the protection of a nation-state, and therefore losing access to human rights, which, for the most part, are rights guaranteed only by the institutions of the nation-state in the absence of any other supranational bodies able and willing to do so. One of her most poignant and resonant observations about this situation is her recognition that this statelessness—the fact of growing millions of people turned into rightless refugees—is a problem not of *space* but of *political organization*.

This account of how the modern system of nation-states has produced statelessness for millions of people in the mid-twentieth century is newly relevant today. Indeed, Butler draws upon and extends Arendt's analysis to reveal how war and nation-states can create "precarity": "Precarity designates the politically induced condition in which certain populations suffer from failing social and economic networks of support and become differentially exposed to injury, violence and death."[88] In *Graphic Migrations*, I remain alert to the complexities of the dissonance between juridico-legal categories deployed in the system of nation-states when addressing the precarity of statelessness and the messiness of the lived practices through which those rendered stateless (and cultural narratives about them) can appropriate, engage, or reject those categories to assert their rights and forge belonging.[89] At the intersection of Postcolonial Feminist Studies, Critical Refugee Studies, and Asian American Studies, I map the transnational cultural impact of decolonization's legacies for statelessness and secularism for India and for South Asian America. In Yến Lê Espiritu's *Body Counts: The Vietnam War and Militarized Refugees*, Cathy J. Schlund-Vials's *War, Genocide, and Justice: Cambodian American Memory Work*, Upamanyu Pablo Mukherjee's *Postcolonial Environments: Nature, Culture, and the Contemporary Indian Novel in English*, Rob Nixon's *Slow Violence and the Environmentalism of the Poor*, Saskia Sassen's *Expulsions: Brutality and Complexity in the Global Economy*, and other works, new scholarship on refugee experience and displacement has radically invited us to recognize how contemporary statelessness is intertwined with multiple forces: with neoimperialist power, gender hierarchies, global capital, ecological expulsions, and the degradation of nonhuman worlds by war and capital in the twenty-first century.[90] I draw upon this rich archive to think through the aesthetics and politics of post-1947 South Asian migration and conflict, and to map the insurgent imagination of resistance to hegemonic ethno-nationalism and to the depredations of the postcolonial state in South Asia and its diasporas.

#rememberingpartition: Unpacking the Archive

Like the Voices of Partition event in Philadelphia discussed above, participants in several public events organized in India have also revisited and remembered the Partition migrations through memory work. For example, on August 4–6, 2017, a landmark event called "Remembering Partition" was organized in Mumbai, India. On the eve of celebrations that would commemorate the seventieth anniversary of India's freedom from British rule, this event comprised a series of exhibits, installations, film screenings, panel discussions, and music performances revolving around the 1947 Partition migration, its memories, and its legacies. The packed schedule of discussions and performances over three days and nights of "Remembering Partition" focused on refugees' experiences. It also invited dialogue on the contemporary stakes of rethinking the historical experience of citizenship for those who are religious minorities in India and Pakistan under governments that espouse extremist religious nationalist views. Simultaneously apparent was the shared aspiration to work toward geopolitical peace between India and Pakistan. As India celebrated the seventieth anniversary of its independence on August 15, 2017, this event was a public invitation to remember that this independence came with a price—displacement, paid by the millions who lost homes, lives, families, and a sense of belonging in 1947.

Organized by a progressive and secular-activist organization called the Godrej India Culture Lab, "Remembering Partition" was the first sustained multiday, multidisciplinary, and multimedia public dialogue that reckoned with the Partition—not only in India but anywhere in the world. The Godrej Group is one of India's leading industrial conglomerates, with its roots in the Indian anti-colonial swadeshi movement.[91] Founded in 1897, it is largely managed and owned by the Godrej family, members of India's minority Parsi community. Envisioned and curated by the India Culture Lab's visionary director Parmesh Shahani and catalyzed by a dynamic team that included manager Dianne Tauro and senior associate Kevin Lobo, "Remembering Partition" was hosted at the state-of-the-art Vikhroli campus in suburban Mumbai.[92] The programming involved more than seven exhibits of art installations, some of which displayed refugees' letters, objects, and fashion, that explored the Partition migrations from a transmedia perspective. As Shahani recalls, "In our collaborative museum of memories, we had invited citizens of Mumbai to bring their own objects for display—things that their parents or grandparents had brought with them, and it was so moving to see the everyday ordinariness of these objects."[93]

"Remembering Partition" also included panel presentations and luminous dialogues over three days with guest speakers and Partition witnesses who shared memories about the mass migrations as well as reflections and research on their legacies. The speakers included Indians, Pakistanis, and Bangladeshis from a range of fields; activists, filmmakers, scholars, teachers, performance artists, musicians, fashion designers, photographers, writers, actors, and others participated in the robust, heartbreaking, and fiercely passionate conversations that unfolded over those three days. Including Sharmeen Obaid-Chinoy, Lalita Ramdas, Salima Hashmi, Nandita Das, Vishwajyoti Ghosh, Anusha Yadav, Nina Sabnani, Tanvir Mokammel, Guneeta Singh Bhalla, and Ramesh Sippy, the speakers traversed geographies from South Asia to the United Kingdom and the United States. Local undergraduate college students sporting jeans and red T-shirts with "#rememberingpartition" printed on them volunteered over the three days to help set up, guide, troubleshoot, explain, and manage the various events and exhibits. The hashtag #rememberingpartition trended on Twitter for several days after the event, realizing the Culture Lab's goals to extend its critical conversation online. About the transnational heterogeneity of cultural performances, screenings, and panelists, Shahani explains, "It was important to us that the performances were representative and inclusive in terms of genre as well as the feelings they evoked. Hence the conscious decision to invite Askari to perform a Soz Khwani—a lamentation, and to end with Kabir Café on an optimistic note—Kabir's mystical poetry infuses the entire subcontinent, irrespective of geographical boundaries." Gesturing to the activist, pro-peace, and transnational commitment of the memory work that "Remembering Partition" wanted to create, Shahani states that his goal was to generate a dialogue "about linkages and possibilities that continue between the now three countries—hence we made sure that voices like Sharmeen Obaid-Chinoy, a Pakistani film-maker and activist with two Academy Awards, and artist Salima Hashmi, who is also the daughter of noted poet Faiz Ahmed Faiz from Pakistan, were heard, as was filmmaker Tanvir Mokammel, the nine times National Film Award winner from Bangladesh, who screened the first worldwide preview of his film *Simantorekha* (The Borderline) here, about the effects of Partition on both sides of Bengal."[94]

For me, one of the surprising dimensions of this event was that, daily, it drew more than six hundred attendees from across four generations; it was standing room only at the state-of-the art auditorium, as people huddled on the floor and steps to listen. People from all walks of life, from scholars and artists, to activists, senior citizens, students, and schoolchildren showed up to hear and participate in this important, and long-overdue dialogue on the 1947 Partition. These creative and path-breaking three days of dialogue and artistic exploration that honored refugees' experiences also identified

Figure I.2: "Well of Remembrance" installation at "Remembering Partition" event. Photo credit: Godrej India Culture Lab.

Partition's many legacies of war and conflict in India, Pakistan, and Bangladesh. Many speakers reflected on the enduring legacies of Partition, from India-Pakistan wars to the violence in Kashmir; others also highlighted feminist and queer perspectives on the Partition migrations. The focus on gender and sexuality was complemented by the central art installation at "Remembering Partition," called *Well of Remembrance* (see Figure I.2). The installation partially re-created a brick well, but it was painted black. White fabric suspended from the ceiling memorialized the fact that thousands of women jumped into wells during Partition to avoid sexual violence and lost their lives in the process. The fabric symbolized the long scarves or sarees women often wore in northern India, its suspension in the air violently halting space as well as time as it invited us to contemplate the women's free falls to death. The installation served as a stark reminder of the differential price that women paid around 1947.

The heterogeneous representational modes employed to remember Partition here illustrated the persistent interest in, and new spaces for, dialogues about Partition refugees that had not yet happened in such a public, collective mode, across four generations, in India. This event unveiled the "thick transnationalism" of the memory and legacy of Partition migrations.[95] The following week, an exhibit at Bikaner House in the capital New Delhi was launched and curated by people behind the 1947 Partition Archive and Aanchal Malhotra, a granddaughter of Partition refugees. It drew nearly a thousand viewers daily, who encountered video oral histories, installations, and photographic displays that crossed religious, ethnic, caste, class, gender, and national borders. More recently, the public conversations created through pop-up exhibits by the 1947 Partition Archive in Berkeley (California), New Delhi (India), and Madison (Wisconsin) have generated large audiences, testifying to the resonance of Partition stories in the present. In a different context, Jennifer Green-Lewis notes, "we re-create the past in response to popular demand—that much seems clear."[96] *These new public cultural initiatives, I suggest, re-create the past and reflect on the prevailing sociopolitical crisis of secularism to perform an imaginative response to this crisis through memory work.* They also signal how cultural forms are being mobilized to challenge ongoing political violence and the state's discursive erasure of South Asia's shared cultures. Through various methods of historicizing discursive practices that constitute collective publics for memorialization, people on the ground are working toward an alternative future *beyond* extremism and nuclear war and *for* secular cohabitation in South Asia.

Resonant with the transnational and mixed-media nature of these intrepid new dialogues, the chapters that compose this book are organized in ways that map postcolonial migration stories and secularism across different media, texts, genres, and geographies from 1947 until 2019. Chapter 1, titled "'Partition Is Still Happening': Transmedia and Graphic Secularism," maps the visual economy of citizenship and statelessness through popular and subaltern images of migration and secularism in graphic narratives and vernacular print culture. I discuss hegemonic graphic representations of a statist idiom of Indian secularism in the *Amar Chitra Katha* (*ACK*; Immortal Picture Stories) comics and in contemporary educational charts from Mumbai print culture. Examining these popular educational prints as graphic narratives in conversation with Chris Pinney's, Kajri Jain's, Karline McLain's, and Sumathi Ramaswamy's work on the imagination of selfhood and nation in Indian print cultural practices, I suggest that the *ACK* comics and the charts seek to play a pedagogical role in the public cultural imagination of national secularity while evacuating, for the most part, migrants from their representations of Indian citizenship, community, and history. They reproduce heteronormativity and erase minorities in ways that reproduce caste, gender, and religious hierarchies. In contrast, I explore the visual economy of Partition graphic narratives and photography that offer a counterdiscourse by narrating the nation through the refugee. I include in this discussion the aesthetically experimental and ecocritical feminist representations of migrant experiences and their legacies in the 2013 graphic narrative anthology curated by Vishwajyoti Ghosh,

This Side, That Side: Restorying Partition. This anthology gathers twenty-eight stylistically varied graphic narratives by more than forty writers and illustrators from three countries: Pakistan, India, and Bangladesh. A truly transnational and transmedia graphic archive that also includes photography, it does memory work that bears witness to displacement in conflict by documenting how displacement shapes middle-class everyday life and media culture, with a substantial focus on women's experiences. It also depicts the multigenerational poverty of refugee camps and instigates new conversations about war, rights, intimacy, displacement, and secular affiliation. I draw upon Jennifer James's theorization of ecomelancholia to trace how the anthology ruminates on the minor voices, memories, and experiences of refugees and migrants (and their descendants) of the 1947 Partition, Kashmir, and the 1971 War of Bangladesh. If some of these graphic narratives draw upon Mughal aesthetics to explore the material memory of Partition migrations, others, such as the story "Welcome to Geneva Camp," use photography to encode the multigenerational unbelonging of three female Urdu-speaking descendants of refugees in Bangladesh still living in refugee camps and reveal, as Eric Tang notes in a different context, "that refuge is never found."[97] Together, I suggest, the anthology's short narratives present a minor archive of how Partition is past and ongoing to critique the failures of the postcolonial state. I engage this powerful feminist graphic representation with the disruptive representation of migrants in the American photographer Margaret Bourke-White's searing, and by now iconic, black-and-white photographs of the 1947 Partition taken for LIFE magazine. Bourke-White documents the migrations of 1947 through photographs that vividly foreground refugee suffering and embodied violence. This work has played a foundational role in establishing photojournalism as an ethical practice of witnessing the expulsions produced by political partitions and conflict. Chapter 1 thus uncovers how this photojournalistic archive places the Partition refugee at the center of the story of national becoming, decolonization, and independence. Central to my analysis is how gender orients these varied media representations of refugees and citizens, many of which are by women and focus on women, embodiment, and the patriarchal representation of family and country.

In Chapter 2, titled "The Ethics and Aesthetics of Witnessing: Refugees, Literary Modernism, and the American Diaspora," I discuss two recent South Asian American modernist literary representations that unveil the precarity of the refugee experience produced by decolonization. I draw upon Ulka Anjaria's theorization of colonial realism and Schlund-Vials's conceptualization of "Cambodian American memory work" to analyze how Bapsi Sidhwa and Shauna Singh Baldwin return to the Partition migrations in their novels. I argue that Sidhwa and Baldwin write aesthetically experimental novels revolving around female protagonists that renegotiate the terms of remembering Partition and offer a political counterpoint to its official histories. Sidhwa's novel *Cracking India* (1991) is a postcolonial *bildungsroman* revolving around a young Parsi girl in Lahore named Lenny who has polio and who witnesses Partition from multiple minority perspectives: as a member of the Parsi community, as a child, and as a polio survivor. The novel connects different forms of minoritization around able-bodiedness, gender, age, ethnicity, and citizenship; simultaneously, it identifies a practice of subaltern secular affiliation across these differences. Baldwin's novel *What the Body Remembers* (1999) continuously punctures its realism with the modernist interior monologues of its Sikh female protagonists Satya and Roop from mid-twentieth-century India. When Roop becomes a Partition refugee, the novel, like *Cracking India*, shows how she performs an affective secular intimacy in the midst of violence to critique how decolonization unfolded. My analysis illuminates how, in both novels, citizens and refugees eschew ethnic hatred and invent an ethico-political subaltern secular. Attentive to the nuances of caste, Dalit experience, capital, and gender, the novels become hybrid aesthetic practices that bear witness while imaginatively constituting a subaltern secular response to political division.[98] This chapter concludes with a discussion of Arundhati Roy's novel *The Ministry of Utmost Happiness* (2017), whose free-wheeling and transnational geography links South Asia and the United States through multiple migration stories. In the process, the novel identifies and criticizes the disappearance of secularism and the violence against minorities that inhabit many societies in South Asia as well as in the United States in the present. Taken together, these novels present scenes of precarity and precariousness, even as they identify practices of subaltern secularism enunciated by refugees and minor citizens who survive the ethno-nationalist state and racial nationalisms.

In Chapter 3, titled "Melodrama, Community, and Diasporas in Popular Hindi and Accented Cinema," I theorize how melodrama animates the representation of migration, secularism, and public culture in Indian art cinema (Shyam Benegal's *Mammo*), contemporary Bollywood cinema (Rakeysh Omprakash Mehra's *Delhi-6*, Kabir Khan's *Bajrangi Bhaijaan*, and Meghna Gulzar's *Raazi* [Agree]), and what Hamid Naficy calls "accented cinema" (Sabiha Sumar's *Khamosh Pani* [Silent Waters], a transnational Pakistani-German collaboration). I select these five films because, in different ways, they depict minor subjects—migrants, refugees, and immigrants, many of whom are women—negotiating the lived secular in the face of hegemonic religious nationalism in India, Pakistan, and America. Engaging scholarship on melodrama as a narrative and stylistic gesture as well as Priya Joshi's analysis of Bollywood cinema as indexing a public fantasy of the Indian nation, I show how melodrama enables the film's critique of the postcolonial state, the crisis of secularism, and globalized media. Benegal's realist art film *Mammo* (1994) revolves around an eponymous, widowed, lower-middle-class Muslim protagonist who leaves India for Pakistan with her husband during the 1947 exodus; when her husband dies, his relatives expel her to seize his property. Childless, Mammo (Farida Jalal) returns to India to live with the only family she knows: her sister and sister's grandson. The film uses melodrama to poignantly mark Mammo's multiple displacements as well as the disjunction between her familial intimacies and her unbelonging as a nonreproductive female, a Muslim, and a Pakistani. Mehra's award-winning *Delhi-6* (2009) criticizes the sensationalizing politicization of religious identity in contemporary India through the perspective of an immigrant Indian American couple and their son, Roshan (Abhishek Bachchan). Its subtle exploration of secularism and nationalism is linked to how it reinvents a common trope of Hindi cinema: the diaspora-homeland antagonism. For instance, in *Delhi-6*, the immigrant couple moves to the United States due to familial and social opposition to their interreligious Hindu-Muslim marriage. Thus, the United States becomes a refuge for this exiled interreligious intimacy, reversing popular and nostalgic Bollywood depictions of the diaspora that fetishize India as an ideal community. Later, as the Asian American Roshan moves to Delhi with his grandmother, he witnesses how mass media and ethnic politics destroy an intimately secular community; the film unveils how ethnic violence takes over the religiously diverse Old Delhi neighborhood, and articulates Asian American diasporic masculinity with the production of subaltern secularism. I extend this discussion of Bollywood melodrama as it articulates an ethico-political secular to two more recent films. The representation of India-Pakistan border crossings, gender, and secularism in Khan's blockbuster *Bajrangi Bhaijaan* (2015), is juxtaposed with Gulzar's *Raazi* (2018), a quiet, female-centered spy thriller set in the background of the imminent 1971 war between India and Pakistan over the independence of what would become Bangladesh. These two films revolve around transnational border crossings that, like Ghosh's graphic anthology *This Side, That Side*, reinvent secular citizenship via protagonists who create Indian-Pakistani romantic and familial intimacies and, from there, new political affiliations. Thus, they offer new imaginative visions of humanity and empathy as alternatives to geopolitical conflict between the Indian and Pakistani nation-states. Gulzar's *Raazi* is based on Harinder Sikka's novel *Calling Sehmat* (2008), which is based on a true story about a female Indian spy in Pakistan during the 1971 war. The transformation of its Kashmiri Muslim protagonist, Sehmat (Alia Bhatt), from a normative, fiercely patriotic Indian soldier-spy into a traumatized anti-war subject over the course of the film offers a powerful critique of statecraft and India-Pakistan conflict. Unlike the Hindi melodramas discussed above, in the temporally experimental aesthetics of the international production *Khamosh Pani* (2003), directed by Pakistani filmmaker Sumar, state-sponsored Islamicization wreaks havoc on the family life and friendships of its female protagonist, Ayesha. Ayesha is a Sikh Partition survivor in rural Pakistan who converts to Islam and marries her abductor. The film shows how Ayesha ekes out a living teaching the Quran to young schoolgirls and becomes a silent spectator to the increasing radicalization of her son, an unemployed teenager with few opportunities. In the process, many intimacies are shattered by violent political conflict. Across these films traversing the registers of art and popular cinema, India and Pakistan, the United States and Europe, the cinematic representation of intimacy graphically unveils the failure of state secularism and the minor aspiration to a secular humanist vision of community.

In Chapter 4, titled "Transnational Asia, Testimony, and New Media," I analyze the growing multiple digital archives of testimony about migration and South Asian conflict that enact a mode of secular memory work. Connecting with Chapter 3's discussion of the uses of melodrama, I begin this chapter by considering Google's recent contribution to Partition Studies. Beginning in 2013, Google created several advertisements aimed at South Asian markets that thematically revolved around Partition. The first one, "Reunion," is about two friends, Baldev and Yusuf, separated in childhood by the Partition migrations and reunited in their old age by their grandchildren. Engaging melodrama, testimony, and technology in the representation of their Hindu-Muslim intimacy, the commercial fashions what Lauren Berlant calls "national sentimentality," while simultaneously inviting a global affective investment in peace, aspirational consumption, and cross-cultural secular intimacy.[99] Released first on YouTube before being telecast on Indian television networks, its positive reception globally—from viewers not only in South Asia but also in the Middle East, Eastern Europe, and elsewhere—evinces the reach and resonance of this migration story about loss, memory work, and secular reconciliation. I show how this commercial is part of a subgenre of what I call "border-crossing" advertising popular in India and Pakistan, and juxtapose its representation of traumatic memory and subaltern secularism with the intergenerational testimonies I have collected from people in Mumbai and the diaspora in the last decade. These testimonies, I suggest, offer knowledge about the refugee experience often elided in other registers: they are intimate, fragmented stories about post-47 Bombay/Mumbai, Hong Kong, and the United States. They unveil the images, spoken and unspoken, of loss, survival, and secularism with which second- and third-generation members of refugees' families live. By engaging Veena Das's attention to the texture of narrative silences in everyday life, I show that the everyday familial intimacy of Partition variously resonates for this new generation: it generates a desire to forge a conversation about peace with Pakistanis or Indians, it evokes the loss of Sindhi language and cultural identity, or it becomes an incitement to express humanist empathy with other refugees of division and conflict. On the one hand, the migrant narratives tell of the material hardships of displacement and resettlement, the struggle to survive economically and to find a dwelling. Simultaneously, they also bear witness to how women and men experienced this migration differently, as well as to the traumatic ancestral loss and cultural ambivalence they felt in their unequal assimilation into Indian citizenship. I link these narratives to other new media initiatives, such as 1947PartitionArchive.org, that invent new, transnational publics by gathering and disseminating video testimonies of migrant experience through those its Bay Area–based founder Bhalla calls "citizen historians." I also discuss here the installation *Open Wound* by Asian American photographer and artist Annu Palakunnathu Matthew as well as Mumbai-based Anusha Yadav's 2016 Partition-related exhibit through her Indian Memory Project. These new archives, I suggest, are institutions that memorialize the 1947 migrations and performances of remembering (as per Espiritu) that reinvent, on the ground, the secular movement toward peace in the subcontinent.

In the Conclusion, I connect how these different aesthetic archives mark the subaltern secular, teasing out the links between discriminatory displacement and geopolitical conflict. In this book's archives, although a key focus is the narration of the Indian nation, some of the texts and objects that represent post-47 migration as well as citizenship are also created by, or in collaboration with, Pakistani and Bangladeshi artists, cultural workers, scholars, and critics. This transnational memory work, I suggest, is part of the intellectual labor necessary for provincializing the nation form, as I have argued elsewhere.[100] It also reframes the political divisions and related migrations that accompanied mid-twentieth-century decolonization and pre–Cold War politics in South Asia, in the period that Leela Gandhi and Deborah Nelson call "around 1948," to uncover the hidden intimacies of what have traditionally been seen as unconnected histories.[101] Turning to a digital oral history of Chinese/Taiwanese/American displacement in 1949, I gesture to how our understanding of post-47 Asia remains unfinished. This narrative of familial separation during the 1949 separation of mainland China and Taiwan evokes many of the tropes that haunt Partition migrants' narratives. Through this chronicle, I most explicitly argue that studies of World War II and decolonization must engage with a truly global inquiry, so that we can better illuminate the textured public cultures of the transnational partitions that mark mid-twentieth-century Asia and its diasporas. Such an engagement is urgent; it also demands that we redraw the boundaries of how we tell the story of modern world history and the intricately interwoven, intimate production of statelessness and citizenship across the world's communities. As Vazira Fazila-Yacoobali Zamindar also notes, by uncovering these alternative histories and accounts of the Partition, we can "make other forms of belonging and politics available to the memory of Partition—and thus shift the very possibilities of how its future unfolds."[102]

1

"Partition Is Still Happening"

Transmedia and Graphic Secularism

> Without a critique of state violence and the power it wields to construct the subject of cultural difference, our claims to freedom risk an appropriation by the state that can make us lose sight of all our other commitments.
>
> —Judith Butler, *Frames of War*[1]

Among my aims in this book, as mapped in the Introduction, is to examine Partition refugees from several vantage points as they appear in South Asian fiction, film, and public discourse: as objects of political discourses that seek to define the rights of refugees and the norms of citizenship after political independence in India; as subjects of a democratic Indian state's institutions of gendered redress and rehabilitation; as political actors and speakers who assert individual "rights" in modes that invoke the emergent international language of human rights; and as figures who are not conventionally stateless, insofar as the refugees are ambivalently and unevenly welcomed as "citizens" by institutional actors and in public sphere accounts. In the Introduction, I argue for a fresh understanding of secularism, beyond the critique of Enlightenment universalism; I draw upon the theorization of subalternity by Subaltern Studies scholars and of secularism and modernity by Talal Asad to analyze how the secular appears in migration stories about citizenship and community in post-Partition India and the South Asian America diaspora. In this chapter, I turn to different media forms and objects—from print culture and graphic narratives to photography—that visualize gendered citizenship and the secular as they narrate the nation and Partition. Upamanyu Pablo Mukherjee argues that "it would not be possible for works of Indian, or indeed, any literature, to constitute their own singularities without [the] symbiotic and mobile relationship with the non-literary forms that surround them."[2] While in the next chapter I address the literary representation of South Asian migrations in 1947 and after, here I first gather an eclectic set of nonliterary texts and material objects that constitute the public sphere imaginary in which South Asian literature circulates: for example, I discuss the visual grammar of Indian educational charts that depict citizenship, and popular nationalist prints from the mid-twentieth century that map the Indian nation, in dialogue with the counterdiscourse of South Asian graphic narratives and photography that represent Partition refugees. By juxtaposing them, I track across media and historical moments their unique and ubiquitous imagination of secularism as well as their critique of state power through the representation of refugees' perspectives. I admit that my choice of certain prints and objects may appear arbitrary; however, I hope to show that even in the distance and dissonance between these objects, we can see lines of convergence and resonance in the collective, cultural negotiation of norms around national citizenship, state power, and refugees' memories. Placing heterogeneous images and media into conversation, in this chapter, I foreground the ongoing and necessary labor of the images of history that surround us and the political stakes of their critical analysis. In the afterword to her study of Walter Benjamin and his Arcades Project, Susan Buck-Morss writes, "The responsibility for a 'theological' reading of the *Passagenwerk* (one which concerns itself not only with the text, but also with the changing present that has become the index of the text's legibility) cannot be brushed aside. This means simply that politics cannot be brushed aside. By way of concluding this study, the following images provide material for such a reading, urging that readers begin this interpretive project on their own."[3] In this chapter, I draw upon current scholars of South Asian visual culture to enact a new interpretative project for the present crisis of the secular.

Deborah Poole argues that instead of the term *visual culture*—which suggests homogeneity and unity—we should use the term *visual economy* to refer to representational domains. She offers two reasons. First, it allows for the consideration of unequal flows, exchanges, and power relations within which images circulate. As Christopher Pinney notes, "She states that economy 'suggests that this organization has as much to do with social relationships, inequality and power as with shared meanings and community.' . . . We must not lose sight of the extraordinary circumstances of inequality (encompassing the range from cultural, political, and economic hierarchy to systematic genocide) that gave rise to the vast majority of images that inhabit the colonial archive."[4] Second, it allows us to stress the global circulation of images over the local fixity that the term *culture* implies, foregrounding "how visual images move across national and cultural boundaries."[5] Thus, in this chapter, I analyze the visual grammar of citizenship, statelessness, and the secular across a range of media objects and institutions linking South Asia and the United States. The questions this chapter explores are:

How do visual representations of Partition figure the secular, the nation-state, and the gendering of the refugee experience? How do they produce (or not produce) stories about displacement and nation formation that chronicle and reconcile us with the past? How do they explain the losses and challenges faced by Partition refugees, and what aesthetic traditions do they engage to chronicle their legacies? What stories about state power, living with difference, and citizenship and its discontents do they offer? I assemble here a network of literary, official, and visual practices that have unfolded in the context of the Partition migrations. By doing so, I illuminate how those migrations have shaped gendered subject formation and the secular in postcolonial India as well as in South Asia. My analysis shows how some public cultural images reproduce heteronormative, hegemonic state ideas about gendered citizenship, intimacy, and family; others resist them, offering feminist counternarratives that do memory work, critique geopolitical conflict and refugee experiences in the postcolonial state, and illuminate the subaltern secular. I first draw upon the work by Christopher Pinney and Kajri Jain on Indian visual culture to extend their insights to an analysis of two popular, everyday objects that represent the nation: educational charts and prints. I then analyze the transnational representation of gendered refugees in graphic narratives and photography to discuss how they reveal the violence of statelessness and geopolitical conflict produced by British decolonization and the postcolonial state in South Asia.

Drawing Embodied Secularism: Religion and Pedagogical Nationalism in Print Culture

In this section, I address how Indian citizenship and secularism appear in popular print culture. In his extensive work on commercial Indian print and photographic practices in colonial and postcolonial India, Pinney convincingly argues for "a new historiographic practice grounded in the study of popular visual representations" that would challenge the narratives of elite historiography about Indian nationalism.[6] This practice, he contends, would allow us to deprivilege the text-based histories of Indian nationalism that dominate South Asian Studies. Exploring how certain chromolithographic images and offset printing practices constitute spaces where "intensities are felt," Pinney suggests that these representational practices "take the form of a popular historicity configured by . . . a dense 'semioticity.'"[7] Taking up this approach, I explore how "the materiality of representation creates its own force field."[8] This practice entails a different type of analysis, "one in which images are treated as unpredictable compressed performances, caught up in the recursive trajectories of repetition and pastiche, whose dense complexity makes them resistant to any particular moment."[9] Thus, I approach the question of aesthetics not by discussing high or low art but by attending to the sensory, sensual dimension of aesthetic experience, as Benjamin urges. I turn to the visual and material artifact to "map the political and moral economies and forms of social distinction with which it is enmeshed,"[10] as Jain suggests, to identify what kind of sensory and conceptual response it invites from us. Examining some visual images that figure the secular thusly, I consider two different material visual representations of the "national secular" and Partition: (1) a print titled *Kalpa Taru* that visually maps secular national community in pre-Partition India and (2) the ubiquitous, printed educational "charts" of everyday life and ethno-religious difference in modern India.

Very few prints or maps depict Partition refugees, to my knowledge; however, many prints that depict India around 1947 address and imaginatively present images of secularism and Partition. One print that has long fascinated me bears the date 1946 and is titled *Kalpa Taru: Independence Is Our Birth Right: Galaxy of Congress Leaders Who Wrought for Independence for Sixty Years* (see Figure 1.1). It was published in three languages (English, Hindi, and Telugu) in Secundarabad in southern India by M. Thimmiah Sresty, Batchu Ragavaiah, and Jonnala Pentaiah.

A copy of this print also exists in the extensive Priya Paul Collection (most comprehensively archived at Heidelberg University in New Delhi) and can be found in the digital visual archive Tasveer Ghar with this accompanying commentary:

> This tri-lingual poster (in English, Hindi and Telugu) appears to suggest that the leaders of the national movement are the various fruit of the wish-fulfilling tree (*kalpa taru*), culminating in Nehru's interim government (September 1946). Rare among such political prints, we see the faces of several women—Kasturba Gandhi, Annie Besant, "Captain" Lakshmi, Sarojini Naidu, to name the most prominent—embedded amongst the vast majority of men. . . . [A]t the top of the print, and the words *Jai Hind* (Hail India) and *Vande Mataram* (I Worship the Mother), alongside verses and phrases from the *Bhagavad Gita*, are also inscribed.

The dense semiotics of this poster depicts a smiling Mahatma Gandhi framed by the symbol for "Om" at the center of a tree symbolizing community. Around Gandhi are crowded images of male and female political leaders and activists from different religious and ethnic backgrounds as well as different historical moments in the nationalist struggle. In this sense, the print appears to have two pedagogical aims: to educate the viewer about all

Figure 1.1: "Kalpa Taru: Independence Is our Birth Right: Galaxy of Congress Leaders who Wrought for Independence for Sixty Years." Published by M. Thimmiah Sresty, Batchu Ragavaiah, and Jonnala Pentaiah, Secunderabad, circa 1946–1947. (Kavita Daiya and Sunny Rao Collection).

those who have contributed to the anti-colonial Indian nationalist movement, and to depict this community as diverse and, paradoxically, secular within a Hindu-majority milieu. The print thus establishes Hinduism as the center of the imagined Indian national community, even though Parsis, Hindus, Muslims, Sikhs, and Christians appear here alongside linguistic and regional communities from the north, south, east, and west. This composition only makes sense if we recall Asad's point: that the secular and the religious must be read not as simply binary, antagonistic, and exclusive domains, but as mutually constituted through representational acts and embodied practices. The map of undivided India above this "tree of life" image is green—a fact suggesting that India's division and the association of green with Pakistan was not yet in place, although Muhammad Ali Jinnah, the leader of the Muslim League and founder of Pakistan, is absent here (surprising, given that he was a prominent member of the Indian National Congress in the first decades of the twentieth century).

Sumathi Ramaswamy's discussion of this print illuminates how the print represents the nation as mother and goddess, reinforcing the popular cartographic print representation of the Indian nation as Mother Goddess in colonial India.[11] Extending this analysis, I am interested in contemplating the articulation of ecology and embodied diversity across the rest of this print, in which faces, names, and, in some cases, dates create a cartography that has less to do with territory than with embodied diversity.[12] The print reflects in part what Pinney describes as the unofficial canonization of Gandhi that had begun in print culture during the 1920s, in which popular visual representations of him acquire an "auratic potency." The goddess adjacent to Gandhi's face and his encircling by the halolike "Om" seem to reinforce this intention. Yet the overwhelming sense of this fairly popular print's semiotic density is its ethnic, gender, and regional inclusiveness and its visualization of an ecology of embodied secularism—albeit one that is ultimately delimited by its own centralized privileging of Hinduism, insofar as the Hindu word *Om* is placed in the center of this imagined community. This print exemplifies the possibilities and the limits of the popular national secular as imagined in public culture at this historical moment.

In Pinney's discussion of popular visual representations of Gandhi before his death in 1948, he notes that while "chromolithography generally positioned him within the 'empty, homogenous time' of the documentary photographic image," local photographic practice, with the use of artisanal montage techniques, was able to reject "a disenchanted chronotope" and situate Gandhi within a "messianic space" popular on the streets.[13] Insisting on the deity's efficacy alongside a corporeal relationship to the "darshan" of Gandhi at the center, this image in *Kalpa Taru* is magical realist, as it performs an anti-colonial resistance or refusal (not only in the text at the bottom asserting that "Independence Is Our Birthright") of the geometry of colonial reason and a certain technology of representation, inviting instead what Theodor Adorno calls "somatic solidarity,"[14] a corporeal relationship with the image. Through this place of somatic viewing practices of India's vernacular modernity—or what Pinney calls "corpothetics"—we might also understand the aesthetic labor of Indian graphic narratives of the 1947 Partition assembled by Vishwajyoti Ghosh, which I discuss shortly. Both offer practices that posit an alternative or vernacular modernity that seeks to draw or redraw South Asian imagined communities. Suffice it to say that the prints depicting the map of India after Partition that I have seen—in the Priya Paul collection, Tasveer Ghar, and the Center for Indian Visual Culture—look nothing like *Kalpa Taru*. They tend to be like *New India* (see Figure 1.2): the corporeal density is evacuated, the statist cartography is evident in the depiction of linguistically demarcated states, and although the Mother Goddess is now absent, between one and four Hindu male political elite leaders' faces frame the national map of clearly etched borders and boundaries.

The troubling, imagined secularity of the *Kalpa Taru* print for me links in complex and interesting ways to the visual iconography of ethnic citizenship in prints used as educational "charts" in independent India. These charts were (and still are) mass produced and cheap, and they can, even today, be purchased from street vendors as well as from shops in cities and villages. These are similar to "lottery sheets" in London, described by Andrea Immel as "a type of print for children that had been on the market since at least the late seventeenth century. Lotteries were small engravings covered with little pictures laid out in rows, depicting such subjects as the social ranks, trades and professions, caricatures, humorous subjects, animals, birds, fish, plants, the seasons, and sports and games. . . . According to the printsellers' catalogues, lotteries were 'chiefly intended for children to play with.'"[15] By the mid-eighteenth century, these lottery sheets were also seen as "an educational aid,"[16] and it is in this form that similar, image-text-paneled, graphic prints acquired their mass circulation in modern India. While chromolithographic printing was established in India by the 1880s and dominated through the 1920s and 1930s, the arrival of offset printing in the 1930s in India shaped the life of similar lottery sheets. Their twentieth-century Indian counterparts, called "charts," are designed around a variety of themes—from types of birds/fruits/vegetables/vehicles/dwellings to numbers, the alphabet in multiple languages, "good habits," "bad habits," "famous temples," "festivals of communities," and "morals."

The images in these pedagogical charts educate children as citizens and create a visual iconography for the Indian nation and normative citizenship that points to Asad's argument about secular modernity. They materialize the state's conception of secular citizenship, indexing a lexicon in which

Figure 1.2: Print no. 400, "New India." Priya Paul Collection @ TasveerGhar.

religious/ethnic difference organizes the discursive articulation of sameness and difference that, Benedict Anderson notes, produces the nation as an imagined community.[17] This presentation is not about the evacuation of religion (or religious difference) from the national secular but about its affirmation—the affirmation, recognition, and performance of religious difference. One of the most prolific publishers of these educational charts is the Indian Book Depot (Map House). Among its products are children's books, cut-and-paste books, maps, charts, and atlases. The Indian Book Depot (Map House) was established in Lahore (Pakistan) in 1936 by Nawnit Rai Chawla. After Partition, Chawla moved his business to Sadar Bazaar, Delhi; it became one of the most successful print businesses in India. It continues to be controlled by Chawla's descendants, as it disseminates its products across India's twenty-eight states and seven union territories. The bright colors and style of imagery popularized by the India Book Depot can be seen in the charts produced by other printers too, including Mumbai-based Spectrum (which only publishes education charts), established in 1991.

In her analysis of *Amar Chitra Katha* (*ACK*) comics, Nandini Chandra argues, "It is possible to draw an analogy between the photographic image and the iconic/mythic image on the one hand, and the cinematic image and the narrativizing/historicizing impulse of the comic on the other."[18] I suggest that Indian education charts straddle the divide that Chandra posits: individually, each panel in the chart reproduces iconic and dominant images of community and identity; in their sequential arrangement in a chart, they create a narrative (albeit dehistoricized) about national citizenship and belonging in modern India. A typical vintage chart, called "Children of India," depicts two things: first, we see the gendered nature of this imagined pluralist citizenship (all the children are boys); and second, homogenized in their facial and embodied features, the boys can only be differentiated by their clothes. Their dress signifies regional, occupational, or religious differences, thus creating a taxonomy of Indian modernity that visualizes secular national diversity through sartorial performance (see Figure 1.3). Like the caste charts of colonial Mexico that delineate the intricate taxonomies of racial difference described by Ben Vinson,[19] Indian charts offer similar taxonomies or frameworks of ethno-religious difference: these unevenly depict such differences as language, religion, and region, while largely erasing caste difference and the Dalit experience from view. These images straddle the space between the action-oriented *ACK* comics that purportedly repurposed tradition in the early national period toward secular aims and the flat iconic images of ethnographic photographic representations. I also include examples of contemporary charts that, in similar normative ways, map religious community onto the citizen's body to present a performative, secular diversity (see Figures 1.4 and 1.5).

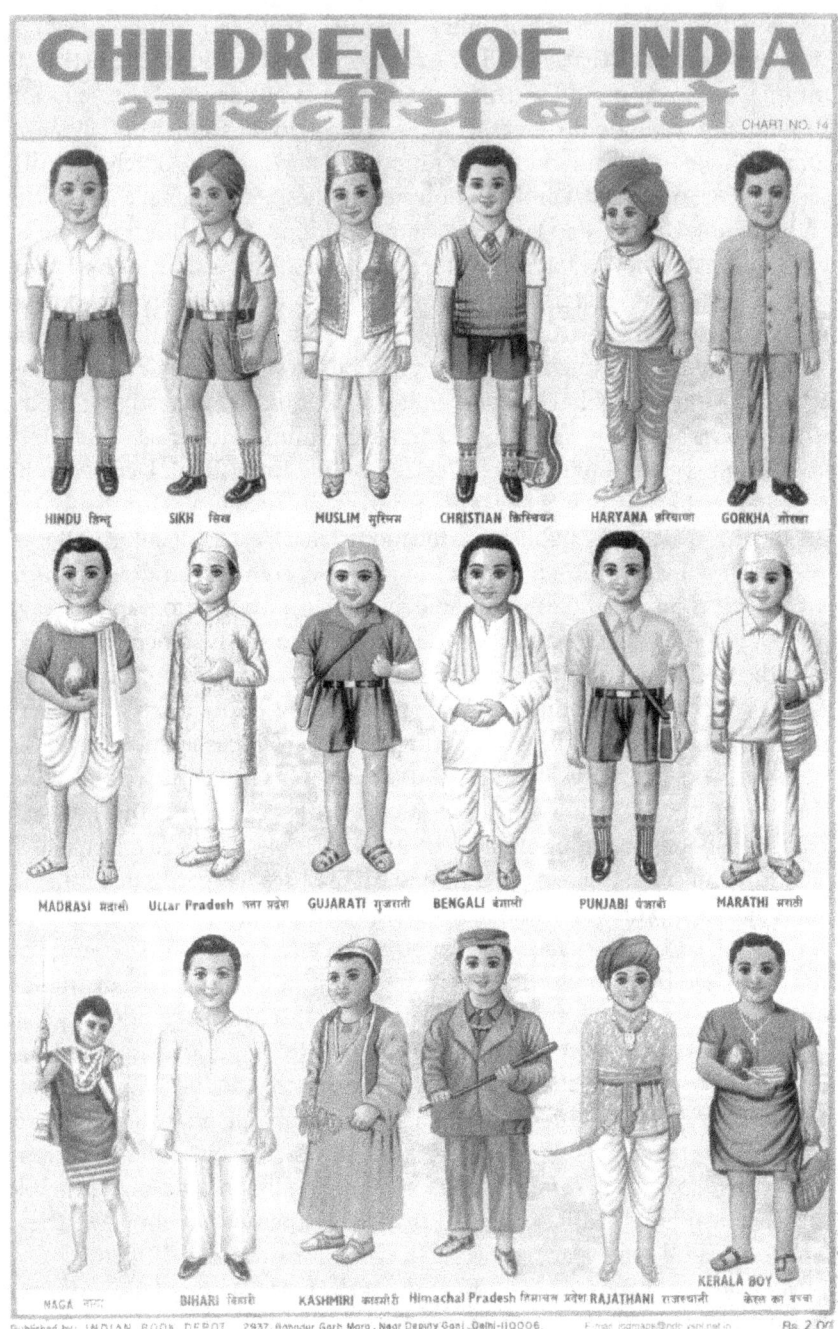

Figure 1.3: "Children of India." Courtesy of India Book Depot (Map House).

Figure 1.4: Spectrum chart no. 157, "Family and Religion." Spectrum Charts.

Figure 1.5: Spectrum chart no. 111, "Festivals of Communities." Spectrum Charts.

In all these charts, we see a rigid and organized graphic arrangement of panels. Each panel frames a static image, accompanied by a caption that anchors it and becomes "an occasion to display the overt ideology conforming to the dominant social/political morality."[20] It is important to acknowledge here that in the contemporary chart titled *Family and Religion*, the graphic representation of political subjectivity and communities does two things: first, it reiterates the centrality of religion to the imagining and fashioning of modern cultural identity in India, and second, it reproduces the taxonomic categories of colonial administration that homogenized the diversity of India's religious and cultural practices to political groupings of "Hindus," "Muslims," and so on. Some charts erase from view smaller ethnic communities, such as India's ancient Jewish community—so beautifully represented in the fiction and memoir of Ahmedabad-based author Esther David (e.g., *Book of Esther, Shalom India Housing Society, Book of Rachel*)—even as they leave no space for acknowledging interethnic or atheistic subject positions in their depictions of citizenship.[21] Through their assembly of graphic panels, I suggest that these charts create a "narrative/secular frame":[22] in this narrative, we see a static, heteronormative conception of inclusive, secular community that is secured through the institution of the extended family and through the sartorial performance of dominant modes of religious identity in contemporary India. In the process, they reproduce discourses of colorism, sexism, and heteronormativity, while erasing from view caste hierarchies as well as the Dalit and indigenous communities. They also render invisible the millions of refugees who arrived in India after 1947 and dramatically transformed its urban centers economically, educationally, and culturally. In the chart titled *Festivals of Communities*, graphic panels assemble illustrations that depict a range of religious holidays celebrated by Hindus, Christians, Sikhs, Muslims, Parsis, Buddhists, and Jains; enumerated willy-nilly alongside these images are the celebration of the nation's independence day and nonreligious collective events, such as fairs. This chart indexes some of India's notorious heterogeneity of festivals and celebrations, even as caste and indigenous differences often remain under erasure. It is important to note that, given that Islam prohibits the embodied depiction of God, these visual iconographies (which often include frontal depictions of Hindu, Sikh, Parsi, Jain, and Christian gods) must work around this restriction to include India's minority Muslim community within their visual representations.[23] Today, many vintage charts from the 1950s and 1960s are sold in India as well as in the United States (serving more as quaint wall décor in the latter).

I realize that my discussion of charts here is eclectic; I have not mapped here the history of the production of these charts, nor have I offered an in-depth discussion about the development of this print industry and these charts' uses. Indeed, a thorough study of the historically changing iconography of these educational charts is beyond the scope of this chapter. It would also be interesting to compare charts from Pakistan and Bangladesh with those from India, as well as from different regions, or to consider those from the early national period to the present day in a more thorough manner. My aim here is to gesture to the popular, sensuous, and graphic depiction of secular community and citizenship in these ubiquitous charts. I do so to explore how we might put into conversation the different genres of graphic representations—literary and popular—such that we can track the differential imagination (normative as well as subaltern) of embodied secularism in their visual iconography of citizenship, religion, and refugees in postcolonial South Asia. In the next section, I map how new transnational graphic narratives articulate a visual and political counterdiscourse to these prints' hegemonic, heteronormative iconography of secular community and national citizenship in India. These representations rely on the figuration of the family to represent and contain national diversity, even as they erase the refugee from view; in contrast, as I discuss below, the aesthetic of comics places refugees, memory, and historical loss center stage to bear witness to the production of statelessness and survival in the nation.

Gender, Displacement, and Ecologies of Loss in Vishwajyoti Ghosh's Graphic Anthology *This Side, That Side: Restorying Partition*

In 2013, the first graphic narrative anthology about the 1947 Partition—*This Side, That Side: Restorying Partition*—curated by acclaimed Indian graphic artist Vishwajyoti Ghosh and published by Yoda Press in India was released. *This Side, That Side* offers migration stories in black and white that interrogate hegemonic narratives about modern South Asian history, articulating, in the process, a critique of the postcolonial state, decolonization, and their expulsions. I approach the concept of expulsion through Saskia Sassen's analysis of "the systemic edge" whose key dynamic is "expulsion from the diverse systems in play—economic, social, biospheric."[24] Arguing that the diverse processes, conditions, and channels for producing expulsion are all acute, Sassen seeks "to make visible the crossing into the space of the expelled—to capture the visible site or moment of expulsion, before we forget."[25] In what follows, I show how this anthology also makes visible the diverse modes of expulsion that have inhabited South Asia since 1947, born of the Partition. Ghosh is billed as the "curator," not editor, of this collection. He was previously known for being one of the most important graphic chroniclers of postcolonial Indian history: his graphic novel *Delhi Calm* (2010) depicts the repressive emergency (1975–1977) that Indira Gandhi imposed on India. Ghosh himself grew up in a refugee colony in Delhi, learning about the refugee experience firsthand as he saw his grandmother work in rehabilitation services in the government.

This Side, That Side is a groundbreaking work: it is the first collection of graphic representations of the multiple Partitions that have fragmented South Asia since 1947 (see Figure 1.6). This 366-page black-and-white volume offers a hitherto unprecedented and profoundly unique cross-border artistic exploration of Partition in experimental graphic narratives produced by transnational collaborations. Through an open call for contributions, Ghosh gathered more than forty writers and artists from three countries—Pakistan, India, and Bangladesh—and, putting different writers and illustrators together (often from different cities and nations), commissioned them to create the twenty-eight narratives about Partition and its legacies included in this book. In one sense, the anthology presents occluded perspectives of decolonization. It includes poetic and moving experimental pieces by many women writers, activists, illustrators, and photographers, including Beena Sarwar, Bani Abidi, Mehreen Murtaza, Syeda Farhana, Priya Sen, and others, some in collaboration with counterparts from across the border. The pieces included vary aesthetically, and many experiment with conventions of comics as well as literature, Mughal art, indigenous art forms, and photojournalism as they comment on migration, media, memory, gender, environment, and war. Arguably, more than any other artistic work, this anthology vividly addresses the links across South Asia's modern history of conflict: from the memory and trauma of 1947, refugee experience, the 1965 India-Pakistan war over Kashmir, the 1971 War of Bangladesh, and India-Pakistan hostilities, to contemporary joblessness in Dhaka, the ongoing multigenerational poverty of millions of refugees, and state violence. Although most of the narratives were originally written in English, several have been translated from Hindu, Urdu, and Bangla. When this edited collection was released in August 2013, Ghosh asserted in an interview that Partition was not over—that "Partition is still happening."[26] This melancholic sense of division and displacement as something that remains, as an ongoing psychic and sociopolitical condition of life in South Asia, is perhaps what unites the contributors to this volume.

This Side, That Side critiques statelessness and provincializes the nation in several ways. First, urban experience and media appear here in radical new ways: Delhi, Karachi, Kolkata/Calcutta, and Dhaka are recast as refugees' cities. Second, the anthology does memory work that foregrounds desires, histories, intimacies, and affects tied to border crossings. Often, these border crossings are rooted in secular, eco-critical memory. Finally, several contributions' critiques of the nation-state's ongoing production of statelessness exemplify the anthology's investment in redirecting the

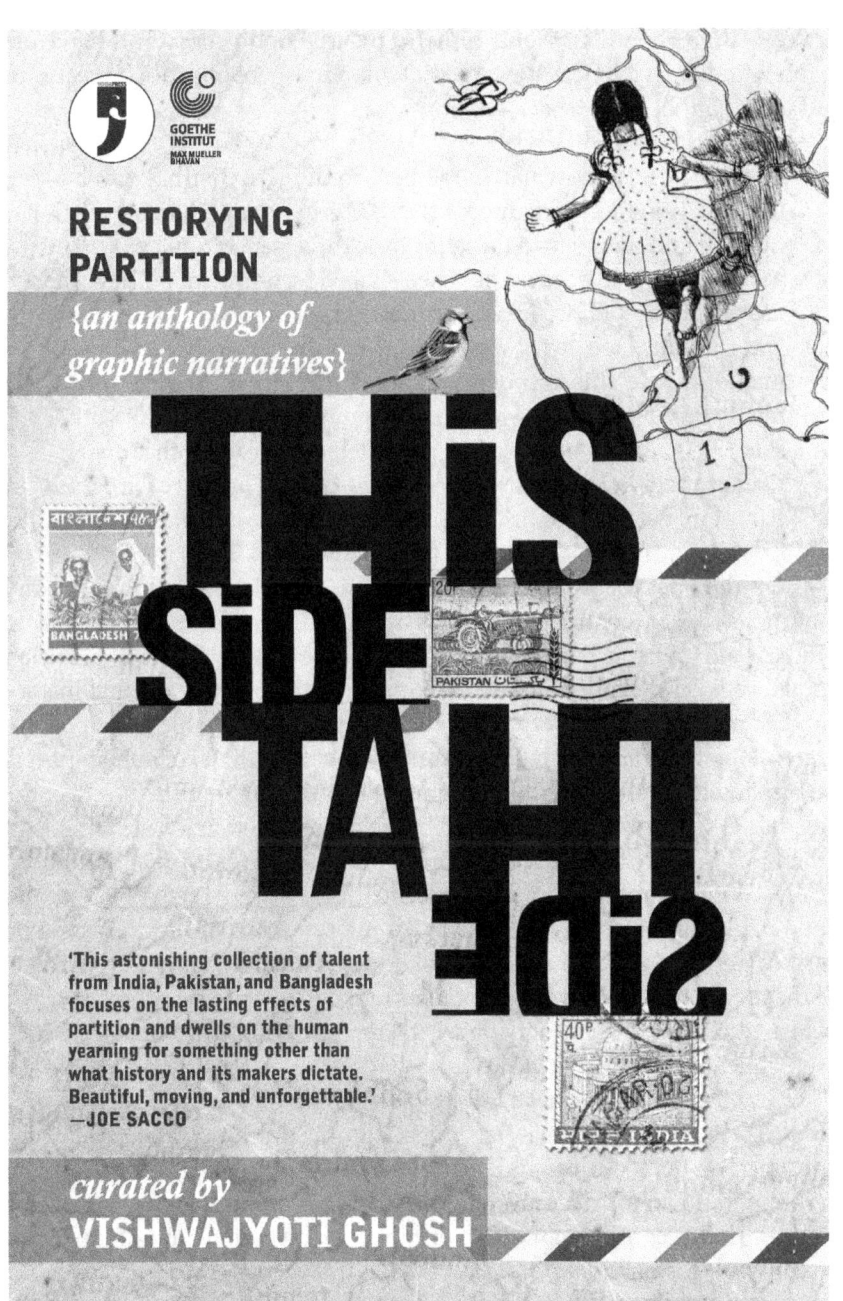

Figure 1.6: *This Side, That Side: Restorying Partition.* Courtesy of Yoda Press.

conversation about Partition—hitherto focused on memory and survivors who witnessed violence—toward contemporary geopolitical connections. As stated on the book's back cover:

> The most decisive formative moment in modern South Asian history, Partition has remained a site of constant engagement, investigation and memory-making for over three generations. Over the years, Partition discourse has been shaped by prevalent politics, the use of faith for political reasons, a nod to nostalgia, a cocktail of facts and rumours laced with speculation, and the scholarly exchange of memories.... This anthology explores a dominant theme in contemporary South Asia—an enduring curiosity about the "other side." Poignant, contemplative, and often even playful, these narratives are creative explorations by those who may not have witnessed Partition, but who continue, to date, to negotiate its legacy.

On the book's cover, acclaimed Maltese American graphic artist and journalist Joe Sacco proclaims, "This astonishing collection of talent from India, Pakistan and Bangladesh focuses on the lasting effects of partition and dwells on the human yearning for something other than what history and its makers dictate. Beautiful, moving, and unforgettable." The positive reception of *This Side, That Side* in transnational South Asian public spheres traversing India and Pakistan is impressive. Although some believe that the terrible ethnic violence of Partition is given less attention in this anthology than it is due, critics praise the transnational, collaborative, and aesthetically diverse graphic narratives presented here as moving, resonant, and powerful. Ghosh's own response in an interview in part addresses some critics' reservations about the anthology's approach to Partition violence: "The idea here was to use a graphic narrative to explore the whole concept of Partition, not to focus only on what happened back then but also on how subsequent generations negotiated with it."[27]

Graphic narratives have a long history in India, dating back to premodern sequential art that accompanied oral traditions and largely did not include text.[28] In the nineteenth century, the circulation of colonial representational forms, especially the British magazine *Punch*, generated a lively tradition of cartooning in print media, including but not limited to its Indian version, *Oudh Punch*. As Bharath Murthy notes, subsequently, imported British and American superhero comic books largely dominated the consumption of graphic narratives. In the 1960s, the Hindi comic strip made its appearance in Indian newspapers and, with Pran Kumar Sharma's "Chacha Chaudhary" character, quickly became popular. However, only when the *ACK* series was launched in 1967 by Anant Pai's India Book House did Indian sequential art, or graphic narratives, become firmly established in Indian cultural life.[29] Today, more than ninety million copies of *ACK*'s more than four hundred titles in twenty languages have been sold; an app also disseminates its comics about major religious, historical, and mythological figures (which range from Gandhi, the Rani of Jhansi, and Akbar to Mother Teresa, Kabir, Zarathustra, and Shivaji) and historic events (such as the establishment of the Mughal empire, the anti-colonial freedom struggle, and the 1965 Indo-China War); stories from the Hindu epics Ramayana and Mahabharata; and stories from folk parables (such as Jataka Tales and Panchatantra Tales). (See Figures 1.7, 1.8, 1.9, and 1.10.)

Several scholars, including Karline McLain and Nandini Chandra, have well illuminated the historical development of *ACK* titles and their peculiar negotiation of the comic form toward an indigenous nationalist idea of culture. Chandra's analysis tracks the historical emergence and transformation of the *ACK* books as aesthetic practices in "the skein of the national," cultural commodities, and pedagogical objects that invented new rhetorics about religion, nationalism, and modernity in India. Among her arguments is that, although the *ACK* series "may represent an ideal Hindu state underwritten by the ideology of feudalism . . . it derives its profit from the bourgeois capitalist state."[30] As I note elsewhere, the pedagogical goals of the *ACK* comics, with their investment in disseminating Indian historical, folk, and mythological stories to reinforce a bourgeois Hindu nationalism, meant that the modern Indian graphic novel—intended for adult consumption and deeply linked to the project of political critique—would not emerge until 1994.[31] In 1994, the Indian state's Narmada Dam Project (with its ecological devastation and mass rural displacement) inspired Orijit Sen's graphic novel *River of Stories* (1994), which was followed by Sarnath Banerjee's *Corridor* (2004). These and other works that followed, including Amruta Patil's *Kari* (2008), Vishwajyoti Ghosh's *Delhi Calm* (2010), Durgabai Vyam et al.'s *Bhimayana* (2011), and Malik Sajad's *Munnu: A Boy from Kashmir* (2015), are considered among the most important Indian graphic narratives. Indian graphic novels' deep commitment to the horizon of the public and the political aligns them with the work of such artists as Art Spiegelman, Marjane Satrapi, and Joe Sacco. As Ghosh notes, "I think Indian graphic novels have made brave choices in terms of content, picking up the Narmada Dam, picking up urban queer movements, sex, politics, the Emergency, caste. I don't think there is a specialized readership for graphic novels in India. They are readers who become readers of graphic novels as well."[32] The Indian comics scene has grown exponentially in the last decade, and comics are published by established presses like HarperCollins as well as new entrepreneurial publication houses like Blaft and Yoda Press; ComicCon was held in India in 2012, as was the Anime Convention in 2013. Ghosh himself is part of

Figure 1.7: Amar Chitra Katha, *The Great Mughals* cover. Courtesy of Amar Chitra Katha Media.

Figure 1.8: Amar Chitra Katha, *Jesus Christ* cover. Courtesy of Amar Chitra Katha Media.

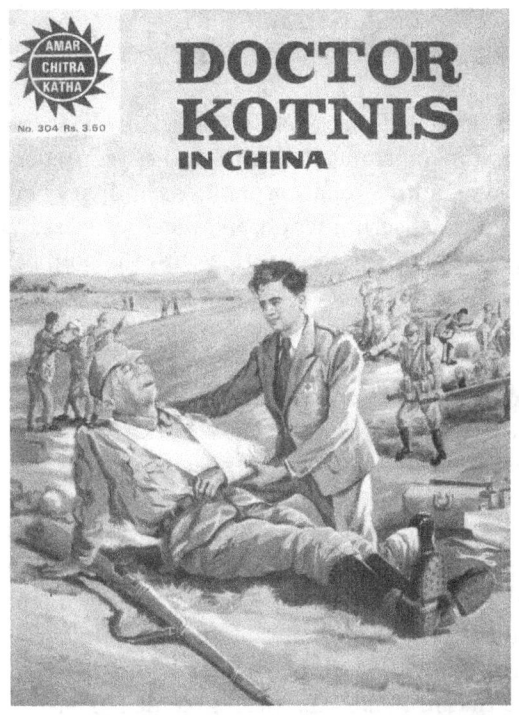

Figure 1.9: Amar Chitra Katha, *Doctor Kotnis in China* cover. Courtesy of Amar Chitra Katha Media.

Figure 1.10: Panels from *Kumbhakarna*, Amar Chitra Katha vol. 528. Courtesy of Amar Chitra Katha Media.

two collectives—the Pao Collective and Inverted Commas—that produce graphic narratives in several languages, including English, for a variety of contexts.

In a different context, I have argued that what is distinctive about the contemporary South Asian graphic narrative is "its critical edge: gender-based violence, forced migration, multinational corporations, military violence, caste oppression, ethno-racial discrimination, and water wars fissure social experience in this archive."[33] This preoccupation with the political anchors *This Side, That Side* as well. Several scholars working on diverse national cultures have analyzed the relationship between comics and political critique, exploring how comics bear witness as they represent history. While Monica Chiu shows how many Asian American comics also function as "ethnic stories,"[34] Hillary Chute suggests that American feminist and queer graphic narratives represent traumatic intimacies in ways that "put the body on the page."[35] Extending this argument to Satrapi's *Persepolis*, Chute argues, "*Persepolis* is about the ethical visual and verbal practice of 'not forgetting' and the political confluence of the everyday and the historical: through its verbal and visual witnessing, it contests dominant images and narratives of history."[36] Indeed, Chute later insists, "comics is a form *disposed* to witness [italics original]."[37] Similarly, Martha J. Cutter and Cathy J. Schlund-Vials argue that in Asian American graphic narratives, "the past is evocatively renarrated, provocatively reconfigured, and strategically remade in multiethnic graphic novels." As a result, they note, graphic narratives "have the ability to return to the traumatic past and construct a new reality that acknowledges the dehumanizing nature of much of what we consider history."[38] These insights about how American and multiethnic graphic narratives represent history and bear witness inform my approach to the intervention of *This Side, That Side*. Below, I consider the following questions: How do the narratives in this anthology bear witness? What kind of work—documenting, witnessing, reimagining, or translating—do they do? How does this visual-verbal form intervene in South Asian public sphere discourses about gendered displacement, the crisis of secularism, and loss in the postcolonial nation-state? What fugitive knowledge does the book offer about what remains after Partition—about survival and geopolitical conflict?

I proffer that the anthology's intervention lies in how its diverse image-text negotiations restory Partition in the public imagination. They instigate us to rethink subjectivity and embodied trauma in the midst of world-historical and violent conflicts; challenging elite historiography about the pastness of its migrations, they unveil Partition's legacies and its ongoing violence for people who are still fighting to belong, to have citizenship, and to have access to a safe, dignified life. *This Side, That Side* does so by revisiting the momentous historical "events" of 1947 and 1971 and by challenging their "pastness" in conventional historiography. The anthology argues that the events of 1947 and 1971 are very much alive, and still happening. Its diverse narratives put the human body on the page through an eco-critical frame; further, the anthology's visual testimony about statelessness emerges through its eco-critical representation of the embodied experience of violent conflict, past as well as present, as well as its intergenerational inheritance and transmittal. Finally, in the transnational and often feminist provenance of its contributors as well as of the protagonists of its migration stories, these narratives envision and enact the subaltern secular under siege in contemporary South Asia.

Aesthetically, the heterogeneity of style and technique across *This Side, That Side* is unique. Some of the stories follow a conventional layout of horizontal and sequential panels in a grid format, with evenly spaced gutters. But in most stories, the layout of panels is unconventional and unpredictable. Sometimes, a panel occupies a whole page; at other times, following Will Eisner's preference for unframed panels that then allow for a fluid dialogue between them, the frames for juxtaposed panels are missing. In some, the gutters are laid out diagonally, disorienting our perspective as we attempt to follow the story's chronological narrative arc, thus muddling our sense of time and space as if inscribing the disorientation of Partition's displacement. Several narratives use photography to assert a documentary realism or invoke mass-media technologies. In many stories, the protagonists are not centered mid-ground; they often occupy the peripheries of the full-page frame, appearing in the foreground or background. Further, in some panels, their bodies are only partially visible in the frame. This divided, partial, and peripheral embodied presence suggests that refugees and citizens alike are rendered peripheral by national history. In some stories, the use of graphic weight through shading, shadows, and patterns accompanies subjects perched precariously on the boundaries of the frame, bleeding into the space beyond the page. In the story "A Letter from India," written by Mahmood Farooqui (adapted from an Urdu story by Intizar Hussain) and illustrated by Fariha Rehman, the use of shading, of light and dark, creates perspectival depth, suggesting that this refugee story is being recovered from the dusty recesses of time. "The Red Ledger" by Ankur Ahuja invokes the melancholic grief of Ahuja's grandfather, a refugee in Delhi. The story ends with a drawing of an official government document affirming his refugee status. The presence of this object as the concluding image of this story bears incomplete witness to his traumatic displacement, inserting the past in the present. "An Old Fable" by Tabish Khair and Priya Kurian draws upon biblical imagery to offer a searing allegory of decolonization. Here, the Partition of India is depicted as the murder of a newborn by a British king. The nation is allegorized as a baby murdered, and the image depicting this fragmentation is so abstract—suggesting that representing it would be impossible—that only by reading the accompanying text can we decipher the outcome. This story on the one hand speaks to how embodied trauma focalizes so many transnational graphic narratives. However, here, the nation is materialized as a child's unrecognizable body, mutilated and murdered by a British king, to symbolize the collective trauma created by decolonization.

In his study of the Indian graphic novel, Pramod Nayar argues, "The graphic narrative, with its verbal-visual and critical literacy, is the medium India *needs* to address contemporary concerns and provide a politically edged cultural critique [italics original]."[39] *This Side, That Side* is politically engaged, with narratives that revolve around border crossings, geopolitical conflict, refugee experiences, and the failures of the postcolonial nation-state. The anthology, however, eschews a focus on ethnic violence (something that has been well documented in Partition Studies thus far) to reflect on the refugee experience and its legacies. This focus on migration and border crossing from 1947 to 2012 opens a new approach to Partition: it invites us to explore what has been created, and what remains, after 1947. It is my contention that in telling these migration stories, the anthology animates a subaltern secular that contests the hegemony of the postcolonial state. It illuminates the perspectives and memories of Partition refugees and of their grandchildren, contemplating their inheritance of loss; and, later in the anthology, of the refugees and descendants of the 1971 War of Bangladesh—many of whom are working-class teachers, housewives, and poor students still living in a refugee colony called "Geneva Camp" in Dhaka.

I comment primarily on three dimensions of the aesthetic and cultural intervention of this anthology, although I hope that future scholarship will further explore the multiple interventions it offers. The first is that many narratives are preoccupied with the fraught relationship between refugees and citizens on the one hand and the postcolonial state on the other. As such, they articulate a critique of the state, as this chapter's epigraph invites; further, they resonate with Hannah Arendt's critique of the mid-twentieth century's state production of statelessness and internment by rendering precarity sharply and poignantly visible. For instance, Ghosh contributes an autobiographical narrative called "A Good Education," in which he depicts his own childhood education about refugees through his grandmother Amiya Sen, also an early Partition refugee. (See Figure 1.11.) Sen's story and voice are framed for us by the child who listens, hears, and so bears witness to refugee history. For instance, several panels depict Ghosh as a child listening in and looking at her: through him, we hear snippets of conversations between Sen and her husband, and we learn of her nightly diary writing, through which she pours out her contradictory feelings about her

Figure 1.11: Panels from "A Good Education," in *This Side, That Side*. Courtesy of Yoda Press.

work as a rehabilitation officer. Through both, we learn of Sen's compassion for other refugees like her as well as her deep ambivalence about her job.

Evident in this narrative is her sense of her complicity with the state's ethical violence in addressing refugees from the 1965 and 1971 wars: her assignment is to separate Bengali refugee children from their mothers to place them in orphanages in Delhi with the promise of "a good education" and a good life. In a two-page panel that has no frame, Ghosh radically draws the nation's map as one made up of multitudes of refugees; the words and images combine to depict refugees' bodies as constitutive of the nation (in the image) and as subject to violent governance, poverty, and the failures of the postcolonial state (in the text). (See Figure 1.12.)

As in many other comics, the meaning of the narrative emerges in the dissonance between the image and the text. Under the image is epistolary text, which constitutes a palimpsest presenting Sen's writings about her work. On the previous page, Ghosh as our narrator reveals that in the night, after work, Sen would take refuge in writing about her experiences: "And once I slept, would begin Didu's second life, her writing. Late into the night,

Figure 1.12: Two-page depiction of a refugee camp from "A Good Education," in *This Side, That Side*. Courtesy of Yoda Press.

when the world slept, her stories based on her daily encounters would awake to light and freedom. Passionate and possessed, writing was her only refuge from a clerical, ruthless world of files and forms."[40] This refuge appears in the epistolary text under the image of India as refugee nation, as Sen's voice describes the arrival of refugees in Mana Camp as part of the Dandakaranya Project, on the outskirts of Raipur, where she also worked. The Dandakaranya Project was established in 1958, as the Indian government took over at least twenty thousand square miles of water-rich "tribal" or indigenous land on which to house refugees of the 1947 Partition arriving from East Pakistan:[41]

> I am told that right now 35,000 are living here in Mana Camp. Farmers, sweet-makers, blacksmiths, potters and cobblers from East Bengal. Unlike us, the privileged who moved at the very outset, these are the real lambs of partition. Pushed by the unanticipated attack of death, they've reached the Indian border. The very sight of them made the West Bengal government scream. "There's no space here—we can't accommodate them." Despite being unlettered and

helpless, they show such dignity! But who will understand! We are such a self-oblivious race.[42]

Here, Sen has a double voice: she speaks as a refugee who recognizes her own material privileged circumstances in her relatively early arrival to India, and as a state representative who sees the government's cruel and deliberate failure to help the impoverished incoming refugees. This moment importantly recasts Partition: contra the tendency to discuss it as an event of 1947, it reminds us that the enactment of decolonization through Partition generated migrations that continued even a decade later in South Asia. Further, it gestures to the transnational response to this unfolding history in South Asia through its mention of the U.S. international aid efforts. On the far right of this two-page unframed panel, we see an image of a man wearing a hat with stars and stripes, standing by a single drum with a label reading, "USAID." This American figure says, "I want you to have US milk." Adjacent to him, a female figure, probably Sen, is depicted as holding up a cup and saying to the emaciated refugee children looking up at her with wide eyes, "This is a result of America's magnanimity. While others got Patton tanks, we got unlimited milk powder. We should remain grateful to America. Please bring your cup and stand in a queue!"[43]

The contrasting images in this spread—a small, single drum of milk and the large numbers of refugees depicted across the page (in the shape of the country)—powerfully suggest how vast the challenge was, and how tragically limited the resources and aid were, to assist refugees. Panels covering an entire page or sometimes two pages are often used to make a dramatic point in the narrative, to add weight and details that would be impossible to render in a smaller panel. This two-page spread effectively draws our attention to individual expressions (many look bewildered and lost) as well as the embodied details of a large number of refugees of different ages, genders, and classes. Many look emaciated, and many children are naked, depicting the precarity and poverty of these migrants. Sen's words in the caption also ironically acknowledge the two dimensions of U.S. foreign policy as part of the Cold War, which had dramatic legacies for international relations between India and Pakistan: weapons sales and humanitarian aid.

The narrative's critique of the state is further marked in the confessional epistolary text underneath, wherein Sen recognizes the violence and trauma generated by the family separations she enacted on behalf of the Indian state:

> Simply put, my job is to counsel and convince mothers to send their kids to Delhi. . . . They would have to let go of their children for years! That's exactly how it was meant to work. These boys and girls

wouldn't be returning before they could be on their own. We are talking of 15–20 years. Here, their world changes within minutes; who knows if Mana Camp will exist when they return? Even if it does, these destitute women might get lost in the deep crannies of the forest.[44]

Here, Sen acknowledges that the family separation policy she is implementing will likely permanently separate mothers from their children; through her, the multiple modes of ongoing state violence generating precarity in the name of "rehabilitation" experienced by women and children become visible in a popular visual medium. This double-page panel poignantly bears witness to the forgotten history of the state and its refugees in South Asia. The narrative makes visible the mid-twentieth-century history of and the modern internationalization of family separation policies. That such family separation policies continue to be deployed for migrants and refugees on the U.S. southern border signals the entrenched nature of global internment regimes naturalized by the modern nation-state system, which Arendt warns us against. Here, as in other contributions in the anthology, refugee stories contest and disavow ethno-nationalism, even as they foreground, at times, the failures of the postcolonial state.

Like this narrative's foregrounding of Sen's work with female and child refugees, the second fascinating dimension of this anthology is that many of its stories dwell on the shape and texture of Partition's losses and legacies for female subjects across South Asia. This attention to how gender inhabits migration stories and marks specific forms of precarity resonates with the focus of literary fiction on Partition, including Shauna Singh Baldwin's *What the Body Remembers*, Arundhati Roy's *The Ministry of Utmost Happiness*, and Bapsi Sidhwa's *Cracking India*, which I discuss in the next chapter. For example, Malini Gupta and Dyuti Mittal's "The Taboo," Syeda Farhana and Nitesh Mohanty's "Little Women," and Maria M. Litwa's "Welcome to Geneva Camp" are stories about the gendered precarity of multigenerational female refugees and citizens, as girls and women lose family members to migration, dream of getting an education, struggle to find work, and battle the loss of land—negotiating persistent discrimination and statelessness. In some of these works, as I discuss later, everyday life becomes the site for the enunciation of the subaltern secular by the minor, gendered migrant/refugee/citizen. Within the rhetoric of colonialism and ethno-nationalism, as many feminist scholars from Radha Kumar to Sangeeta Ray have shown, the female subject is constructed as patriarchal object and communal property. Feminist historiography as well as literary and graphic narratives have challenged these hegemonic narratives that subject women to specific, gender-based violence in moments of political conflict.[45] In *This Side*,

That Side, the female subject, as stateless or citizen subject, rejects ethnonationalism. Through the articulation of aspirations, critiques, and memories, female subjects in these migration stories enact a subaltern secularism that belies official narratives about nation, rehabilitation, and belonging. Given that women have largely been marginalized in the historiography of Partition, the illumination of women's stories is central to the graphic and literary political intervention across these texts (and, more broadly, across the archive of South Asian and South Asian American literature). By illuminating the heterogeneous experience of gendered migrants and survivors as they perform the secular in mid- and late-twentieth-century South Asia, these works constitute a counterarchive that challenges the elisions of dominant national histories.

Gupta and Mittal's "The Taboo" revolves around women's lives in Cooper's Camp in 1999, narrating the diverse forms of enterprise, survival, and agency that a microfinance officer witnesses in women's personal and economic lives. Across several two-page spreads that depict a refugee camp humming with activity and refugee life, speech bubbles introduce us to the history, ecological challenges, and state failures that plague the camp's denizens. As one speech bubble reads ironically, "Cooper's Camp is one of the largest refugee transit camps in West Bengal. Established in 1950, we were registered in the Ranaghat transit camp. A lot of us here still think this is a transit camp. That we will be rehabilitated."[46] By depicting women's voices from different religious and class backgrounds, this narrative bears witness to the failed promises of state rehabilitation and the bias and discrimination from local citizens that refugees face. Yet the narrative presents "a couple of thousand women" who are busy, struggling, and surviving in varied ways in the camp: we encounter Lily, an independent and successful garage owner admired by all the women; a woman "running for panchayat elections"; Sumati, whose husband throws her out of her home "again"; and more. As the narrator, Malini, explains in response to her own question, "What were the women doing?": "They were saving money, taking loans, buying and selling everything from school books to goats, cultivating land on lease, arguing with banks that refused to allow them accounts, attending gram sabhas. And every woman was fighting her own private battle."[47] Gupta and Mittal thus inscribe the complexity of female refugees' lives with an ethical commitment that recognizes them as active agents who rebuild and survive in the camp, while criticizing the postcolonial state's failure to offer them rehabilitation and redress. In one of the panels, one Cooper's Camp resident poignantly says, "Maybe nothing happened here for we were refugees from the backward castes? Who knows. . . ."[48] This narrative is one of the few that gestures to how caste, in addition to gender, shaped refugee experience and the government's rehabilitation practices.

While caste is acknowledged unevenly in many visual representations of the Partition migrations, class, gender, and religion occupy a more prominent space as forces that shape citizenship and displacement. For instance, "Karachi Delhi Katha" by Sonya Fatah and Archana Sreenivasan is set in post-liberalization Delhi and follows its protagonist, Sonya, as she shuttles back and forth between Karachi and Delhi. Fatah's biography reveals that she discovered the complications of Indo-Pak identities after she moved to India with her husband in 2006 from Pakistan. Presumably then, the narrative is set at this time, in the early twenty-first century. The secular and the state appear in this narrative in two ways: through a focus on gendered experience and domestic space. The narrative moves spatially back and forth between Karachi and Delhi; after every two pages, we see the protagonist—the upper-class Muslim housewife, Sonya—in a different city. In both cities, Sonya's conversations with domestic workers reflect how citizenship and everyday life have become increasingly ethnicized in India and Pakistan, in ways that diminish equal rights and secular inclusion. In the panels set in Karachi, Sonya's conversations with a Hindu couple Paro and Hemu who work in her mother's Karachi home reflect the vulnerability and anxieties of Pakistan's Hindu minorities. Paro and Hemu are shown as continually debating whether they should stay in Pakistan or go to India. At one point, Hemu tells Sonya that he would like to take their children to visit their "homeland" of India. When Sonya asks, "Isn't this [Pakistan] your homeland?" he replies, "Well, you know, the Hindu homeland. Here, it's becoming increasingly difficult for us."[49] Paro describes to Sonya the shrinking public space for equal citizenship and secular inclusion in Pakistan for its Hindu minorities: "Array Sonya, you'd remember there was a time when we wouldn't think twice about wearing bindis and saris. We went around town, and went to our mandirs ... all that's gone. Now we dress like that only for our family weddings."[50] Thus, the narrative presents a Pakistani Hindu woman as she mourns the loss of sartorial freedom that signifies Hindu identity; indirectly, this concern constitutes evidence of the growing discrimination against a visible ethnic minority in Karachi's urban public sphere, when difference is recognizable through dress. In the next panel, Sonya is depicted as sadly acknowledging to them, "I know. It's terrible, terrible."[51] This panel's illustration suggests that she recalls Jinnah's asserting when Pakistan was formed in 1947, "You are free to go to your mosques, you are free to go to your churches and to your temples."[52] Even as Jinnah's past aspirations for religious freedom and secular inclusive community in Pakistan are recalled, this narrative acknowledges the loss of those freedoms and the growing crisis of secularism on *this side and that side*. Its transnational story, about a protagonist who goes back and forth, unveils the experiences of minoritization that have accrued to Hindus in Pakistan and to Muslims in India since the late twentieth century.

"Karachi Delhi Katha" bears witness to the crisis of secularism in India differently: it presents Sonya's engagement with the story of a poor Bangladeshi woman named Syeda, who is living in Delhi. Syeda changes her name to the more Hindu-sounding name Vimla to pass as Hindu. She also starts wearing a bindi. As a destitute refugee in Delhi, she needs a job, and she knows that her Muslim name will invite discrimination. Sonya hires Syeda (as Vimla) as a domestic worker. Eventually, Syeda discloses her Muslim identity to Sonya. As the narrative traces their interactions, an unlikely intimacy seems to grow between them. However, in the visual embodiment of the characters, Syeda's face is the only face that is given no detail: in fact, it is curiously pixelated, unlike the other protagonists, whose clearly defined faces and expressions convey such feelings as anxiety, worry, joy, and so on. Halfway through the narrative, in one panel, Syeda finally announces that she has a "ration card"—that much-coveted state-issued identification (ID) card signifying legal status. (See Figure 1.13.)

The ration card materializes her faciality and, by extension, her embodied humanity: from this panel on, her face is no longer pixelated. This aesthetic strategy vividly calls attention to the dehumanization of modern governmentality. Simultaneously, it depicts the melancholic refugee as a canny survivor of these discriminatory milieus. The cross-class, interethnic friendship between Sonya in India and Paro and Hemu in Pakistan, across the borders, also makes visible a subaltern secular affect that lives on in everyday life in the postcolonial nation-state. Sonya becomes a reluctant interlocutor in this couple's confused discussions about whether they should uproot their lives and move to India; central to this discussion is the fact of gendered violence and the abduction of Hindu women and girls by Muslim men in Pakistan. Although accurate data on the issue is hard to find, journalistic reports about the abduction of Hindu women and girls suggest that there is some truth to Paro's fears. Staring directly at the reader, a close-up of Paro's face shows an expression of fear that her daughter Kanika will be abducted: "It's just that things have become so difficult here. I fear for Kanika. The horror stories about girls being kidnapped. . . ."[53] In the next panel, Sonya is shown as looking away and saying, "God, I know. This is becoming a sick, bigoted society."[54] This narrative thus criticizes the gendered dehumanization experienced by religious minorities in India and Pakistan and foregrounds how violence against girls and women in the form of abduction, sexual assault, and forced conversion, which was widespread during the 1947 Partition migrations, persists in present-day Pakistan. In this way, "Karachi Delhi Katha" extends the critique of the

Figure 1.13: Panels from "Karachi Delhi Katha," in *This Side, That Side*. Courtesy of Yoda Press.

dehumanization of minorities in Bangladesh, also evident elsewhere in this anthology. Paro, Hemu, and Sonya's cross-religion, cross-class dialogue thus refracts multiple subalternities, as does Sonya and Syeda's relationship. Articulating India, Pakistan, and Bangladesh, it also traces how Sonya and Paro hold on to and perform a subaltern secular bond in the midst of growing religious extremism.

Chute argues that "comics is powerful precisely in how it intervenes against the trauma-driven discourse of the unrepresentable and ineffable"; for her, the "current prominence of comics, especially in our twenty-first-century age of global wars and endemic violence, indicates desire for forms of aesthetic expression that do face history and trauma, that even document it visually—as opposed to sacralizing its absence."[55] Extending this argument, I suggest that Ghosh's comics anthology faces the persistent, hidden violence of mid-twentieth-century decolonization and its legacies of transnational displacement; it bears witness to memory, grief, survival, and secular formations in the everyday lives of refugees and their descendants across South Asia as well as in the United Kingdom.

Thus, for instance, Maria M. Litwa's narrative "Welcome to Geneva Camp" is set in 2011 Dhaka, Bangladesh, and illuminates the refugee experience of women and girls living there. Its panels include black-and-white photographs accompanied by text to represent the lives, aspirations, and disappointments of people still living in a refugee camp since the 1971 war. (See Figure 1.14.) These photographs are drawn from Litwa's photo film *Inside Geneva Camp* (2012), which focuses on the Urdu-speaking Muslim people ("Biharis") who were expelled during the 1971 war and became internally stateless, living in ghettolike refugee camps in Dhaka for thirty-seven years. (Toward the end, the text informs us that approximately 250,000 stateless "so-called Biharis" in Bangladesh were finally allowed to apply for national ID cards in 2008). In Geneva Camp, approximately twenty-five thousand refugees live in an area the size of three football fields. Focusing mostly on women through a mix of close-ups as well as portrait-style photographs, Litwa draws upon a documentary realism in her photography to present the perspectives of three female residents of the camp: Rina (fourteen, a housewife), Shabnam (twenty, a student), and Putul (twenty-four, a teacher). In the process, the narrative invites readers to engage its postcolonial feminist critique of how gender, language, war, and nationalism intersect to produce the precarity of Geneva Camp's girls and women. For example, Rina, a child bride who is not a Bihari, is nonetheless stuck in Geneva Camp. The first-person textual narrative accompanying the photographs indicates that she would like to get an education. However, that dream is impossible, given the poverty of her sixteen-member family. In the photo collage about Rina, the ninth panel shows a photograph of a caged

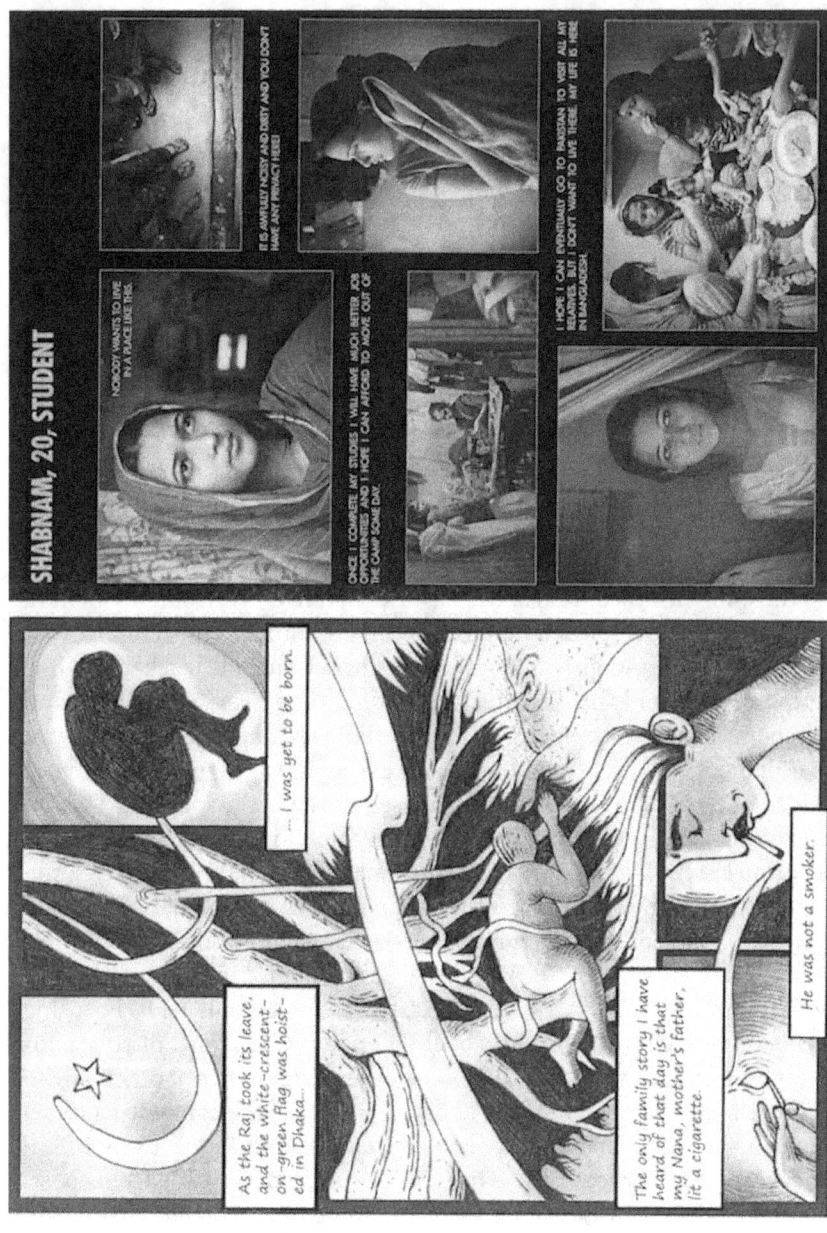

Figure 1.14: Panels from "Profit and Loss" and "Geneva Camp," in *This Side, That Side*. Courtesy of Yoda Press.

parrot looking to the left, into the distance.⁵⁶ On this page, it functions in dual ways: first, it evokes a popular image in the iconography of middle-class and working-class domestic life in South Asia, as many people keep caged birds as pets. Second, because the last panel on this page presents a close-up photo of Rina's sad face, with her unsmiling eyes looking into the distance in the same direction as the parrot, the collage draws an analogy between the parrot's entrapment in the cage and Rina's entrapment in Geneva Camp, bequeathed by the events of 1947 and 1971. Both lives are inextricably linked in postcolonial ecologies of unfreedom.

"Welcome to Geneva Camp" next presents the story of twenty-year-old college student Shabnam. The caption that accompanies the photographs in this section is in Shabnam's voice: her words indicate that she has some freedom from being assimilated into marriage as Rina has been. She imagines education as the only way to escape the camp and her precarious existence, and she aspires to be integrated into the national-social fabric of Bangladesh. She also says that although she would like to visit her relatives in Pakistan, "my life is here in Bangladesh."⁵⁷ Finally, the twenty-four-year-old schoolteacher Putul reveals in her story that the government has not paid her salary for four months. Putul worries that the school will close if this nonpayment continues, leaving the stateless children of the camp bereft of an education. This narrative ends with a collage of photographs of an old lady, a young girl, a father holding two toddler girls, and, among others, a sign atop one of the camp's structures that reads, "Stranded Pakistanis General Repatriation Committee." As Mahruba Mowtushi notes, "The spatial disarray inside the camp reflects the women's emotional disarray."⁵⁸ These snapshots, when juxtaposed, document the vulnerability and poverty of everyday life for these stateless people abandoned by nation-states (Pakistan and Bangladesh); they also illuminate the double displacement of Muslim Biharis, who fled from Bihar, India, to what was then East Pakistan in 1947 to escape violence against Muslims and then were forced to run again in 1971, when Bangladesh seceded from West Pakistan, to escape violence against those who speak Urdu. Litwa notes that the "Urdu-speaking community of Bangladesh has remained stateless for 37 years." It was not until 2008 that "they were finally allowed to apply for the national ID card of Bangladesh."⁵⁹ This modern production of statelessness, a legacy of the 1947 Partition, bears out Arendt's critique of the nation-state system. It also illuminates the complex contours of refugee experiences and the causes of statelessness that turn on not only religious differences but also language, caste, class, gender, and so forth.

Cutter and Schlund-Vials observe that "given the visual registers of the medium and historical preoccupations of form, as well as the focus on collecting and archiving experiences that have been fissured and broken," many multiethnic graphic narratives engage photography in diverse ways: "Integral to many multiethnic graphic novels is a re-seeing of history, and central to these revisionist works is an archival project of reassemblage."[60] This archival project of reassemblage is also at work in "Welcome to Geneva Camp," as its photographs renarrativize the history of Bangladesh by reassembling the disparate fragments of Urdu-speaking migrants' stories. These stories unveil the trauma and dispossessions of experiencing recurring displacement from 1947 to 1971 due to religion and linguistic minoritization. This expulsion endures for those economically impoverished migrants' families across generations, well into the twenty-first century. By unveiling it, Litwa's narrative demonstrates the failure of the Bangladeshi state to protect and offer redress to its own minority citizens. Because of its use of photography, this narrative does not share the playful aspect of hand-drawn illustrations of a majority of the anthology's pieces. As Mowtushi observes, "However poignant and striking in its execution, Litwa's depictions of camp life eschew the precariousness of critical issues such as the safety and security concerns of women seeking asylum in internment camps."[61] Although Litwa's ironically titled "Welcome to Geneva Camp" does not address sexual violence or its threat, the visual economy of its multilayered collage of photojournalistic as well as abstract images that depict three stateless female subjects' migration stories bears witness to their gendered struggles and stasis in the face of nationality and patriarchy. It indexes their precariousness and invites empathy for their individual stories, aspirations, and labors.

The third dimension that links many of the stylistically different narratives as an archive of the subaltern secular is the restorying of the relationship between human and nonhuman worlds. Their recasting of national history through an eco-critical frame is striking: if land is at the heart of Partition, then trees, roots, rivers, flowers, and especially birds (doves, crows, pigeons, sparrows, and vultures) often populate the frames in which gendered bodies feel trapped or free, lay down or reach skyward as if in agony, as if enumerating what is lost and imagining flight to an alternative life. If Partition divided societies by creating borders, nonhuman forces like trees, rivers, birds, and roots have repeatedly defied these political borders and crossed them as well as the panels' frames. In some narratives, they embrace and envelope gendered bodies fleeing violence outside the frame, as if attempting to protect and shelter them. Taken together, these experimental narratives emblematize what Suvadip Sinha and Amit Baishya call "postcolonial animalities," which "is a call for a radical erasure of the bar between human and non-human animals." As they explain, "Postcolonial animalities, as a methodology or conceptual framework, promises to provoke an ontological and political miscegenation that constantly alerts us about the need of a multivalent reading of violence and precarity."⁶² Many of the narratives in this anthology enact such a multispecies miscegenation of life-forms; in them, the refugee subject is an embodied self in an ecosystem that intricately binds human and nonhuman animals with the state, memories, and the secular. In this sense, they visualize "embodied memories" and make visible "a multiplicity of overlapping bonds and identities" that articulate a subaltern secular under siege in the homogenous time of the postcolonial nation-state.⁶³

Multispecies life-forms—especially birds—appear as important actors in the works across this anthology. One of the most vivid instances of image-text negotiations in which birds play a central role is found in Farhana and Mohanty's "Little Women." In many panels, birds represent an invitation to cross the border, as the protagonist, Tara, whose name means "star," narrates her experiences of exile. The first panel of the narrative contains this text etched on a black background, with an image of the moon that represents nocturnal time: "I want to be a Tree."⁶⁴ The tree represents rootedness and belonging, for the text across the panel under this line reveals, "Tara, the star in Bengali, never came from the skies above. . . ." Then, the second panel allows for the continuity of this origin story, with an illustration of a photograph of a man and a sketch of a woman. The text accompanying this illustration completes the sentence of the previous panel: ". . . but from a Bihari father and a Bengali mother who lived below them."⁶⁵ In the third panel on this page, the image is a centered photograph of a young woman as she hugs the roots of a tree to the right, while she is flanked on the left with an illustration of fish in watery waves. The accompanying text in this panel presents her voice to us: "So who am I? A Bengali or a Bihari?"⁶⁶ In the midst of this multispecies ecosystem, the postcolonial subject Tara is adrift due to her hybrid regional-cultural as well as linguistic Bihari-Bengali heritage—one that centers the conflict in Bangladesh in 1971.

The critique of statelessness and life in refugee camps in "Little Women" appears in complex and poignant ways. We see Tara displaced as a refugee due to her heritage; in one panel, Tara explains that she finds herself "in this refugee camp, engrossed in a daily struggle for survival"⁶⁷ (see Figure 1.15). However, the illustration depicts her as flying above and out of the camp, arms outstretched, surrounded by birds, as if flying away with them across the borders and out of the entrapment of refugee camps. Resonant with the opening panels that present Tara's desire to become a tree, a later three-panel page contains an illustration that superimposes a photograph of a tree and Tara's hands (see Figure 1.16). The accompanying text signals

Figure 1.15: Single-panel page from "Little Women," in *This Side, That Side.* Courtesy of Yoda Press.

Tara's intergenerational trauma as well as her articulation of a multispecies mode of being that rejects ethnic and linguistic differences that ground postcolonial nationalisms:

> *I have no past and*
> *don't know if there's any future ahead.*
> *I know I have a present.*
> *If I close my eyes, I can see my roots*
> *Entering the soil, this land I stand on.*[68]

The precarious refugee survives the nation and claims the land she stands on. In some panels across many narratives, the illustrations resonate with the text; in others, their dissonance produces "an effect of disjuncture."[69] If birds in flight sometimes link with humans in flight, they also challenge, in some panels, the ideas of partition and nationalism. In "Which Side?" by Ravish Kumar, Ikroop Sandhu, and Shveta Sarda, the illustrations of anthropomorphized insects and birds cast Partition as absurd, as when an illustration of a swanlike figure is accompanied by this caption: "What?

Figure 1.16: Multi-panel page from "Little Women," in *This Side, That Side*. Courtesy of Yoda Press.

Are we going to be divided as well?"[70] Invoking mythical as well as mystical elements, these narratives articulate a subaltern secular that amalgamates embodied memories and an ecomelancholia. The disruption embedded in these narratives is, then, aesthetic and political.

"Little Women" also bears witness to how war destroys interethnic intimacies, families, and communities. It depicts the intimate alienation of women separated from family members—fathers, sisters—on the other side. We learn that Tara's younger sister lives in the refugee camp with her, and she hopes to educate her so that she does not have to live in the camp forever; her elder sister, she later reveals, left on a boat for India. Tara says, "We haven't heard from my sister ever since. Who knows if they're alive or dead?"[71] By unveiling these refugee experiences, these graphic narratives also critique the history of nationalism in post-1947 South Asia. At the bottom of one page from "Little Women" is this caption: "A few years after the Liberation War of 1971." In the two panels above this text, we see illustrations that represent what remains after the liberation war. Startlingly, the first panel includes a sketch of many human skulls; in the second panel, we see an image of vultures waiting on desiccated trees and circling overhead

Figure 1.17: Panel from "Little Women," in *This Side, That Side*. Courtesy of Yoda Press.

in an arid landscape (see Figure 1.17). Again, the birds are drawn within the borders of the panel as well as flying over and beyond them; the border of the panel becomes a metaphor for the national border.

The meaning of this sequence emerges from the disjunction between the images (of death) and the text (about the "liberation war") on the page as well as the placement of the text as a caption under the image. This disjunction ironizes the nation-state's war of "liberation" by bearing witness to the "unfreedom" of death. Stella Oh suggests that "the aesthetic representations of the traumatic event as expressed through cultural practices of art and literature allow for the possibility of memory and mediation. Our acts of reading trauma are affective movements that cannot but fail. In reading, seeing, interpreting, and repeating through the medium of the graphic narrative, we interrogate social and political histories and its various traumatic ruptures."[72] Similarly, "Little Women," I suggest, visually interrogates the nationalist histories of our Anthropocene. It reveals the material effects of nationalist wars on a multispecies system, showing that the large-scale human death they create gives the lie to the nomenclature of liberation.

Writing about African American literature, Jennifer James identifies a form of "ecomelancholia" in some narratives. These narratives mark how the "recovery of lost love objects—disappearing land, species, finite resources, ways of life—would prove impossible."[73] Ecomelancholia "responds to the cumulative losses of nature, land, resources, and to traumas tied to those losses, such as death, deracination, and dispossession; it is activated by ongoing and interrelated social and political violence, including the catastrophe of war, genocide, and poverty."[74] This conception of ecomelancholia is resonant for our understanding of the remarkable intervention of *This Side, That Side*; in this anthology, ecomelancholia is tied to storytelling. Across its very different narratives, an ecomelancholia appears in the images of birds and trees that sometimes embrace human bodies as if comforting them; it also appears in the images of people becoming rivers to defy the new national borders of Partition and crossing over from this side to that side. For example, in "Water Stories" by Arundhati Ghosh and Appupen, the narrator opens the piece by explaining the significance of water for her father, a Partition migrant: "In all her father's stories about the land he came from, there was water."[75] By the end of the narrative, we learn, "Many years later, after her father's death, she went looking for the river in the other land."[76] This story unveils intergenerational ecomelancholia, even as it personifies the river in the land left by this family as an animate force. Yet because the narrator also reveals her stigmatization socially for not bearing a child, this trauma intersects with the intergenerational trauma of the refugee experience, culminating in her death by suicide when she enters the river.

Similarly, "Making of a Poet" by M. Hasan and Sukanya Ghosh begins with river memories. Set in 2009, it opens with the narrator explaining how he is traveling to a border checkpoint between India and Bangladesh to meet an Indian poet, Nitya Malakar, who was once a refugee: "An overnight bus journey to the northern Changrabandha–Burimari border, crossing the Teesta twice. The legendary Teesta, over which governments fight, elections are won, looked splendid that new year morning."[77] The narrator then recounts the poet's migration story: he left Bangladesh for India as a small child with his father in 1957. What strikes the narrator almost immediately about this migrant-turned-poet from India is this: "And as I looked at him talking to me with his smiling face, I could smell it in him. The Bangladesh inside him flowing like a small river, a very personal one, much cherished and well taken care of."[78] Here, the remembered community is likened to a river, flowing within the refugee and animating his life. Under this text, an unbordered panel features graphic shading over an image of crows perched on the ground, looking toward the edge of the page, as if contemplating flight. When people become birds, trees, and rivers in these narratives, then, like memories, they transgress the walled states built by Partition. Indeed, when the interviewer asks, "What does it mean, the land to a poet?" the poet replies, "*The birds, the trees, don't belong to some particular land. There is a real land that exists outside, and there is one in the imagination* [italics original]."[79] The migrant's memory work intertwines with ecomelancholia here to instigate our narrator to critically contemplate the power of nationality over one's identity: "This got me thinking . . . at least I have a passport, an identity, a nationality. Until I met this man, I hadn't realized that a few papers could be so powerful."[80] The narrator thus attempts to disengage identity with nationality, creating a narrative space for the refugee-poet's memory work that links two nations and generations. An important dimension of this story and others is the many secular intimacies they depict through the act of border crossings. Like "Making of a Poet," Beena Sarwar and Prasanna Dhandharphale's "Milne Do" (Let Us Meet) showcases efforts by Indian and Pakistani journalists and activists to create dialogue and ease visa restrictions between the two countries. It opens with a panel showing two nearly identical men hugging, standing on top of a globe and flanked by winged cherubs on both sides releasing flowers. Centered under this large square panel is a frame with text that asserts an international and shared secular intimacy: "So here we are, two neighbours. Same people. We share a history and general culture. We love the same music, the same food, the same films. When we meet in a third country, we become best friends, burying our same differences. But in our own neck of the woods, we could be aliens at opposite ends of the world, 'othering.' The hawk eyes ensure the lack of interaction between the peoples."[81] Thus, Sarwar and Dhandharphale describe the distinctions between the political establishment of India and Pakistan on the one hand (as fostering alienation), and the secular practice of ordinary people on the ground to forge transnational relationships on the other. The casual mention of meeting in a third country gestures to how, in many accounts, it is in the diaspora that Indo-Pak friendships become possible. This opening also resonates with the representation of diasporic experience in the more optimistic autobiographical account "90 Upper Mall or 1 Bawa Park" by Ahmad Rafay Alam and Martand Khosla. Here, they describe how Alam, a law student, and Khosla, an architecture student, become friends in London as they live in the same boardinghouse. Very soon, they discover an older connection between their two families: their grandparents migrated due to Partition, and Alam's home in Lahore once belonged to Khosla's family. This material connection for the two of them instantiates their secular friendship, rooted in the recognition of a shared history: "Martand and I tell this story every time we meet people together. We've gotten quite good at it. For us, the story is interesting because of the sheer coincidence of it all. Every time we tell it, we also rediscover the absurd and arbitrary nature of Partition."[82] Further, Alam illuminates how third-generation refugee descendants can perform the secular and survive Partition's historical legacies: "The rhetoric of Partition has always been characterized by loss and violence. Yet, in writing this or reflecting on the story, I can't but think of Partition in terms I'm familiar with: the story of 90 Upper Mall. Maybe this has been our buffer against the prejudices of history."[83] The intensely autobiographical first-person narrative combines with illustrations that resemble architectural drawings of a large home on several pages with the reproduction of photographs that depict the artists' grandparents and parents; it concludes with a photograph of Alam in conversation with Martand's grandmother in New Delhi, in 2010. In this account, the two men's gender and class privilege of being able to pursue higher education in the United Kingdom turns the diaspora into a generative space that enables new secular intimacies and journeys.

Across many of these narratives, as well as others addressing memory, the traditional sequential, horizontal arrangement of panels in conventional comics is eschewed. Instead, we see panels that sometimes have no frames, that vary in size and shape juxtaposed on the same page, or that are placed at odd angles on the page, such that their temporal sequence is not clear. Sometimes, there are no panels at all, as the page presents a dense and intricate series of illustrations overlaid with text that enables a less linear encounter with the story. For instance, Nina Sabnani's remarkable "Know Directions Home?" is illustrated through motifs of Kutchi embroidery from the region of Kutch (a princely state that was absorbed into the state of Gujarat after independence) that depict experiences of refugees living in a border village in Pakistan who flee to India in 1972 following the 1971 War of Bangladesh. Sabnani depicts their trauma and struggles, as every time they are escorted in government trucks and think that they are going to be settled safely in India, they realize that they are being taken back to Pakistan. A combination of patchwork and embroidery imagery combines with text and describes how they resist their deportation, are moved from one camp to another in Kutch, are offered arid land without water resources in Kutch, and face political uncertainty and neglect. Thus, "Know Directions Home?" vividly depicts hidden stories of refugee-state encounters and ironically bears witness to the loss of home due to war. It also shows how these refugees eventually survived and rebuilt their lives in this new land: "Today we are a collective and we use our art not only to support ourselves but also to tell our stories."[84] Sabnani offers us a lesser-known story about how some refugees survived by assimilating into an unfamiliar artistic landscape and practice in Kutch; her panel-less two-page spreads communicate through illustrations that resemble a tapestry of traditional Kutchi embroidery. Each spread depicts Partition refugees arriving in army trucks, waiting for information; being visited by untrustworthy politicians in their camps; and being forced to settle in a harsh and arid landscape. The accompanying captions express their fear, hunger, grief, settlement, and, eventually, survival. Because the illustrations resemble an embroidered Kutchi tapestry, we encounter each two-page spread as a nonlinear object, "one in which the eye wanders and assembles moments without clear beginning or end—in which we as readers build the pieces of a life together out of fragments—fragments of images, like in the process of memory itself."[85]

The dizzying array of graphic creativity across the narratives also renders this anthology unique. Here, we encounter a visual economy of images of Partition migrants that connects multiple media, traditions, and artistic practices in insurgent and hybrid stories that critique the state and do memory work. In some narratives, standard gutter spaces separate mostly evenly placed panels; in others, the panels bleed into one another. On the one hand, this variation suggests disarray and is disorienting. On the other hand, it creates space for readerly engagement and interpretation, allowing us to examine what is created by this history of border drawing and border crossings that is being remembered and reframed.[86] Above all, these illustrations interrupt the teleological narrative of history and the homogeneous time of the nation; they rupture that time, break it open, and gesture to how it is constituted by the modern production of statelessness.

Finally, *This Side, That Side* offers narratives that create visions of the secular as being rooted in intimacy as well as in political practices and aspirations. The collection challenges the geopolitical interstate conflicts that have transformed everyday life for refugees and citizens in post-47 South Asia, and it offers an insurgent counterknowledge to hegemonic narratives about those conflicts. It critiques the state as well as state-sponsored media institutions and the production of "news" in the subcontinent. For instance, Bani Abidi's satirical "The News" offers a witty look at the sameness on this side and that of India and Pakistan: she places adjacent black-and-white photos of two TV newsreaders—one Indian, one Pakistani—on each page. However, the women posing as newsreaders are actually the same person—Abidi herself—dressed in different ways to reflect the dominant sartorial conventions of government-sponsored news media in the two countries in the 1980s and early 1990s. At the bottom of each photograph is a transcription of their reportage: the Indian reports "Confrontation between Indian and Pakistani," and the Pakistani reports "Confrontation between Pakistani and Indian."[87] This item is followed by "Pakistani takes egg laid by Indian's hen" and "Indian takes egg laid by Pakistani's hen."[88] This juxtaposition of the different ways in which each country's representative tells the story calls attention, through irony, to how nationalism shapes the representation of conflict in news media in India and in Pakistan. By performing ethno-nationalist difference through sartorial and linguistic practices in these photographs, Abidi ironically gestures to the identity of statecraft on both sides. Eventually, both reporters say, "Situation is tense but under control"—a familiar refrain for anyone who has watched TV news in the subcontinent.[89] And so it goes, this side and that side.

While Abidi's narrative uses humor to offer critique, the relationship between the state and media comes under more serious scrutiny in Sajad's coming-of-age graphic narrative *Munnu: A Boy from Kashmir*. Munnu lays bare the complexities of local and international media institutions as they bear witness to, or erase from view, state violence and minority citizenship in Kashmir. Indeed, several scholars, including Sreyoshi Sarkar and Amit Baishya, have analyzed how *Munnu* offers an eco-critical history of pre-Partition and postcolonial Kashmir as a militarized conflict zone that challenges the human-animal divide when it represents Kashmiris as the endangered hangul (a species of deer native to Kashmir). They also illuminate how *Munnu* unveils Kashmiris' experience of subaltern citizenship through the transmission of intergenerational memory and storytelling.[90]

It is beyond the scope of this book to offer an exhaustive analysis of the diverse narratives that populate *This Side, That Side*. However, I hope that I have illuminated how the anthology invents and performs a brilliant, new, cross-border dialogue on the Partition migrations and their legacies of geopolitical conflict that reimagines the secular. Perennially interested in both sides, *This Side, That Side* asks us to look askance at the idea of the nation-state, to see the nation *from the vantage point of its refugees*. This perspective could not be more resonant for our times. In *The Other Side of Silence*, Urvashi Butalia observes that "the particular is harder to discover."[91] Ghosh's anthology maps this particular, and its heterogeneity, of what happens after Partition—on all sides—for the generations who inherited the 1947 Partition as well as its legacies, from the 1971 war to the Kashmir conflict. In the next section, I juxtapose how refugee experiences in heterogeneous spaces—internment camps, rivers, fields, and cities—are drawn across these graphic narratives with how they appear in photography from around 1947.

Photojournalism and Bearing Witness in Margaret Bourke-White's Photography

> Let the atrocious images haunt us.
> —Susan Sontag, *Regarding the Pain of Others*[92]

I conclude this chapter with a resonant reminder—from a very different context—of the ongoing and necessary labor of our work on the images of history that surround us. Toward my interpretive project about the Partition migrations in this book, I am interested in an earlier visual archive: some of the most searing and iconic visual representations of the Partition refugees are found in the black-and-white photographs of the pioneering American photographer Margaret Bourke-White. Born in 1901, Bourke-White is considered America's first female photojournalist and first war photographer, and she was an industrial photographer who was one of the first four staff photographers (and the only woman) hired by Henry Luce at LIFE magazine in 1936. She went on to photograph some of the most traumatic moments of the mid-twentieth century, from Nazi death camps in 1945, to India's decolonization from 1946 to 1948, to Mahatma Gandhi's assassination, the Korean War, and South Africa's political conflicts. Bourke-White is widely credited with the invention of photojournalism; more than any other photographer of her time, her work is marked by an unflinching, humanist eye that is committed to revealing the terrible traumas of the mid-twentieth century.

How can we understand the economy of Bourke-White's images of the 1947 migrations as they circulate across national, regional, and cultural boundaries in the mid-twentieth century and in the present moment? Bourke-White arrived in India in March 1946. She went back and forth between the United States and India through 1947 on assignment for LIFE, taking photos of South Asian political leaders like Gandhi and Jinnah while also creating an archive of mass migration and refugee experiences. Fewer than one hundred of these images were printed in LIFE magazine, but many were reprinted in the fiftieth anniversary edition of Khushwant Singh's novel *Train to Pakistan*. Asma Naeem has analyzed Bourke-White's life and photographs of the Partition experience in a comparative conversation with the prints of South Asian American artist Zarina.[93] For Naeem, this comparison shows "how these artists negotiated identities through their work that are at once global and American, and, further, that international events such as Partition spark artistic responses that extend beyond national borders and religious/ethnic categories to entwine seemingly unrelated cultural forms."[94]

For Benjamin, the photograph in modernity becomes standard evidence for historical occurrence, establishing what is photographed as a scene of crime and thereby acquiring a hidden political significance. Taking as axiomatic Pinney's claim that "photography is a cultural practice with no fixed outcome" and drawing upon the resonant writing on photography by Benjamin, Butler, and others, I suggest that Bourke-White's graphic photographs of the mass migrations of 1947–1948 should be recognized as historical evidence of the Partition mass migrations while also offering a political critique of decolonization as a scene of war and carnage. By recording the genocidal upheavals of Partition migrations, these black-and-white photographs constitute an important archive of the refugee experience, stories that would subsequently be effaced in other media in the public sphere. The camera in this moment becomes an instrument for evidence, participating in what Jennifer Green-Lewis calls a "culture of realism."[95] This archive of the refugee experience has become a "shadow archive" that has had a lasting impact on the field of photojournalism and its visual discourse about statelessness.[96]

Aesthetically, many of the photographs construct the refugees as if situated in a tableau; these index older visual representational forms of portraiture, paying attention to perspectival depth. Some are situated indoors in built spaces within the refugee camps; others are outdoors in city streets strewn with charred remains of people and objects, or they are set in the countryside, showing refugees pausing to cook meals or to rest. If we examine the wide range of Bourke-White's photographs of the Partition migrations, several features emerge. In some photographs, we see a reproduction of the colonial gaze, as refugees are situated within the lexicon of passive, colonial objects fixed in time by the still gaze of the photographer. In this reading, the photographs of the migration and the plight of the dead or dying refugees depicted might be read as an extension of colonial surveillance. As the precursor of late-twentieth-century photojournalism, this reading exemplifies what David Spurr problematizes: "Western journalism is filled with situations where the observer, from an exterior position, views the bodies of the captured, imprisoned, incapacitated, or dead."[97] In this sense, particular photographs resemble, or appear to be part of the same family as, ethnographic photography in the colonial period. In her analysis of the mutually constitutive relation between Victorian fiction and realist photography, Nancy Armstrong argues, "Whenever it refers to the world beyond itself, a photograph refers only to images rather than to things as they were before they were reduced to visual information."[98] Thus, at least some of these photographs participate in the reproduction, identification, and classification of Indian bodies as image-objects in a stable system of realist representations that make up that shadow archive of colonial modernity.

However, as Christopher Wright argues, "what is important is not so much what the image contains, a meaning that resides within it, but what is brought to it, how it is used, and how it is connected to various trajectories."[99] I suggest, then, that we connect Bourke-White's photographs with this chapter's graphic archive of that which remains after Partition. In doing so, I find resonant Butler's suggestion that "to confirm that a life was, even within the life itself, is to underscore that a life is a grievable life. In this sense the photograph, through its relation to the future anterior, instates grievability."[100] Seen through this point of view, I argue that Bourke-White's photographs invite us to grieve for the lives and losses of refugees displaced through decolonization. Naeem draws upon Bourke-White's own writing to similarly suggest that her "empathy for the devastation she is witnessing" is evident in her stylistic decisions while framing her photographs. For instance, she places "the camera low to the ground in barren landscapes or in the midst of the suffering bodies ... for, as she later wrote, she was profoundly moved by the 'travail of a people divided by pen strokes.'" For Bourke-White, Naeem suggests, the condition of India and Pakistan was analogous to that of the United States when it fought for independence from Britain.[101] Thus, Bourke-White's perspective on photographing India's decolonization is intimately tied to her own nationalism and to America's own history of British occupation, suggesting that her photographs are yoked to a transnational, anti-colonial memory. This anti-colonialism is, of course, one that nonetheless elides the colonization of Native Americans.

For the purposes of this chapter, I am primarily interested in two modes of representing refugees that emerge across Bourke-White's prolific documentation of the Partition migrations. One is the monumental image of large groups of refugees as they trudge on foot, alongside bullock carts laden with personal belongings or small children, toward an unseen horizon. There are also photographs that frame and capture the overcrowded trains, teeming with refugees sitting not just inside but also on the roofs of trains or hanging off their doors and windows, as they ferry people across the new borders between India and Pakistan. The second is the profile of the traumatized and grief-stricken refugee's face, where the eyes suggest distrust of the camera's gaze or often look into the distance with a glazed expression. In these photographs, the facial and bodily gestures signify loss, trauma, hunger, exhaustion, disease, anger, and frustration. In *Frames of War*, Butler reminds us that how suffering is represented intimately affects our response to it.[102] We must therefore, she says, try to "understand how the frames that allocate the recognizability of certain figures of the human are themselves linked with the broader norms of what will and will not be a grievable life."[103] I consider this question about whether the photograph constructs life as grievable when reviewing the range of Bourke-White's archive of the 1947 migrations. Many of these photographs frame South Asian refugees through frontal shots of their faces, in which we see a range of emotions, in all their complexity. These photographs bear witness to those violent migrations and demand that we, as viewers, encounter the refugees' pain and empathize with their plight.[104] They establish refugees' lives as grievable and precarious. Sometimes captions accompany the photographs; at other times, they stand alone, inviting us into the interpretive field. While we never learn the refugees' names or their stories, we are nonetheless confronted by their embodied presence and therefore invited to reckon with the human as well as nonhuman suffering of mass migration. As Butler points out, the photograph operates at the "affective register" as well as through "instituting a certain mode of acknowledgement. It 'argues' for the grievability of a life: its pathos is at once affective and interpretive."[105] Now preserved through the Getty Archive, Bourke-White's photographs, in their renewed circulation in South Asian public spheres through republication, can activate genocidal memory that interrogates nationalist histories (a concept Schlund-Vials uses in her analysis of Cambodian American cultural production). Like the graphic narratives discussed earlier, these photographs' visual economy of refugees' precarity indicts British decolonization and invites us to a vivid encounter with precariousness.

Bourke-White's effort to depict the precarity of those who are stateless and to instigate empathy is evoked today by the contemporary photography project called *Where the Children Sleep* (2013) by Swedish photographer Magnus Wennman, produced in partnership with the United Nations High Commissioner for Refugees (UNHCR). *Where the Children Sleep* calls attention to the abjection and dispossession of Syrian and Iraqi refugees in Europe. In this series of color photographs, Wennman presents images of refugee children in Europe, in various states of repose—in the field, in the forest, in a hospital bed, on a ripped mattress in a street square, or on the sidewalk under huddled blankets. Accompanied by a brief paragraph that shares with us the children's first names, ages, locations, and a memory about where they are from or about what they dream of or fear, each photograph invites us to empathize with stateless children being dehumanized in mainstream media accounts as refugees.[106] In presenting fragmentary information about their past, like where they originally lived, what they liked to do in their leisure time, what forced them to move, and what they fear today, the project also does the memory work of instantiating their historical lives, their pasts, before their displacement. Each photograph like this, whether by Bourke-White or Wennman, "brings us close to an understanding of the fragility and mortality of human life, the stakes of death in the scene of politics."[107]

Analyzing Victorian photography, Jennifer Green-Lewis acknowledges that

> we have found the Victorians accessible thanks to their appearance in photographs, and that sense of access has been enabled by the cultural indivisibility of the photograph *as* a photograph. . . . And just as other historical artifacts affirm a connection with human beings from earlier generations, so old photographs, their negatives (and subjects) along gone, now assume the aura of originals, not merely in terms of their economic value but as points of reference or departure.[108]

It is in this sense that I return to Bourke-White's photographic archive of the Partition migrations—to affirm a connection with refugees long neglected in histories of postcolonial nationalism as well as to constitute a point of departure from which we might historicize the ongoing production of statelessness in South Asia and the Middle East. These photographs as material artifacts of Partition refugees' experiences, I suggest, constitute a connection with them; they must be brought into our contemporary, ongoing dialogue about media, decolonization, and statelessness. That Partition remains a residual frame through which South Asians understand migration is evident in recent media discourse: this discourse invokes Partition to describe the scale of the recent exodus of impoverished migrant workers from Indian cities, who walked hundreds of miles to their native villages, starving and sick, when the Indian government abruptly declared a national lockdown due to the pandemic on March 24, 2020. Photojournalistic reporting of this mass exodus also recalls, as many commentators observe, the visual economy of Bourke-White's Partition photographs.[109]

From Bourke-White's Partition photography, recently published in a volume with Singh's seminal Partition novel *Train to Pakistan*, to the recent pop-up audiovisual exhibit *Refugees of the British Empire* hosted by the 1947 Partition Archive in California, visual objects in public culture have been mobilized in creative ways to critique the statelessness and violence of decolonization around 1947. At times, as with the work of current diasporic and subcontinental artists like Annu Palakunnathu Matthew and Anusha Yadav (discussed in Chapter 4), they also do the memory work that uncovers a subaltern secular history of these migrations. To be sure, my discussion of Partition-related photography is not exhaustive; however, I hope it serves as an effective starting point for us to consider the interrelationships and afterlife of gendered refugees' representations across media. Like the literature, film, and testimonials I consider in this book, the stories our visual archives tell us about statelessness have, as Butler argues, "political consequences."[110] It is beyond the scope of this chapter to do justice to related photographic work by Henri Cartier-Bresson, although this comparison would certainly be fruitful. I have been especially interested in Bourke-White's work and mobility as a female photographer, an American, and a cultural producer; like many of the female authors and filmmakers I consider in this book, Bourke-White offers us unique insights into the refugee history to which she bears witness, and activates remembrance of an experience erased under nationalism. It is important to note that Bourke-White's American identity facilitated her ability to be in public spaces, camps, and streets, and therefore to document this mass migration. India's own pioneering and brilliant photojournalist Homai Vyarawalla notes that she was never able to take photographs during the Partition. She was busy working, taking care of her family, or hiding with her family in the home (trying to keep it safe) of a Muslim friend in Delhi, as violence raged on outside:

I didn't take pictures of Partition because I was working in the office and couldn't go out. Another reason I couldn't go out was that we were living in a Muslim's house in Connaught Place. People wanted to burn that house down, to loot the furniture in the landlord's shop downstairs. So one of us had to be there. At the same time, we had to work in the office. My son was four years old. We had to take turns saving our house and family, and at the same time we were working. Those were difficult times. We had to be dressed all the time, never knowing when we would have to move. People used to throw burning rags. It was a very posh furniture shop where maharajas' furniture was made. We had to be on the alert. Fortunately, because we were Parsi, we were saved although Muslims were hiding in our house. They had to arrange to move out because so many killings were taking place all around. They had to shift to Purana Killa.[111]

This excerpt from her 2005 interview reveals Vyarawalla's challenges during this violent time and its complexities, when people tried to affirm secular ties in the midst of precariousness. I began this chapter by discussing how colorful popular nationalist prints and charts visualize the secular nation through organized, graphic taxonomies of heteronormative, embodied, ethnic diversity. In contrast, a counterdiscourse emerges in the visual economy of Ghosh's graphic narrative anthology and Bourke-White's black-and-white photographs; this counterarchive does memory work that makes the refugee experience visible and grievable. It documents the 1947 migrations and violence as they affected all involved, across gender, religion, caste, class, age, and country. It also constitutes a secular archive that critiques decolonization and resonates with the project of the 1947 Partition Archive that would begin a half century later in the United States, discussed in Chapter 4. As scholars and teachers, we must continue to engage these representations. This work entails retelling the stories about nations and nationalisms we have been so preoccupied with, since the work of Anderson, but through the perspective of those expelled to their border zones. This approach might perhaps equip us to find a new way to live, a way to reinvent the politics of the present in Asia and in the United States.

2

The Ethics and Aesthetics of Witnessing

Refugees, Literary Modernism, and the American Diaspora

> Women carry with them incorporated traumas swallowed whole.... Political failures have brought about a disidentification with the nation that fails to represent women.
>
> —RANJANA KHANNA, *"Ethical Ambiguities and Specters of Colonialism"*[1]

> The fact that decolonization is a temporal project of emergence becomes especially clear once we grasp that cultural genocide is a consequence of colonial domination.
>
> —PHENG CHEAH, *What Is a World?*[2]

In the previous chapter, I discuss the heterogeneous representation of post-47 migrations and secularism in graphic narratives, popular print culture, and photography from South Asia and the United States. Here, I turn to the literary representation of post-47 migrations, beginning with the representation of Partition migrations in the South Asian American diaspora. This choice is not accidental—representing a contemporary return to, and reckoning with, a historical moment that has largely been forgotten in public discourse, two of the most powerful recent novels about the South Asian legacies of decolonization have been written by feminist writers in South Asian America: Bapsi Sidhwa's *Cracking India* (1991) and Shauna Singh Baldwin's *What the Body Remembers* (1999). These works invite dialogue on how art bears witness to the genocidal violence and mass migrations of mid-twentieth century decolonization and on the role of literature in rendering legible the gendered experiences of war and displacement not always accounted for in nationalist historiography. Additionally, they tell us stories about *what remains* and illuminate how critical resistance is fashioned by minor subjects in the midst of violent displacement. As Ranjana Khanna's words in this chapter's first epigraph suggest, women's alienation from and disidentification with hegemonic nationalism needs to be acknowledged; emerging across these novels in heterogenous ways, in this chapter I trace how this disidentification, as Khanna argues, "allows for coalitions between women internationally where a concept of justice is forged in the full knowledge of the thorniness of the spectre of colonial relations and 'local' abuses of women."[3] These novels not only vividly show how gendered subjects differently experienced modern histories of decolonization and nation formation in South Asia as they became refugees or citizens of India and Pakistan; they also, to use Crystal Parikh's words in a different context, constitute a minor literature "that gives voice to the complex desires of [its] subjects and how such desires—sexual as well as social—mediate the subject's experience of vulnerability and agency."[4] I conclude by turning to India-based writer and activist Arundhati Roy's novel *The Ministry of Utmost Happiness* (2017), which is set in the contemporary moment and therefore stands in contrast to the diasporic novels set in and around 1947. *The Ministry*, I show, paints a wide canvas in which the sweep of post-47 national history in South Asia is situated in the broader context of world history, from the vantage point of the present and of those who are minorities in the nation. The novel indicts the postcolonial nation-state for its role in sustaining discrimination, violating human rights, and engendering harm for those who are religious, caste, gender, indigenous, and sexual minorities. Taken together, these three novels reveal how capital, debt, nationalism, and heteronormative patriarchy work on minor bodies and minor subjects, even as they identify the embodied and ideological performance of resistance—and one such mode of resistance, I argue, is the invention of "the subaltern secular." Each novel offers a new understanding of how gender, religion, and statelessness have been historically intertwined since the mid-twentieth century in South Asia.[5] In this chapter, I ask: What is the role of literature in a world saturated by different forms of violence and border making—religious, sociopolitical, ecological, or psychic? Indeed, what is the relation between our literary and cultural representations of statelessness and secularism and our hope for social justice?

Many important women writers have written fiction that bears witness to South Asian women's experiences during the Partition migrations. The literary archive of this violent displacement includes a vast body of Hindi, English, Urdu, Punjabi, Bengali, and Sindhi fiction, prose, and poetry; in its fold, it gathers writers based in the subcontinent as well as those settled in diasporas in the United Kingdom and North America. In this chapter, I do not offer an exhaustive account of the range and diversity of this vast archive. Instead, I am interested in how two contemporary writers return to the constitutive past of Partition migrations from the new spatio-temporal vantage point of the diaspora in the 1990s. In her ethnography of Indian migrants in Dubai, Neha Vora notes the historical bias in the study of modern Indian migration, where diaspora studies have focused on post-47 emigration "to western countries enabled by postcolonial policies and globalization."⁶ Within this field, the artistic production of these two diasporic writers gains importance for two reasons: they tell mid-twentieth-century migration stories about gendered subjects who cross borders within South Asia, and they join earlier diasporic writers, such as Santha Rama Rau, who lived in the United States but created works that were invested in the project of decolonization, nation formation, and freedom.⁷ Sidhwa's *Cracking India* and Baldwin's *What the Body Remembers* depict the 1947 migrations in narratives that historically begin well before 1947 and follow minority female protagonists, young and adult, as they witness and experience the transformations wreaked by Partition on ordinary people in urban and rural India and Pakistan. This literature can be seen as "worlding" this history at the same time that it bears witness to it: in one sense, both novels fissure the boundaries of the nation, *reframing migration and the crisis of secularism in postcolonial nationalism*.⁸

In her discussion of acclaimed and canonical Anglophone novels from the late twentieth century, Ankhi Mukherjee asserts that their personal stories are always imbricated with "transnational structures and global forms of power."⁹ Similarly, the novels by Sidhwa and Baldwin raise questions about the politics of form that also engage with the aesthetics of transnational historical oppression; simultaneously, they "supplement forgetting with new narratives of affirmation and presence."¹⁰ If decolonization and nation formation constitute the most pervasive political changes of the global twentieth century, as European empires were dismantled and new nations emerged across Asia, Africa, and the Caribbean, then this Asian American literature of decolonization returns to the past to account for the violent displacement that decolonization created. In this sense, Sidhwa and Baldwin are "remembrance activists" or "memory workers" who rewrite this imagined national community from the vantage point of those who became its refugees.¹¹ In the absence of "unrealized juridical processes"¹² that might enact an institutional, reparative justice (or even reckoning) for those who suffered this division, these writers retell traumatic migration stories to memorialize the refugee experience, unveil inequity and violence before and after Partition, and invent new ideas about secular, just community in postcolonial South Asia. My analysis of Sidhwa and Baldwin's memory work concludes with India-based writer Roy's novel *The Ministry of Utmost Happiness*, which represents the manifold, fragmented legacies of the 1947 migrations through stories that chronicle the abjections of minority citizenship in postcolonial India and its diaspora. "Reenlivening political aspirations for solidarity and justice" like the many other American writers of color Crystal Parikh analyzes, Sidhwa, Baldwin, and Roy offer us new feminist stories about surviving migration and nationalism in decolonization and its aftermath.¹³

Both *Cracking India* and *What the Body Remembers* revolve around female protagonists occupying middle-class and working-class subject positions; in both novels, these female protagonists have an ambivalent relationship to elite nationalism and are critical of Partition. Without idealizing pre-Partition India or the interwoven lives of its different minority communities, these writers poignantly depict how Partition shatters interethnic friendships and intimacies, with very violent consequences for girls and women. These works' various female protagonists and characters—young and old, rich and poor, Parsi, Muslim, Hindu, Christian, and Sikh—bear witness to traumatic sexual violence unleashed on women and children, the shattering of interethnic secular communities, and the forced displacement of millions. Thus, they call into question the ethical and moral claims of empire and nation in the conflict zone of Partition. Simultaneously, these novels illuminate how minor, gendered subjects create and perform the subaltern secular. This subaltern secularism, at times, emerges in relation to ethico-political memory work; at other times, it emerges as a counterpractice that criticizes statelessness in the postcolonial state.

It is interesting to note the aesthetic resonances across these two works. Baldwin and Sidhwa experiment with the form of the novel, weaving together elements of realism and modernism. They intertwine the conventions of both as they struggle to restory women's experiences of embodied violation, the loss of community and belonging, and becoming rightless and stateless because of how decolonization was implemented. As such, both novels offer fractured narratives that present multiple points of view, from multiple narrators, as the empire unravels. Baldwin's *What the Body Remembers*, for instance, moves back and forth between a linear realist narrative and stream-of-consciousness monologues that represent the female protagonists Satya's and Roop's interiority. Sidhwa's *Cracking India* is a *bildungsroman* that incorporates a modernist alienation to unveil the disjointed unreality of 1947's forced migrations. However, in both novels, the story of migration and secularism is part of a longer story about the inextricable economic and social-cultural violence that saturates women's lives in colonial and post-Partition South Asia. In the process, they invite us to consider the continuities and discontinuities in women's experiences of citizenship and power in post-47 South Asia and who gets written as the normative citizen subject in the postcolonial nation in South Asia. In Ulka Anjaria's analysis of colonial realism, she identifies "a critical, aspirational energy of 'realism in the colony,'"[14] rooted in its "detachment from and continuing skepticism toward the nationalism of the public sphere."[15] Engaging this, I suggest that these novels' apparent aesthetic indeterminacy marks a postcolonial skepticism toward the hegemonic myths of South Asian ethno-nationalism. Sidhwa's and Baldwin's diasporic novels throw the idealized mythical origins of the Pakistani and Indian postcolonial nations into doubt through their migration stories (as Tahmima Anam's novel *A Golden Age* does for the origins of Bangladesh). Roy's novel brings that critique full circle in its representation of the postcolonial state as continually engendering violence, displacement, and the loss of human rights then and now. In the following sections, I argue that for all three novels, aesthetic form is tied to the project of illuminating embodied experience and *secular intimacy*—of the female and hijira protagonists and characters. Engaging these novels in dialogue, I map how minor subjects encounter and survive the crisis of secularism that accompanied decolonization. I trace what is illuminated about refugee experience and minority citizenship in the postcolonial nation-state, in these stories about gender, belonging, and the futures of ethno-nationalism. They invite a reckoning with the subaltern secularism that emerges in and through migration, and rehistoricize post-47 South Asia in ways that hold the state accountable for its failures to prevent gendered and ethnic violence. Their stories about how those displaced survive the state are also stories about the creation of a resistant subaltern secular under siege in the contemporary moment.

Disability, Patriarchal Violence, and Witnessing in Bapsi Sidhwa's *Cracking India*

> "No!" I scream, unable to bear the thought of an able-bodied future.
>
> —BAPSI SIDHWA, *Cracking India*[16]

Cracking India describes the traumatic upheaval of the 1947 Partition of India through the eyes of the young child narrator, Lenny Sethi, a Parsi girl living in Lahore. Lenny has polio, and her negotiation of the norms around able-bodiedness, along with the novel's representation of her multiple marginality—as a child, female, and belonging to the minority Parsi community—intimately inhabits its critical account of forced migration. This peripherality is in fact central to the novel's critical memorialization of decolonization and migration that accompanied nationality for men and women in South Asia. Anupama Jain ably explains how the ancient history of forced displacement of Parsis or Zoroastrians from Iran to India inflects Sidhwa's representation of this modern displacement in 1947.[17] In what follows, I hope to illuminate how Sidhwa's feminist critique vividly problematizes not only the patriarchal contours of this migration but also the politics of nationalism in the intimate forms of family and community.

Sidhwa's novel depicts India's deliberate division by showing how political debates about Partition manifest in and fragment the syncretic interethnic community in Lahore, of which Lenny's Parsi family is a part. Lenny is five years old when the narrative opens in 1942, and because of polio, she walks with a limp. When the novel begins, we encounter a fragile interethnic community where interracial and interethnic intimacy is a fact of colonial social life in Lahore. Although she is part of a conventional upper-middle-class Parsi family, Lenny's attachments to other female figures in her life, from her godmother to her nanny, Shanta, help her survive "the perplexing unrealities" of her own home—and, later, of the Partition.[18] Her days are spent in the company of Shanta, whom she calls Ayah; their intimacy offers Lenny access to Ayah's subaltern community of servants and traders in Lahore, allowing us to encounter how Partition's politics played out in ordinary lives, across class, caste, gender, and ethnicity.

That Lenny belongs to the economically elite but tiny minority community of Parsis, descendants of the Zoroastrians who migrated to India in the A.D. eighth or tenth century from Iran, complicates this relationship: its very peripherality to the dominant political processes of nationalist struggle is implicitly cited as a politically neutral perspective—a kind of secular practice—on the Hindu-Muslim-Sikh antagonisms that were said to structure the nationalist struggle. Sangeeta Ray notes:

> The term "partition" implies a neat, cartographic creation of a new geographic entity that elides the personal and political vicissitudes accompanying such remappings. Yet, Sidhwa's use of the gerund "cracking" evokes the tortuous birthing of new nation-states through hacking, splintering, and breaking.[19]

The largely first-person narrative of the novel follows Lenny and Ayah as they witness how ethnic political rhetoric and violence around the imminent Partition change their lives in Lahore's Warris Road, Queen's Garden, and other local haunts. As some friends get killed and others flee across the border to India, the birth of the nation generates the fracturing and loss of multiple intimacies for Lenny and Ayah. Ayah's Muslim lover Masseur is murdered, and, subsequently, her one-time friend and admirer Ice-Candy Man arrives with a murderous mob to abduct and rape her. When he tricks the unsuspecting Lenny into revealing Ayah's hiding place and then abducts her, Lenny and Ayah's deep bond is irrevocably and traumatically destroyed. The novel ends by depicting many scenes of unhomeliness and intimate loss: for instance, the family's erstwhile Hindu neighbor's home is turned into a recovered women's camp where female refugees are housed and aided. When Ayah is abducted, Hamida, one of the women from this refugee camp, is hired to be Lenny's nanny. Once Ayah is rescued from a brothel in Lahore by Lenny's godmother, she is also placed in this camp. She eventually decides to go to her family in Amritsar and becomes a refugee. A lovelorn Ice-Candy Man follows her.

In my first book, *Violent Belongings*, I discuss the representation of bodily violence in this novel and how it unveils the complexity of violence that comes to be named ethnic, even when it was often more about other things: caste, class, desire, property, and debt.[20] In this chapter, building on the preceding discussion of graphic representations of gendered refugees' experiences, I want to call attention to how literature locates the secular through a feminist commitment to illuminating gendered experiences in *Cracking India*. On the one hand, as the historian Partha Chatterjee[21] and critic Sangeeta Ray show, Indian nationalist discourse often deploys the middle-class Hindu woman as the embodied representative of national culture. Ray adds that Indian nationalist literature does this through the figure of the upper-caste Hindu woman. The idealizing image of the Hindu upper-caste woman as embodiment of cultural tradition in turn allows Indian nationalism to assimilate into the discourses of Western modernity while preserving its autonomy through the assertion of cultural difference. *Cracking India* interrupts this rhetoric. Unlike the centrality of the allegory in Salman Rushdie's depiction of Saleem Sinai in *Midnight's Children*, and although Lenny's eighth birthday falls on Pakistan's independence day— August 14, 1947—her multiple marginality, in terms of able-bodiedness, age, gender, as a Parsi, and so forth, disrupts any allegorical reading. Instead, in *Cracking India*, Lenny is colonial subject and national critic—a peripheral protagonist at odds with colonialist and nationalist discourses.[22] For instance, the former is evident when her family doctor Colonel Bharucha roars to Lenny's mother, who is blaming herself for Lenny's polio, "If anyone's to blame, blame the British! There was no polio in India till they brought it here!"[23] This enunciation historicizes Lenny's difference, implicating colonial power in the intimate production of colonial embodiment. Further, Lenny's first-person account of how ethno-nationalist politics violently destroys the people she loves—Ayah and her community of friends—becomes, as I show below, a powerful indictment of postcolonial ethno-nationalism.

Elsewhere, I discuss the representation of Lenny's disability.[24] She is a peripheral and perceptive child protagonist whose observations about everyday life enfold social and political critique. Further, she represents her embodied difference as one she desires and fiercely protects. While she understands, even as a five-year-old child, that her mother feels responsible for her polio, Lenny likens having polio to "being born under a lucky star."[25] When her "valuable deformity" is not much altered by Dr. Bharucha's cast,[26] she is delighted: "My leg looks functional but gratifyingly abnormal—and far from banal!"[27] Following Partition, Lenny's embodiment anchors her solidarity with others displaced within the conventional gendered construction of normalcy and citizenship. As she says one evening in the Queen's Garden in Lahore about her new, melancholic nanny Hamida (who herself is a Partition refugee who cannot return home to her husband and children because she has been raped), "Like Hamida, I do not fit."[28] Lenny's hypervisible and counternormative body becomes a site of affective affiliation with the various subaltern figures in the novel as they experience violent displacement: the forcibly drugged and married-off servant child Pappoo, the abducted and raped Shanta and Hamida, and the Sikh childhood friend Ranna, who loses his family to horrific violence in rural Punjab. It is important to acknowledge that to some extent, Lenny's construction of her polio as a "valuable deformity" is also shaped by her age and class privilege. Her family's wealth ensures that she continues to have access to education (through a private tutor), the pleasures of leisure in the park (through the nanny who pushes her there daily in a stroller), and to intimacy.[29] Nevertheless, the novel illuminates non-normative intimacies that disclose the subaltern secular as India is divided by the British, and things fall apart in Lenny's fragile world.

The representation of Partition refugees in the novel is multidimensional, illuminating how class and caste shaped this mass migration. On the one hand, we witness the departure of her parents' Hindu and Sikh family friends, including the Mehtas, the Malhotras, the Guptas, and the Singhs; their class position allows them to arrange conveyance and safe passage for themselves and their belongings across the border. But also present in this story are the many women, Hindu and Muslim, who are raped and abducted under this violent decolonization. Lenny hears and inscribes into the narrative the grief of abducted women and refugees in the freshly abandoned homes around hers: "The mystery of the women in the courtyard deepens. At night we hear them wailing, their cries verging on the inhuman. Sometimes I can't tell where the cries are coming from. From the women, or from the house next door infiltrated by our invisible neighbors."[30] Even as she is awoken nightly by the crying and wailing of the female refugees around her, she articulates a critical recognition about the problematic discourse of fate that is often proffered as an explanatory narrative for the women's state. One night, when a female refugee's crying wakes her up again, Lenny says, "My heart is wrung with pity and horror. I want to leap out of my bed and soothe the wailing woman and slay her tormentors. I've seen Ayah carried away—and it had less to do with fate than with the will of men."[31] Here, the novel interrogates the ideology of fate or karma that is often cited to explain human suffering to instead articulate a political critique of sexual violence as generated by male agency. In an interview with Alok Bhalla, Sidhwa gestures to her apprehension of the difference between women's and men's Partition stories. Discussing the fiction of women writers from the early national period who wrote about the Partition migrations, she argues:

> In all these stories it is the women survivors who were filled with compassion for those whose plight is worse than theirs. They are the ones who reach out to others and offer consolation. Maybe not towards the men who was responsible for the atrocities, but certainly towards each other. . . . I have heard of innumerable instances of women from both sides going out of their way to rescue their sisters. I am talking about Muslim women who helped Hindu women and Hindu women who consoled Muslim women. In fact, the stories these women have to tell were more *intimate* and more touching than the ones I heard from men [my italics]. Men have narrated tales about Muslims or Hindus giving shelter to each other. But the stories told by women spoke specifically about the physical conditions of the refugees and described in detail the places they were forced to live in. They looked at each other as fellow sufferers. . . . [T]hey've recognized each other as victims of the same politics.[32]

Sidhwa's recognition of how these early national narratives from South Asia enunciate an interethnic solidarity from the female refugee's perspective—one that I would call a subaltern secular—is evident in her own representation of intimacy in *Cracking India*.

The representation of intimacy in the novel is multifaceted. Lenny's account of the many women raped and abducted in ethnic violence lies alongside her observations about the violence that saturates marital intimacy for her parents. If, outside her home, Lenny hears the wailing of abducted women and refugees in freshly abandoned homes, inside the domestic space of her home are "the caged voices of our parents fighting in their bedroom. Mother crying, wheedling. Father's terse, brash, indecipherable sentences. Terrifying thumps."[33] In different unhomely homes, then, grief at violence against women is linked; Lenny apprehends that infidelity and domestic violence permeate the apparently successful normative coupledom of her parents when she further hears her mother trying to stop her father from going "to her" and failing: "Father goes anyway. . . . Although Father has never raised his hands to us, one day I surprise Mother at her bath, and see the bruises on her body."[34] Lenny's intimate invasion of the bathroom deprivatizes domestic violence and brings her surprising, new knowledge of her mother's wounded embodiment. Thus, Lenny bears witness to the domestic violence her mother lives with as well as the failure of bourgeois ideologies of marriage.

This knowledge of marital unhappiness shapes Lenny's critique of refugee women's violent experiences. Lenny links the gendered violence experienced by female subjects like her mother, Ayah, and Hamida (representing different ethnic groups) and articulates a secular political critique of gendered violence as generated by patriarchal male agency. When later Hamida cries at Lenny's question about whether she is a "fallen woman," Lenny is devastated: "I get out of bed and press her face into my chest. I rock her, and Hamida's tears soak right through my flannel nightgown. . . . I can't bear to hurt her: I'd rather bite my tongue than cause pain to her grief-wounded eye."[35] This act of intimate embrace embodies and performs the secular, disentangling it from nationalism. It signifies an affective secular intimacy between Hamida and Lenny, across class and age, across political status and religion. The mention of Hamida's "grief-wounded eye" here and elsewhere in the text evocatively connects her to Lenny, signaling their shared, non-normative embodiment. Like her bond with her childless godmother, Lenny's affective intimacy here is queer, as defined by Lauren Berlant and Michael Warner: it eschews the dominant forms of intimacy tied to coupling, kinship, property, or the nation and presents instead a more optimism-sustaining, political vision of intimacy on the peripheries of the nation.[36]

Migration, Reproductive Femininity, and Citizenship in Shauna Singh Baldwin's *What the Body Remembers*

> Novels are, I think, more truthful than historical accounts.
> —BAPSI SIDHWA, *"Grief and Survival in Ice-Candy Man"*[37]

This diasporic investment in telling the story of Partition on another continent is evident in writings by other South Asian writers beside Bapsi Sidhwa, including Salman Rushdie, Amitav Ghosh, Vikram Chandra, Kamila Shamsie, and Shauna Singh Baldwin. Baldwin's novel *What the Body Remembers* (1999) resonates with the preoccupations of Sidhwa's *Cracking India* insofar as it dwells on questions about embodiment, ethnicity, and gender in its account of Partition. *What the Body Remembers* is set in the decade leading up to Partition in 1947 and ends in 1965. It revolves around the life of two female protagonists: Satya is the beautiful and nonreproductive wife of the forty-two-year-old Sardarji, a prosperous Oxford-educated Sikh engineer, while sixteen-year-old Roop is the second wife he marries so that he can have children. Roop is coerced into marrying him by the debt that her father has incurred with the local money lender, who engineers the marriage proposal. The novel traces the lives of both women in Rawalpindi (in what would become Pakistan) in the 1930s and 1940s as well as how they negotiate their location in familial networks of power structured by dominating male figures. It critiques how their lives are indelibly shaped by their differential value as reproductive bodies or laboring bodies in the domestic patriarchal economy. The latter constitutes an adjacent prehistory of the different fates of the women during Partition: some arrive in India as refugees, and others do not. Satya's husband emotionally and physically abandons her as a barren woman, her infertility marking her failure to perform in the regime of compulsory reproductive able-bodiedness. Subsequently, she commits suicide in pre-Partition India by deliberately acquiring a tuberculosis infection. In contrast, Roop, as a beloved wife and mother, migrates to India with Sardarji and their children in 1947. In linking this long socioeconomic history of how reproductive capacity shapes female subjectivity, value, and citizenship with the gendered violence of 1947, Baldwin radically challenges mainstream rhetoric that Partition's gendered and sexual violence against women was unique or exceptional. By extensively using interior monologues to represent the thoughts and feelings of the female characters, she suggests, to use Ritu Menon and Kamla Bhasin's phrase, that Partition's violence was part of "a continuum of violence"[38] against women that inhabited life in colonial and postcolonial India.[39]

Deepti Misri argues that Baldwin's novel absorbs and retells the "stories [about violence against women] told by men from within the feminist framework of its own fictional discourse."[40] I am interested in how the novel's migration story enacts this retelling and unveils subaltern secularism articulated with precariousness; thus, my discussion here focuses primarily on Part 8, which revolves around Sardarji and Roop's dramatic and painful migration to India when Partition is certain. In this account, told primarily from Roop's perspective, an omniscient narrator presents her as one who bears witness to the everyday violence inflicted on precarious female subjects peripheral to the economy of reproductive value, such as Satya (nonreproductive wife), Gujri (the servant woman), Revati Bhua (her unmarried aunt), and Jorimon (her son's nanny). For instance, Satya, as the infertile first wife, does not get to migrate across the border and become a refugee. Realizing her own disposability in the heteronormative patriarchal economy of her family, she deliberately infects herself with tuberculosis and dies. Adjacent to the ironic description of this discursive gendered violence in which nonreproductive women become dispensable subjects and devalued citizens, Roop places a link between her own displacement to India and that of Muslims who are forced to go to Pakistan. For instance, she reads out loud a letter from the manager of their extensive property, Abdul Aziz: "Please not to worry—I have released a king and queen cobra into the godowns to guard your possessions by night. I give them milk each morning so, inshallah, they will sleep during the day and not harm the refugees who shelter in your haveli. Full four hundred people are living here now, both in your wing of the haveli and in your older brother's wing, but only till they can go back to their homes in India."⁴¹ This moment suggestively instantiates the interethnic bond between Sardarji and Abdul; it also reminds us that many, including Partition refugees themselves, thought that they were only displaced temporarily and that they would be able to return to their homes once the violence abated. Few understood that their displacement and their ethnic identity would reinvent them as citizens of new nations and, paradoxically, make a return home impossible.

As in *Cracking India*, where the Parsi Lenny's embodied peripherality incites her to empathize with her nanny, the Muslim refugee Hamida, the Sikh refugee Roop in *What the Body Remembers* also affectively forges an imaginative affiliation with the Muslim female refugee whose house she uneasily inhabits once she has arrived across the border in India. As the narrator observes:

> Roop leaves him, but only to go to the small kitchen. This sagging bungalow holds them in its inner dark till it seems they wander in it always, though their feet be motionless. The Muslim junior official's family it once sheltered before them must now be dead or in some Sikh or Hindu's bungalow in the new Pakistan. Did a Muslim woman feel the fear that lives within Roop, and has she gone to Pakistan, carrying her fear within her? What stories will that woman tell her son?⁴²

In this moment, a secular interethnic affiliation, positing a shared fear, articulates the Sikh refugee Roop and the former Muslim resident who may now be a refugee elsewhere and whose domesticity Roop now inhabits. The home's material space and its household objects metonymically signal Roop's affective state: as if stuck in perpetual movement, she can only forge a contingent, exilic intimacy as a refugee in India. This exilic intimacy is fashioned through her encounter with household objects imbued with memory: "She covers the glass of water at his bedside with a beaded doily a Muslim woman must have crocheted and left behind here."⁴³ This act of remembrance and memory through the material object—the doily—suggests to me what Judith Butler, in *Frames of War*, calls "precariousness," an ethical regard for and recognition of the other's life, when lost, as grievable:

> Precariousness implies living socially, that is, the fact that one's life is always in some sense in the hands of the other. It implies exposure both to those we know and to those we do not know; a dependency on people we know, or barely know, or know not at all. Reciprocally, it implies being impinged upon by the exposure and dependency of others, most of whom remain anonymous. These are not necessarily

relations of love or even of care, but constitute obligations toward others, most of whom we cannot name and do not know, and who may or may not bear traits of familiarity to an established sense of who "we" are.[44]

For Butler, this precariousness entails recognizing that we have obligations toward others and, in turn, acknowledging that any such constructed "we" "is riven from the start, interrupted by alterity, as Levinas has said, and the obligations 'we' have are precisely those that disrupt any established notion of the 'we.'"[45] It is this interruption of alterity, in the migrant's contemplation of self and other marking obligation and connection, that this scene establishes in its representation of Roop's secular recognition of their shared precariousness. In wondering what stories that Muslim woman would tell her son, Roop raises the issues of intergenerational memory, storytelling, and family center stage. The scene therefore presents the subaltern secular through Roop's imaginative and empathetic identification with the female Muslim refugee whose home she inhabits.

Anjaria argues that colonial realism, which appears simplistic or failed, might actually be a deeply political form; indeed, she suggests that the postcolonial realist novel's contribution lies in how it "can account for heterogeneous temporal narratives."[46] This analysis resonates for a deeper understanding of *What the Body Remembers*. The novel's realist narrative is interspersed with sections in which an interior monologue reveals Roop's and Satya's thoughts, feelings, and memories that would be otherwise silenced and that often give the lie to the narrative posited in the realist chapters. Structured thus, the fragmented narrative reiterates in its form the various dismemberments—personal and national—it seeks to represent and, in the process, remember. Within the narrative, storytelling also has a pedagogical dimension: "Why does Papaji tell Jeevan this story? Roop wonders. Whenever Gujri tells Roop a story, she reminds Roop that stories are not told for the telling, but for the teaching."[47] Thus, if the structure of the novel stages multiple perspectives, it also calls attention to its own gaps and silences; this complex structure also reiterates how gendered storytelling constitutes generational memory. This interpretation applies to the stories about women's experiences before and during Partition. For instance, when Roop is reunited with her father, Papaji, in Delhi and asks after the various women in the household, she realizes with horror that each female family member was sacrificed differently in the journey her father made with his grandsons to India. Her single aunt, Revati Bhua, was seen as too old: if she were raped, her father says, "what man would feel dishonored?"[48] Others who die are their servant woman, Gujri, whose feet swell during the long walk across the border until she gives up and refuses to continue, and her sister-in-law, Kusum, who is beautiful and therefore killed by Papaji himself to protect her from the potential/imminent dishonor of rape: all become disposable bodies in the patriarchal economy. Even before Papaji says so, Roop apprehends that Kusum was killed, as so many women were killed, by her own family members—in this case, her own father-in-law: "Roop wants her Papaji to say it, now. Tell this story, just one story of so many. . . . Roop's shoulders hunch beneath the weight of Papaji's stories. . . . His telling is the telling that she will have to tell Jeevan's sons one day: that their mother went to her death just as she was offered it, baring her neck to Papaji's kirpan, willingly, Papaji says, for the izzat of her quom."[49] This moment presents the official patriarchal story about women as desiring death to preserve familial honor while also introducing an instability in its rhetorical claim to veracity through Roop's phrase "willingly, Papaji says." In this way, Roop's voice interrogates the hegemonic patriarchal account of gender-based violence during Partition. Read in dialogue with other diasporic texts that return to post-47 migration, these stories about gendered refugees are powerful performances: "Emerging from scenes of extraordinary subjugation, they remain proof of stubborn life, vulnerable, overwhelmed, their own and not their own, dispossessed, enraged, and perspicacious."[50]

The importance of the telling of these once-silenced stories is reflected in the oral histories that have emerged in Partition Studies. For example, in the introduction to their groundbreaking work *Borders and Boundaries*, Menon and Bhasin note, "For most of the women remembering was important, but as important was remembering to others, having someone listen to their stories and feel that their experience was of value."[51] For me, this desire becomes especially meaningful and resonant in the context of the long history of censorship of refugee voices. Sardarji, one of the key protagonists in *What the Body Remembers*, is depicted as wondering, as he has barely escaped death and made it on a train out of Pakistan, "*Let's see what India brings—let's see if India will be grateful for our sacrifice* [italics original]."[52] Implicit in this musing is the assertion of India's debt to Partition's refugees; thus, a novel that painstakingly maps how debt shapes and mars intimacy and gendered citizenship in colonial India, that criticizes how relations of money lending and socioeconomic debt lead to Roop's marriage to the much-older and much-married Sardarji, now suggestively instantiates a new notion of national ethico-political debt and accountability: the "debt" of the Indian nation for the "sacrifice" of its refugees is established here. This moment vividly recalls Vishwajyoti Ghosh's graphic illustration in "A Good Education," depicting India as a nation constituted by refugees (discussed in the previous chapter). Further, this complex multilayered notion of debt is woven throughout the novel, its gendered impact acknowledged and made visible, over and over. Debt, in Sardarji's imagination, is a nod to the hegemonic political discourse that narrates the Partition migrations and the refugee experience as the "price" of freedom. This notion of debt, as Mimi Thi Nguyen suggests, "points toward a different social order, keeping us in contact with alternate collectivities of others who bear the trace of human freedom that falls apart, or seizes hold, in its giving."[53] Arriving on the literary scene in 1999, more than fifty years after Partition, this novel, through Sardarji's musings, offers an implicit critique of how Partition's refugees have not received recognition or redress for all that they sacrificed at the altar of national independence. In positing this question of the debt owed to Partition refugees in the contemporary moment, and in light of the genocidal attacks on Sikhs in 1984 in India, Baldwin radically offers, from the vantage point of the contemporary diaspora, a powerful critique of how the Indian nation-state has failed its refugees.

Although my discussion of South Asian American literature about Partition here is not comprehensive, I hope it signals how this diasporic and feminist literary production does memory work and animates contemporary reflection on post-47 migrations, as they variously shaped families, intimacy, and national citizenship for women in South Asia. I believe that much scholarship and literature on Partition in the last decade, from the subcontinent and the diaspora, has, in some measure, sought to locate the Partition migrant's silenced voice and to tell the story of what India and Pakistan brought to their refugees. In this context, India-based writer and activist Roy's novel *The Ministry of Utmost Happiness* (2017) is important: perhaps, arguably, more than any other contemporary Indian novel, it connects the ethno-religious divisions of Partition with the contemporary crisis of secularism in the postcolonial state. Its explicit critique of the dehumanization and statelessness generated in and by the ethno-nationalist postcolonial state links it with Ghosh's graphic narrative anthology *This Side, That Side* (discussed in the preceding chapter).[54] Moreover, *The Ministry of Utmost Happiness* situates post-47 India's crisis of secularism in relationship with rapacious capitalism, caste oppression, ecological destruction, and state domination.

Citizenship and Expulsions in Arundhati Roy's
The Ministry of Utmost Happiness

The plot of *The Ministry of Utmost Happiness* revolves around the intertwined stories of two central protagonists: the Muslim hijra Anjum and the Syrian Christian student-and-architect-turned-activist Tilottama (Tilo).

Revolving around Anjum and Tilo's stories are the divergent yet intersecting stories of four male characters, set in India from 1947 to 2017. Biplab Dasgupta, Musa, and Naga are Tilo's friends through college in the mid-1980s. Musa eventually becomes her lover, before he goes underground as a Kashmiri freedom fighter. Biplab (which means "revolution") becomes a staid and cautious official in the Indian Intelligence Bureau and an ambivalent representative of the state. The upper-class Naga, the son of an ambassador, becomes a prominent, left-wing human rights journalist whom Tilo marries for a brief time. The fourth key male character is Major Amrik Singh ("Otter") of the Indian Army in Kashmir. Singh is represented as a sadistic character who deliberately and repeatedly violates Kashmiris' human rights and murders them—innocent bystanders, human rights lawyers, and insurgents—with impunity. Singh eventually flees to Clovis, California, where he seeks asylum and tries to rebuild his life; however, after a few years, tormented by his past and discovered by people looking for him, he murders his wife and two children before committing suicide. This character is based on a real Army officer, Avtar Singh, who was greatly feared in the 1990s in Kashmir. After a particularly grisly kidnapping and killing of a Kashmiri activist, Avtar Singh was transferred to Punjab. He later settled down undercover in the United States after traveling through Canada, until his wife brought domestic violence charges and his cover was blown. In 2012, he killed his family and himself.

Through an omniscient narrator's political commentary and the perspectives of the protagonists, the interlinked stories of these characters from different religious and regional backgrounds depict India in free fall. In an interview promoting the book's release, Roy says, "When everything is collapsing, the only ethical act is to say it, write it, perform it, sing it."[55] This novel addresses the issues of secularism and displacement that I am invested in analyzing; its emergent ethico-political critique sutures the violent histories of the mass displacements of 1947 with those of the 1971 War of Bangladesh, the Kashmir conflict, the 1984 Union Carbide toxic gas disaster, the 1984 anti-Sikh riots, the 1992 Babri Masjid demolition, the 2001 U.S. invasion of Iraq, the 2002 Godhra riots, and other violent moments in world history—enfolding how ethno-nationalism as well as ecological crises, corruption, state brutality, caste oppression, toxic capitalism, patriarchy, and poverty ravage the small and big lives of these characters. This ethico-political critique emerges through an omniscient narrator's voice as well as through the first-person perspectives of different characters.

The 1947 Partition is only briefly mentioned, early in the novel, through the third-person narrator's account of the fortunes of the popular sherbet Rooh Afza, which it describes as "a household name":

For forty years it ruled the market, sending its produce from its headquarters in the old city as far south as Hyderabad and as far west as Afghanistan. Then came Partition. God's carotid burst open on the new border between India and Pakistan and a million people died of hatred. Neighbors turned on each other as though they've never known each other, never been to each other's weddings, never sung each other's songs. The walled city broke open. Old families fled (Muslim). New ones arrived (Hindu) and settled around the city walls. Rooh Afza had a serious setback, but soon recovered and opened a branch in Pakistan. A quarter of a century later, after the Holocaust in East Pakistan, it opened another branch in the brand-new country of Bangladesh. But eventually, the Elixir of the Soul that had survived wars and the bloody birth of three new countries, was, like most things in the world, trumped by Coca-Cola.[56]

This brief and quotidian history of pre- and post-47 South Asia through the commercial fortunes of a favorite sherbet drink—indeed, a household name—is unique; it has a casual air, until it abruptly turns violent. The Partition migrations are described as born of hatred and the "forgetting" of neighbors' interethnic intimacies. The emigration of Muslims and the immigration of Hindus from Delhi in 1947 are then linked to the 1971 repartitioning of Pakistan, described as a "Holocaust." Here, the narrative acknowledges the genocidal scale of these two historical moments of border making and crisis. It does not yet gesture to British colonialism or South Asian nationalisms; it focuses instead on the intimate as that which is lost—on the consumable object in the intimate space of the home and the secular intimate collectivity of neighborly weddings celebrated and songs sung together. This passage mourns both losses—the former felled by multinational capitalism as it spread across Asia in the 1990s and the latter destroyed in 1947.

Although the nation-state and nationalism are not mentioned directly here, as the narrative progresses, the political quickly invades the personal: the life stories of its protagonists increasingly depict a nation-state that produces discriminatory citizenship and secular crisis in South Asia. This discrimination is apparent in Anjum's experiences during the 2002 violence in Godhra and in the representation of multiple characters in or from Kashmir. For instance, the description of the violence against Muslims in 2002 in Gujarat gestures to the complex, multilayered involvement of different institutions in what was officially narrated as "mob" violence:

> The killing went on for weeks and was not confined to the cities alone. The mobs were armed with swords and tridents and wore saffron headbands. They had cadastral lists of Muslim homes, businesses and

shops. They had stockpiles of gas cylinders (which seemed to explain the gas shortages of the previous few weeks). When people who had been injured were taken to hospital, mobs attacked the hospitals. The police would not register murder cases. They said, quite reasonably, that they needed to see the corpses. The catch was that the police were often part of the mobs, and once the mobs had finished their business, the corpses no longer resembled corpses.[57]

This passage suggests the total breakdown of law and order and the statelessness of Muslim citizens in Gujarat at this time. In the aftermath of this violence, "the refugee camps where tens of thousands of Gujarat's Muslims now lived" are depicted, for a while, on TV news: here, as elsewhere, Roy raises questions about visibility and statelessness.[58] In the novel's plot, Anjum survives these riots, because she is a hijra, and the mob is afraid that killing a hijra would bring bad luck upon them. Later, her friend finds her in one of these refugee camps and brings her back to her hijra community in Khwabgah. However, the traumatic memory of this death-filled experience haunts Anjum and drives her to relocate, in retreat, to a graveyard. Here she overcomes her grief and eventually rebuilds her life by creating an alternative imagined community.

The Islamophobia of the postcolonial state depicted here is not unique or new: the novel links it with American politics. Preceding the 2002 Gujarat crisis, the narrator ironically notes that the anti-terrorism measures in the name of national security that swept the United States after September 11, 2001, were expediently deployed in Indian political discourse to justify new anti-terrorism laws in India. Then, the narrative asserts, these laws were used to unlawfully detain Muslims: "The Urdu papers carried stories of young Muslim boys being killed in what the police called 'encounters,' or being caught red-handed in the act of planning terrorist strikes and arrested. A new law was passed which allowed suspects to be detained without trial for months. In no time at all the prisons were full of young Muslim men."[59] Noting the transnational impact of 9/11 on the global spread of Islamophobia, the narrator invites the reader to rethink which actors and institutions engender expulsions. This theme threads through the disparate experiences of the novel's protagonists across South Asia and across the twentieth and early twenty-first centuries—from the 1984 anti-Sikh riots to Kashmir. For instance, Biplab recollects a visit to Kashmir in 1996 ("the sixth straight year of Governor's rule in the state"[60]) and describes the transnational shape of the war zone of Kashmir:

It had already snowed in the high mountains, but the border passes were still negotiable and small legations of fighters, gullible young Kashmiris and murderous Pakistanis, Afghans, even some Sudanese—who belonged to the thirty or so remaining terrorist groups (down from almost one hundred)—were still making the treacherous journey across the Line of Control, dying in droves on the way. Dying. Maybe that's an inadequate description. What was that great line in *Apocalypse Now*? "Terminate with Extreme Prejudice." Our soldiers' instructions at the Line of Control were roughly similar.

What else should they have been? "Call their mothers"?[61]

If Biplab's monologue criticizes the ideological normalization of war, the voices of minority subjects traumatized by state violence, in contrast, bear witness to what remains, and what is created, by the state in the late twentieth century. In diverse ways, the novel's critique of postcolonial reality is rooted in, I suggest, a critique of the nation-state's failure as well as of the global proliferation of war and conflict. Engaging my earlier discussion of Arendt's work, this representation also shows how human rights are lost by minority subjects in the secular state. In this sense, the novel posits that the subaltern has become stateless.

In *The Ministry*, the state's production of death for those who are minorities emblematizes Roy's critique of statelessness as created in postcoloniality. It appears in the poignant or angry reflections of characters like Tilo and Musa and in the recurring accounts of violence and protest in Kashmir. For instance, grieving for his dead two-and-a-half-year-old daughter, Miss Jebeen, Musa writes her a letter:

Babajaana,
    Do you think I'm going to miss you? You are wrong. I will never miss you, because you will always be with me.
    You wanted me to tell you real stories, but I don't know what is real anymore. What used to be real sounds like a silly fairy story now—the kind I used to tell you, the kind you wouldn't tolerate. What I know for sure is only this: in our Kashmir the dead will live forever; and the living are only dead people, pretending.[62]

This evocation of Kashmiris' systemic expulsion as constituting the condition of life in Kashmir recurs at several points in the narrative. It haunts the novel and signals the precarity of statelessness. Undoing all idealizing nationalist rhetorics, as do the graphic narratives discussed in Chapter 1, *The Ministry of Utmost Happiness* offers a critique of the postcolonial condition, marked by secular crisis and "slow violence" for those on the peripheries of the nation-state. In its self-conscious realism, marked by the digressions and disruptions of political commentary, journalistic accounts, and historical information, it also recalls the political realism of exiled Bangladeshi author Taslima Nasrin's novel *Lajja: Shame* (1994).[63] Eschewing the focus on interiority that marks this chapter's earlier novels about migration and loss by Sidhwa and Baldwin, Roy's second novel restories postcolonial India; it chronicles the disintegration of secularism and the failures that attend minor citizenship from the vantage point of its subaltern citizens, marked by caste, religion, sex, indigeneity, and sexuality. To use Jennifer Harford Vargas's words, it "draws attention to the spectrum of domination that dictates people's ability to be fully free."[64]

Noting the turn to realism in Indian fiction in the twenty-first century, Anjaria argues that in contrast to the 1980s' and 1990s' celebration of postmodernism in the work of writers like Salman Rushdie, post-2000 realist fiction embraces an "aesthetic of transparency that verges on the banal, [thematizing] the bearer of 'bare life' rather than the conflicted subject (280)."[65] This transparency gestures to the roots of Roy's novel's political address, which presents the life stories of those rendered subaltern in postcolonial India. Filippo Menozzi notes that Roy's novel defies closure to do "the work of mourning that any idea of art as consolation would provide."[66] For him, the political power of "Arundhati Roy's novels and essays lies in her ability to resist any kind of consolation."[67] Thus, he argues, the novel articulates an "aesthetic of the inconsolable," holding on to the ethical imperatives of realism by eschewing its conventions in favor of a more digressive style that opens up antagonism. This way of reading Roy's aesthetic of the inconsolable as an ethical project resonates; it allows us encounter the novel as bearing witness to the crises that divide the nation *and* as instantiating a just memory of the violence and statelessness produced by the nation-state's institutions. The novel begins with a birth (Anjum's) and ends with one (Udaya Jebeen's); while many relationships in the novel are destroyed by ethnic violence and state brutality, the intimacies and communities that nonetheless survive violence are ethnically diverse. They are built on a shared, secular political solidarity rooted in an ethico-political critique of power relations in India and in its institutions. The novel's survivors are canny and clear-eyed; they forge communities and affiliations through the recognition of their shared dispossessions.

As Chatterjee and others argue, the representation of home and family becomes deeply gendered and linked to the imagination of national culture in Indian nationalist discourse.[68] Relatedly, the space of the home as symbolic of the nation as an imagined community is a trope in many South Asian novels, from Rabindranath Tagore's *The Home and the World* to Salman Rushdie's *Midnight's Children*, to V. S. Naipaul's *A House for*

Mr. Biswas, to Bapsi Sidhwa's *Cracking India*. In *The Ministry of Utmost Happiness*, the space of the home also gestures to political community, but it is resolutely against ethno-nationalism. The structural juxtaposition of two kinds of homes within the novel is itself startling: after witnessing terrible riots in Gujarat, a traumatized Anjum moves into a graveyard in Delhi. Eventually, she settles there, building a community and a ramshackle home that she names Jannat (Paradise) Guest House and Funeral Services. This event is juxtaposed with the image of Kashmir as a region and as a contested homeland. Long described as a paradise/jannat in popular Indian discourse, Kashmir is represented in the stories of Musa, Tilo, and Amrik Singh as riven by war and turned into a graveyard through the 1990s, even as economic liberalization unleashes new urban development in the rest of India: "As the war progressed in the Kashmir Valley, graveyards became as common as the multi-storey parking lots that were springing up in the burgeoning cities in the plains."[69] The narrative's repeated references to graves, graveyards, and funerals in Kashmir signal the growing expulsions in Kashmir that parallel the consumerist growth outside it. What is at stake, the novel suggests, as the graphic anthology *This Side, That Side* also does, is people's aspiration for equal human rights and self-determination in the postcolonial state.

Resonant with Sidhwa's *Cracking India*, children's lives are key in the plot: Anjum's love for her adopted daughter, Zainab; the life and heartbreaking, accidental death of Musa's daughter, the toddler Miss Jebeen Yeswi; and Tilo's adoption of Miss Udaya Jebeen, the baby of Maase Revathy (a gang-rape survivor). Although the novel does not offer the narrative closures of conventional realism or any resolutions for the conflicts and violent statelessness it unveils, it does provide a view of seemingly discrete forms of sexual, ethnic, and economic violence as linked in postcolonial India and imbricated with world history. Joining past and present, it is an act of remembering and witnessing that does memory work. Further, by leaving these antagonisms unresolved, it invites us (as the films *Delhi-6* and *Raazi* do, I suggest in the next chapter) to critique war, religious extremism, and the nation-state's production of statelessness in its drive to consolidate its borders.

As Roy observes in an interview, "All through the book, borders are blurred: between gender, between castes, between human and animals."[70] Elsewhere, I note how Saskia Sassen calls for attention to "the border crossings of contemporary imperialism as systemic processes of 'expulsion' that produce 'astoundingly elementary brutalities'": "today's systemic edge is a space of expulsions," she argues, "from which people, resources, and biospheres are being expelled across the world's geographies."[71] By examining the literary representation of the Partition migrations and displacement in post-47 India in these works by women writers that span the diaspora and the subcontinent, in this chapter, I hope to offer a new account of mid-twentieth-century border crossings as expulsions and of their legacies for refugees and minority citizens in South Asia. In different ways, these novels translate, remember, and witness postcolonial displacement under the modern politicization of religion that unleashes secular crisis. They also, however, illuminate the production of empathy, solidarity, and survival through the practice of the subaltern secular by its minor protagonists. Their focus on female and trans protagonists also queers heteronormative nationalist discourse, revealing how forms of minoritization (ethnicity, religion, caste, indigeneity, sexuality, and so forth) are enmeshed such that their everyday entanglement intensifies disenfranchisement in the conflict zone. Further, like the graphic narratives discussed in the preceding chapter, these novels invite us to consider how the terms we use to narrate transnational histories of modern migration can story subjects as agents of their histories—or fail in that endeavor.

Media, Violence, and Reparations in the Conflict Zone

> Put your ear to the ground in this part of the world and you can hear the thrumming, the deadly drumbeat of burgeoning anger.
>
> —ARUNDHATI ROY, *Power Politics*[72]

> "It reminds me of the days of partition. I sent my young granddaughters to a relative's house after a panchayat was held in our village on September 5. I called their uncle to take them to a safe place," said Rafiqan.
>
> —PEEYUSH KHANDELWAL, *"Muzaffarnagar Riots"*[73]

> Prominent Muslim body Jamiat Ulama-i-Hind on Wednesday demanded . . . a law at the central and state levels against lynching. . . . "Today, the communal situation is worse than at the time of partition but we need not get into hopelessness as this country has a very strong tradition of love and affection," Madani said.
>
> —OUTLOOK WEB BUREAU, *"State of Fear from Kashmir to Kanyakumari"*[74]

The public discourse about Hindu-Muslim ethnic violence in July 2013 following an incident in which a young girl was harassed by men from a different community in the northern Indian city of Muzaffarnagar offers only one of many reminders of the enduring legacy of Partition: it is the residual memory that shapes the interpretation of violence and the failure of the secular in present-day South Asia. The multiple displacements and structural violence that are a legacy of Partition thus continue to reverberate in unexpected ways. Unlike in the early national period, when Hindus and Sikhs from Pakistan were welcomed, even if ambivalently, as citizens in India, Pakistani Hindus and Sikhs arrive in Delhi today only to eke out a precarious existence as refugees in the city's slums. Although mainstream media sympathetically portray their plight and the gendered, ethnic discrimination and violence they are fleeing in Pakistan, the governmental mechanisms for them to actually get Indian citizenship have remained obscure and often inaccessible.[75] In this matter, the new Citizenship Amendment Act, which was passed in Parliament on December 11, 2019, will significantly simplify gaining access to citizenship for these refugee communities. Yet many scholars, protesters, and critics note that it simultaneously institutionalizes new modes (at least in its current form) of discrimination based on religion that undermine India's constitutional ethos of secularism and render Indian Muslims' citizenship rights precarious in historically unprecedented ways. Relatedly, for Partition refugees who settled in the erstwhile state of Jammu and Kashmir immediately after 1947, between thirty and thirty-five thousand families are still struggling for voting rights. Their children do not get birth certificates, and they are denied jobs; the committee president of the West Pakistan Refugees Action Committee says, "Our struggle for the last over 60 years is to get citizenship rights. Children are denied jobs. . . . [O]ur three generations are finished."[76] The reorganization of the state of Jammu and Kashmir in 2019 has created more complications in terms of India's democratic political institutions. The politics of citizenship that ethnicize access to the rights accruing to nationality have only intensified in varied ways across India: commentators from across Asia and the United States have questioned the removal of nearly two million people from the National Register of Citizens voter rolls in Assam in August 2019; most of these voters are Muslim, women, or indigenous peoples whose poverty precludes them from having the necessary paperwork to prove citizenship. Similarly, people feel uncertainty and anxiety about how equal rights and secularism will manifest in the newly organized territory of Jammu and Kashmir.

A substantial field of Critical Kashmir Studies has emerged in which writers, critics, and activists have brought to light the structures of violence that saturate life in Kashmir. This violence, they have shown, has intensified the complex statelessness of Kashmiris. As Basharat Peer, the noted Kashmir journalist who migrated to Delhi in the 1990s, writes in his poignant memoir *Curfewed Night*, when he returned to Kashmir in 2007, "the heady, rebellious Kashmir I left as a teenager was now a land of brutalized, exhausted, and uncertain people."[77] Scholars including Suvir Kaul, Mona Bhan, and Deepti Misri, among others, have called attention to the sociocultural, embodied, and psychic legacies of Kashmir as a war zone since late

1989.⁷⁸ As Kaul notes, "For a decade and more now, observers of Kashmir have noted the high incidence of cases of post-traumatic stress disorder; the psychic and affective wounds of war are visible everywhere."⁷⁹

Precarity thus enfolds minor citizens and migrants' lives; indeed, Srishtee Sethi's ethnography of Hindu Bhil borderland communities as they negotiate various identities—Pakistani, tribal, Hindu, caste—and claim access to Indian citizenship in the wake of Partition and the 1965 war shows how state borderlands transform cultural identities, instigate border crossing in majoritarian contexts, and produce precarity.⁸⁰ It is significant that in November 2017, the Bharatiya Janata Party (BJP) government announced the first historical reparations to be made to refugees of the 1947 Partition currently settled in Jammu and Kashmir. These reparations involve a "one-time settlement" cash award of INR 5.5 lacs (approx. $8,600) to refugees who are from what is called Pakistan-occupied Kashmir (PoK) in India and Azad Jammu and Kashmir (AJK) in Pakistan. "There are 32,000 PoK refugee families and 20,000 West Pakistani refugee families living in Jammu and Kashmir"; however, Partition refugees from West Pakistan, also living in the area, still await reparations.⁸¹ In October 2019, the Union Cabinet of India further announced that fifty-three hundred refugee families who did not get that cash award in 2017 because they had settled outside the state of Jammu and Kashmir would now get this settlement since they had returned to and resettled in that state. However, roughly four hundred thousand Partition refugees from West Pakistan (now Bangladesh) and their descendants remain stateless, and caste inequality is an important factor in this status: "The population of West Pakistan Refugees living in the Jammu region is estimated to be roughly 4 lakh [four hundred thousand] at present. Most of them are Dalits whose families moved to India after partition. Though three generations have lived in the state since then, they were deprived of their rights, including the right to vote during Vidhan Sabha and Panchayat elections, access to central welfare schemes, affirmative action and the right to buy land."⁸²

This contemporary inequity toward the multiple refugee communities created by and in the wake of the 1947 Partition is a stark reminder of how the unfinished Partition continues to manifest in Indian political life and shatter its secular aspirations. As Ghosh's work poignantly reminds us (see Chapter 1), Partition is still happening. It continues to be mobilized in political discourses about citizenship, national community, belonging, and land rights, even as it raises questions about redress, debt, and the monetary value of lives and communities lost. It also shows that the question of how the 1947 migrations resonate for Indian cultural and political life is complex and highly differentiated. It affects many dimensions of contemporary experience for refugees and imperiled citizens alike in the neoliberal, postcolonial state: it influences their material access to shelter, education, political representation, and human rights as well as the collective cultural fashioning of an ethical and just secular. The abjection of the peripheral and precarious refugee communities created by Partition persists even today, three generations later, and speaks to the limits of human rights when conceived in terms of national rights, as noted by Arendt in the mid-twentieth century.

3

Melodrama, Community, and Diasporas in Popular Hindi and Accented Cinema

> The more fruitful approach to melodrama would . . . pick up the threads of a general study of melodrama, as a broadly important cultural form . . . in tension with and transformed by realism and the more realistic techniques of cinema, yet best understood as melodrama, not failed tragedy or inadequate realism.
>
> —LINDA WILLIAMS, *"Melodrama Revised"*[1]

In the preceding chapters, I trace how visual culture, graphic narratives, and literature about South Asia, whether from the subcontinent or the diaspora, have illuminated the transnational and gendered legacies of the Partition migrations, with a focus on the cultural representation of refugee memory and citizenship. In particular, I map some of the tensions inherent in the textual and visual imagination of a performative secular in our received iconographies of refugees and citizens in the nation. By looking at print culture objects, I also gesture to how the popular visual iconography of normative embodied citizenship in the Indian nation changed from the colonial to the postcolonial period and how it became increasingly tied to the visible, embodied, sartorial performance of religious/ethnic difference within the imagined secular space of the nation. My goal is to uncover how the aesthetic strategies of different cultural texts and objects across media—from comics and charts to the novel—enable or foreclose the migrant's performance of an ethico-political secular as a way of relating to the other and enable or foreclose building a secular community in the post-47 period.

I now turn to the medium of film to explore how five different movies address secularism and citizenship during and after the Partition migrations in postcolonial South Asia. In this chapter, I draw upon Linda Williams's work on melodrama as a form incorporating realism to analyze how it shapes the representation of migration, secularism, and citizenship in contemporary Bollywood cinema (Rakeysh Omprakash Mehra's *Delhi-6*, Kabir Khan's *Bajrangi Bhaijaan*, and Meghna Gulzar's *Raazi*), Indian art cinema (Shyam Benegal's *Mammo*), and what Hamid Naficy calls "accented cinema"—Sabiha Sumar's *Khamosh Pani* (Silent Waters), a transnational Pakistani-German collaboration. I select these five films because, in different ways, they stage the sociocultural effects of the Partition migrations at different historical moments of crisis in South Asia. Further, like the literary and graphic narratives discussed in previous chapters, they depict the precariousness that attaches to minority subjects—women, widows, children, Muslims, Dalits—who navigate multiple national border crossings, discrimination, and ethnic citizenship norms in India, Pakistan, and America. One of the many legacies of the 1947 Partition for India, as I argue in my first book, *Violent Belongings*, is that the Indian nation and nationality often become ethnicized as Hindu in the Indian public sphere; as a result, what I endeavor to trace here is how secularism therefore becomes an increasingly anxious idea, a contested commitment, and a precarious practice. The questions that animate this chapter include the following: How do film representations—popular as well as art cinema—about the mid-twentieth-century migrations figure the Partition, the secular, and the national? What stories about the experience of displacement and border crossing do they chronicle, and what aesthetic and affective responses do they invite as they illuminate what is created through displacement? What genre conventions do they mobilize to narrate citizenship and subaltern secularism in the crisis of the postcolonial state?

In this chapter, I argue that some of the mainstream Bollywood films considered here posit one or both of these aspirations: geopolitical peace between India and Pakistan and secular community within these nations. Others, including *Mammo* and *Khamosh Pani* (considered art or accented cinema), depict the forces that render these aspirations impossible to realize; in these films, the nation-state and nationalist politics, articulated with patriarchal institutions, are criticized. Often, they do this by staging, as the Google commercial "Reunion" does (discussed in Chapter 4), border crossings that generate or destroy Hindu-Sikh-Muslim relations of friendship and care—of intimacy. Simultaneously, what emerges in many of these films is a new critique of decolonization, the postcolonial state, and its institutions from the vantage point of the gendered migrant/refugee/citizen. In different ways, these film representations of border crossings signal that "what appears at first blush as the articulation of state sovereignty actually expresses its diminution relative to other kinds of global forces—the waning relevance and cohesiveness of the form."[2] In a recent interview, Wendy Brown argues that today, "new forms of governmentality" in the nation-state are constantly producing "identities that are racialized, ethnicized, and 'religionized,' sometimes in incoherent yet consequential ways." In other words, there is an "intersection between what happens at the borders and what happens within. There are forms of policing, securitizing, categorizing and identity-making that saturate the internal lives of nations engaged in them, and that do not just happen at their borders."[3] The films I consider in this chapter illuminate these new forms of identity making and governmentality in post-47 South Asia from within its nation-states and at their borders, from the early national period as well as the twenty-first century.

Tejaswini Ganti describes some of the ways in which the Hindi film industry has been indelibly marked by the 1947 Partition; for instance, she notes that it has been "shaped by the histories of migration and displacement set in motion by Partition. Many of the prominent actors, producers, directors, and technicians either migrated to Bombay from Pakistan or are descendants of those who did. The predominance of ethnic Punjabis in the contemporary industry is also a consequence of this history."[4] Similarly, Rachel Dwyer delineates how the secular appears in the Bombay film industry, not only at the level of the community of workers who populate it but also in the visual lexicon of identity and community across genres it offers.[5] Arguing that "cinema is the best place" to look for "the secular imagination" in India,[6] Dwyer shows how religion is addressed through different genres of film in Hindi cinema, such as the "mythological film," "the devotional film," and the "Islamicate film." Examining the appearance of religion in the genre of "the social film," Dwyer observes that religion often appears in this genre through an overt or latent invocation of mythology and through the role of fate played in melodrama. I extend this current scholarly discussion of Bollywood's secularism by considering recent films that address secularism in popular and political ways. Drawing upon the writings of Linda Williams, Rachel Dwyer, Tejaswini Ganti, and Ravi Vasudevan on melodrama, I unravel how melodrama frames the encounters among ethno-nationalism, religion, and border crossing in *Delhi-6*, *Bajrangi Bhaijaan*, and *Raazi*.

Film scholars approach the relationship between Indian cinema and public culture in diverse ways. Vasudevan describes "melodrama as a public fictional form."[7] In *Bollywood's India*, Priya Joshi argues that Bollywood cinema articulates a public "fantasy" of the nation and has embedded within it "the iconographies of the nation."[8] Studying the historically "shifting grammar of public fantasies" of Hindi films across the decades, Joshi shows that "Bollywood's blockbusters have conducted a dialogue over the idea of 'India,' recognizing that cleavage rather than coherence is its dominant topos."[9] On the one hand, in this chapter, I examine how contemporary Bollywood films describe the cleavages of migration and border crossing in the public fantasy of the secular they offer. More broadly, I consider Hindi melodrama as a public fictional form that often discloses the public fantasy of secular India. I place into conversation four different Hindi films produced between 1990 and 2018 and Pakistani filmmaker Sumar's

Punjabi film *Khamosh Pani* (2003). Written by Indian writer and activist Paromita Vohra, *Khamosh Pani* was produced through transnational India-Pakistan collaboration, as was Vishwajyoti Ghosh's graphic narrative anthology. Because it thematizes women's experiences during Partition and post-Partition border crossings, it is a critically important intervention in our archive of migration stories that traces what remains, and what has been created, after Partition. I juxtapose these different films to track the heterogeneous iconography of the secular and postcolonial citizenship they create and cite in their stories about migration and intimacies. Among my arguments is that in some of these films, melodrama enables the emergence of a powerful humanist critique of the postcolonial state, the crisis of secularism, and globalized media. As such, the melodramatic representation of gendered intimacies and precarity signal the failures of nationalism and state secularism. Resonant with Arendt's writings, it critiques the modern institution of citizenship as it plays out in the lived experience of urban and rural, male and female Indians, Pakistanis, and South Asian Americans. As an alternative, in many films, melodrama articulates an aspirational and subaltern secular, rooted in and emerging from intimate relationships in the midst of historical dispossessions (as in the literary works discussed in the preceding chapter).

In examining the depiction of religion in Hindi cinema, Dwyer maps how *secularism* is a contested term, especially in India, where it is often used to mean a high and equal regard for all religions.[10] The shifting imagination of secularism across these films is often tied to the central function of the family as well as of the postcolonial state. The films under discussion here represent the Partition migrations in productive and troubling ways. On the one hand, they return to these migrations to rethink the role of religion in the contemporary nation-state in South Asia. On the other hand, they bear witness to how religious ethnicity, violence, and gender increasingly undermine the experience of equal citizenship, social justice, and human rights in postcolonial India and Pakistan. In different ways, they gesture to the political stakes of the recognition or elision of precariousness. In the following sections, I hope to show how recent popular Bollywood cinema uses the Partition and the theme of border crossing to invent new narratives of secularism and secular nationality for minority citizens. Often, these narratives turn to the register of kinship or familial intimacy to reimagine the public fantasy of the Indian nation and secular citizenship. In contrast, art cinema and exilic or third cinema offer a postcolonial feminist critique of the terror of ethno-nationalism in South Asia by representing its violent effects in the minority female citizen's everyday life. Among my arguments, then, is that the contemporary films discussed here use the trope of the family to criticize patriarchal ethno-nationalism, the state, and media institutions.

In my first book, *Violent Belongings*, I track how many Hindi films from the 1980s and 1990s use the trope of "interethnic coupledom" to figure secularism and secular citizenship in Bollywood cinema.[11] There, I describe "interethnic coupledom" as the heteronormative formation of romance between subjects of two different religious/ethnic identities, although in most Hindi films, it is predominantly configured as a Muslim woman and a Hindu man in an intimate relationship/marriage. One of the fascinating aspects of this chapter's filmic archive is that it displaces this formation of heterosexual interethnic coupledom as the privileged site through which power and belonging are negotiated in the nation and through which secular citizenship is invented. Instead, the films about border crossings I consider here reframe intimacies within and beyond the family form to narrate migration, memory, solidarity, and the secular. Vasudevan's analysis of the family melodrama enables a consideration of how familial and civic intimacy narratives overlap; I show how this trait is central to popular as well as art films about experiencing migration and *performing the subaltern secular*, in ways that interrogate dominant public fantasies of the nation.

Asian Americans and Secular Crisis in Rakeysh Omprakash Mehra's *Delhi-6*

Discussing how "the parameters of family, social order, and nationhood" have changed from the "feudal family romance" of the 1930s and 1940s to contemporary Bollywood family films, Vasudevan suggests that while earlier films represent society horizontally as symbolic of the family, later films that foreground the maternal figure should be properly recognized as "vertical" melodrama, insofar as they supplant "the family order with an order consecrating the state form, however ambiguously. In the contemporary epoch, the horizontal form with the father as the authoritative figure of power embeds the political within it."[12] In the process, Vasudevan argues, the state's absence "within the fiction of the globalizing nation" in contemporary Hindi films about family merits attention: "The global frame is crucial: for the contemporary family film is distinguished from its earlier avatars in its bid to reconcile the division between West and East such that a Western upbringing does not make a protagonist ineligible for the national project."[13] This recognition of the global frame of the contemporary family drama is especially resonant for an understanding of how a diasporic Indian American subject—a New Yorker—becomes the central protagonist of a story about the capital of India in *Delhi-6*.

Delhi-6 is a 2009 Hindi film directed by Mehra, who has also made the successful films *Aks* (2001) and *Rang De Basanti* (2006). The film's opening scenes are set in New York City and revolve around the diasporic life of a multigenerational Indian family. In these early sequences, we see an elderly grandmother, Annapurna Mehra, also called Dadi (Waheeda Rehman), informing her son and daughter-in-law that she would like to return to her home in India after five years in the United States—they have all just returned from a doctor's visit, where they have learned that she has a chronic heart condition. Her daughter-in-law, Fatima Mehra (Tanvi Azmi), and son, Rajan Mehra (Indrajit Sarkar), refuse to go to India. Her son vehemently says, "Ma, you know I'll *never* go back to India." As a result, we see her grandson, Roshan (Abhishek Bachchan), offer to accompany her instead, to perform the filial duty that his father rejects. The film's narrative arc then follows the grandmother and grandson as they return to her ancestral home in Chandni Chowk, Old Delhi (zip code 110006), and establish an everyday life together: she, renewing old friendships and ties with her neighbors; he, discovering modern, urban India as well as his own personal history as an Indian American.

Initially, this return to Old Delhi is wonderful and depicted as a return to their "roots"—their neighbors welcome them with open arms, and Old Delhi is shown to be a congested and ethnically hybrid but deeply inclusive and secular community. However, as the film unfolds, an urban legend about a black monkey roaming the city shatters this fragile secular community, alongside the critical unveiling of caste discrimination through the characters of Jalebi (Divya Dutta) and Gobar (Atul Kulkarni). While hyperbolic Indian television media representations proliferating under globalization saturate and shape public discourse about this monkey, political leaders divided on religious lines foment tensions over the mythic monkey until neighbors have turned on old friends along the same religious lines. At the end, police officers influenced by the prevailing media rhetoric instigate Hindu-Muslim riots in Old Delhi, shattering the idyllic representation of secular community set up earlier in the film. As friends and neighbors who have grown up together turn against one another, the film evokes the subcontinent's histories of the 1947 Partition, the more recent 1992 demolition of the Babri Masjid, and the 2002 Godhra pogroms. When the Hindu and Muslim groups are about to attack each other, Roshan heroically tries to stop this tide of violence: he wears a monkey costume and appears in front of them. This bid to defuse the situation and prevent mass ethnic violence works. Both mobs unite to attack Roshan, and the neighborhood is saved; Roshan, as a classic melodramatic victim hero, is almost killed. When his mask is taken off, the warring sides realize that there is no black monkey and that they may have killed their friend. The film ends with the melodramatic near-sacrifice of the diasporic, ethnically hybrid Indian American male subject, which brings a moral lesson for the characters carried away by ethno-nationalist extremism. The film thus reinforces the value of secular community and affirms the emotional bonds that exist across religious (and to a lesser extent, caste) divides in this ancient and densely knit part of Old Delhi.

The reception of *Delhi-6* was complicated. The film won the Nargis Dutt Award for Best Feature Film on National Integration at the fifty-seventh National Film Awards, and its music won music director A. R. Rahman the Best Music Director Award, but it was a box-office flop in commercial terms. Critics said that Mehra had disappointed them after producing such hits as *Rang De Basanti*, which was seen as subtler. Rachel Saltz of the *New York Times* calls the film "a burbling stew of a tale": "You don't have to love *Delhi-6* to admire Rakeysh Omprakash Mehra, a director who has found a way to make personal films within commercial Hindi cinema. His ambitions are vast: *Delhi-6* is nothing less than a referendum on the modern Indian soul.... *Delhi-6* can be maddeningly vague, which robs its ending— a finale as joltingly (melo)dramatic as any in Bollywood—of the impact it intends."[14] Noted critic Anupama Chopra declares, "Ultimately then, the film is a noble failure. *Delhi-6* is ambitious and well-intentioned, but good intentions don't always translate into good cinema. See it if you must."[15] Rajeev Masand's review is more ambivalent: he praises the film's "remarkable cinematography," "inherent beauty," and the "warmth at its centre . . . provided by AR Rahman's spellbinding music." Further, he argues, "at the core of *Delhi-6*, however, are its real heroes, its characters." Yet for Masand, *Delhi-6* has a "muddled message" and a "frustrating climax," and it "isn't great cinema like Mehra's *Rang De Basanti*."[16]

However, I suggest that *Delhi-6*'s apparent "failure," as announced by these critics, also points to what is creative, new, and political in the film's use of melodrama to represent the crisis of secularism in contemporary India. The film has three dimensions as a critical intervention in representations of religion and nationalism in modern India that are worth discussing: (1) it uses melodrama to narrate interethnic intimacy and the secular; (2) it unveils the heterogeneous, historically mobile, and complicated standpoints from which gendered South Asian American subjects may encounter modern India—nostalgically, affectively, and ambivalently; and (3) it criticizes the role of globalized media institutions as well as political leaders in the production of ethno-nationalist violence. Among my arguments is that through the melodramatic unfolding of the hysteria around the mythic black monkey, and through the defamiliarizing perspective of the diasporic, masculine victim hero, Roshan, the film criticizes globalized media, ethno-nationalist rhetoric, and cultural violence (including patriarchal violence) as they shape public culture in urban India.

The film offers three important comments on secularism in contemporary India. First, it presents a unique account of the sensual modes of living religion and performing the secular (as Talal Asad defines it) in everyday life in contemporary India, where interethnic intimacy creates the secular fabric of the community. For instance, in the first half of the film, Roshan's cultural encounter with Indian life in Old Delhi is populated by experiences that are as linked to viewing, performing, and consuming religious cultures as they are to building new friendships and falling in love with Bittu Sharma (Sonam Kapoor). In an early sequence depicting Roshan first arriving in Delhi, we witness his experience at a traditional theatrical performance of the Ram Leela in a large, outdoor venue. The cinematography highlights Roshan's consumption of the aesthetic pleasures of the color, emotion, and drama of the performance itself. It also depicts how attending this performance of a familiar epic story (*The Ramayana*) draws together the locals—across age, gender, religion, and generations—into a familiar, close-knit community. This sensual pleasure in the heterogeneity of India's cultural pluralism is also evident in the dream-and-song sequence "Dil Gira Dafatan": set in New York City, it depicts Roshan's secular fantasy of how the different religious and cultural traditions (and people) that make up his life in Old Delhi blend into his life in the United States.

The film's imagination of the secular, then, is not about the rejection of religion in favor of the embrace of modern, scientific rationality. Instead, as Asad suggests, it insists on the contemporaneity and modernity of faith itself and the plenitude of these heterogenous faiths in the fabric of everyday life in Old Delhi. For instance, in an early sequence where the rickshaw carrying an unconscious Dadi to the hospital gets stuck in a traffic jam, Roshan becomes very angry and frustrated because the cause of the traffic jam—a cow in labor in the middle of the street—is not being moved but instead being treated with reverence. The sequence portrays Roshan's frustration at the situation's apparent irrationality and juxtaposes his irritation with the perspective of the locals, who wait patiently and devoutly pray to the cow (gesturing to the contemporary resurgence of the cow protection movement in India). Indeed, the film then shows Dadi herself regaining consciousness and praying to the pregnant cow, unperturbed and possibly magically healed by her faith, to the astonishment of Roshan. This scene and many others situate different performances of faith and belief alongside Roshan's rationality as diverse ways of life in the heterogeneous city space of Delhi. They reveal competing and contradictory approaches to religion and the performance of faith in public life.

Second, the film proffers the secular as a space-clearing gesture that invites multiple performances of faith as well as atheism—a bold new approach. For instance, in different sequences, Roshan is depicted as praying at the local temple with his grandmother as well as at the mosque in the neighborhood. This melodramatic gesture is not new: in many Hindi films, including *Gadar* (2001) and *Bombay* (1995), the Muslim female protagonist performing the Hindu or Sikh prayer is a trope of the performative secular. But *Delhi-6* differs from these films in two ways: first, the *male* hero, Roshan, repeatedly performs this gesture of prayer in multiple religious spaces; and second, Roshan's parents are Hindu and Muslim. In depicting this hybrid and subaltern secular performance through Roshan's Indian American masculine subjectivity, the film makes visible the cultural hybridities that inhabit Indian society as well as the fact that for many urban Indians, visiting multiple religious sites—Hindu, Muslim, Sufi, Christian—to pray can be an ordinary dimension of their lives. For instance, in Mumbai, several Hindus I know pray not only at the local Ganesh temple on Tuesdays but also at St. Michael's Church in Mahim on Wednesdays and then at the Makhdoom Ali Mahimi Dargah on Thursdays, having heard that praying in each of these spaces on these specific days is auspicious. They see no contradiction in this hybrid way of life between the occasional practice of another's faith and one's own faith as well as cultural identity. Instead, it exists on a continuum of contingent, culturally hybrid subaltern practices that constitute the secular in everyday life.

My third point, however, is that *Delhi-6* wants to create a space in the twenty-first century, as Mani Ratnam's *Bombay* did in the 1990s, to distinguish between the politicization of religion and religious extremism (and the attendant creation of political community on the basis of religion) and the lived hybridity of religion in everyday life and civic society in urban India. Hence, juxtaposed throughout the film are two formations or practices of religious identity: one is everyday, rooted in performance, and reflected in an ethics of regard for the other as neighbor; the other is marked by racism and prejudice toward the different religious community and embodied mostly by those who inhabit the state and political institutions, from the police officers to political leaders in the film. The former is grounded in an affective vision of a hybrid and inclusive community; the latter represents the forces of ethno-nationalism and chauvinism that have increasingly gained power in contemporary India.[17] Given the chilling effects of silencing dissent that recent events have had on cultural discourse, journalism, and even the film industry, *Delhi-6* is an important and landmark film to consider: it bravely illuminates the potential for violence in India's political institutional crisis of secularism in the midst of explosive economic growth and globalization, even as it identifies and celebrates the joy, beauty, hybridity, and ethics of regard that also inhabit the lived performance of the "secular" in the urban modernity of Indian communities like Chandni Chowk.

It is worth acknowledging that *Delhi-6* is also new in that it unveils the heterogeneous, complicated standpoints from which Indian Americans may encounter modern India—nostalgically, affectively, and ambivalently. In this consideration, it departs from the conventional plot device of many earlier popular Dharma Productions and Shahrukh Khan films: these films, when about the diaspora, are structured around an apparent conflict between authentic Indian-ness and the inauthentic diasporic subject and also marked by anxiety over what constitutes authentic Indian-ness as cultural identity. In these films, best exemplified by Yash Chopra's *Dilwale Dulhaniya Le Jayenge*, authenticity is mostly achieved by the diasporic subject when he or she performs Hindu religious identity or behaves in ways that shore up Indian, patriarchal gender cultures and the authority of the father (as Vasudevan notes). In contrast, *Delhi-6* offers a new set of diasporic stories. As the film unfolds, we discover why Roshan's parents are bitterly against going to India: we learn this familial prehistory in the old house in Chandni Chowk (built in 1808), when Dadi tells Roshan that because his parents' love marriage was interethnic (his mother is Muslim, and his father Hindu), Roshan's grandfather refused to accept it. Instead, as the patriarch, he told his son to get out of their house, at which point he left not only the house but also the nation. The couple immigrated to America, never to return except to attend the grandfather's funeral and perform his last rites. In the film, the character of Uncle Ali Baig (Rishi Kapoor) paints this picture for Roshan. He reveals that Roshan's father fought everyone—his parents, her parents, their friends, and the entire community—because of his love for Fatima. Thus, Roshan's parents as exiles and immigrants are diasporic subjects who are definitely *not* nostalgic for the nation. The nation's ideological and official promise of secularism failed them, so they fled to the United States to realize their precarious interethnic coupledom. The film's narrative takes pains to distinguish Roshan's parents' antipathy to returning to India from his: Roshan does not share their bitterness. He is curious and open-minded about India, and his bond with his grandmother allows him to have an affection for many things Indian and, specifically, for Old Delhi. The song sequences are the spaces where you see this interest most vividly, as they etch out the beauty of local life, from the pigeons, the spices, and the warmth of its people to the teeming vibrant "balance" of Indian urban spaces. Living in the close proximity of Old Delhi—and many sequences emphasize the physical intimacy of Chandni Chowk's residents, the crowdedness, and the relentless movement—he falls in love with the local community, its way of life, and Bittu, who dreams of becoming the next winner of *Indian Idol*.

Relatedly, Roshan's Dadi's nostalgic idealization of India changes over the course of the film. As media-stoked Hindu-Muslim tensions escalate in the neighborhood, one scene finds Roshan refused entry into the temple he frequents with his grandmother, ostensibly due to his interethnic parentage. Multiple encounters with Hindu and Muslim extremists disturb Dadi and wash away all her nostalgia: she realizes that ethno-nationalist politics have shattered the secular everyday of life in Chandni Chowk. In a sequence following this understanding, she tells Roshan sadly, "I don't feel like dying here anymore. Roshan, take me back to America." Thus, different characters across the film have diverse and ambivalent feelings toward India and belonging, and these emotions change as the melodramatic plot unfolds.

The film's representation of the diasporic subject breaks with traditional filmic narratives of nostalgia and idealization in several ways. In an early intimate conversation, Baig sighs regretfully that Roshan will leave them all soon and go back to America, to which Roshan gently replies, "Uncle Baig, I'm an American. My life belongs over there." Yet by the end of the film, when Baig urges him to leave the increasingly violent situation for the safety of America, Roshan insists, "I never want to go." Roshan then claims the community—and, suggestively, the nation—as his own: "How can I stay away? This is all mine. Their virtues are my virtues. Their flaws are mine too." When Baig disagrees, Roshan emphatically asserts, "No, Uncle, no. India works. The people make it work. The people are good here. My parents never admit it, but they miss their life here." In this back-and-forth, *Delhi-6* captures the ambivalent desires and affects that can mark diasporic subjects who navigate the complexities of India across generations and negotiate unique journeys of return. In very thoughtful ways, it reverses the typical binaristic representation of India and its British or American diaspora typical of Yash Raj–produced films like Aditya Chopra's *Dilwale Dulhania Le Jayenge* (1995), and Subhash Ghai's *Pardes* (1997). In these narratives, the diaspora is where Indian Americans are "spoiled" or "corrupted" or face the danger of becoming so. They drink alcohol, are sexually promiscuous or disrespectful of elders, and are often required to prove their authentic Indian-ness by performing ritualistic acts or religious traditions that are deeply gendered: touching elders' feet, deferring to parents' wishes, dressing in Indian clothes, putting on the sindoor for married Hindu women, and so forth. These films often idealize India as the land of the golden fields of Punjab and as a source of authenticity, rootedness, and cultural identity—a foil to what Vijay Mishra calls the tropes of "the unhappy, schizophrenic, cultural condition of the diaspora."[18] Indeed, Mishra notes, Hindi cinema persistently represents "its own and India's (mis)reading of the diaspora. Part of this 'misreading' reflects a center-periphery understanding of the homeland-diaspora nexus in which the diaspora becomes a site of permissible but controlled transgressions while the homeland is the crucible of timeless dharmik virtues."[19] In contrast, in *Delhi-6*, set in Old Delhi with architectural evocations of India's Mughal past, populated by subjects who travel back and forth to the United States or aspire to be *Indian Idol* winners, these binaristic stereotypes fall apart. The film thus invites us to recognize how, in India's modernity, as Bhaskar Sarkar says in a different context, "the global and the local endlessly reconstitute each other."[20]

The diaspora-homeland binary falls apart in several ways in *Delhi-6*, such that in the recognition of how the global and the local reconstitute each other, dominant ethno-nationalist ideologies are called into question. For instance, the United States is presented as a safe space for the endangered interethnic secular intimacy of Roshan's parents—indeed, it makes interethnic intimacy possible. Instead of idealizing India, the film's narrative is critical and affirming of modern, globalized India. Most prominently, we encounter India through the perspective of a second-generation, ethnically hybrid, Indian American: Roshan lives in India for an extended time and assimilates into the community in a way rarely depicted in Hindi cinema. Thus, the narrative defamiliarizes everydayness in urban India, holding it up for scrutiny—its caste and gender discriminations, its religious biases, and its extremes of faith and communal warmth.

Like its predecessor *Rang De Basanti*, *Delhi-6* criticizes the role of media and state institutions in engendering violence in the nation. In an early sequence, the freshly arrived Asian American Roshan questions an inspector who is gratuitously slapping a civilian: "Whoa, you don't have the right to do that. What're you doing?" Retaliating against this challenge, the inspector slaps Roshan; when a shocked Roshan slaps him back, he finds himself in jail. This scene ends with Roshan being bailed out by Uncle Ali Baig and the policeman warning Baig to let Roshan know, "This is India. Here, you bow to a uniform. There is no choice in the matter." Here and in several other moments, *Delhi-6* lays bare the corruption in India's law-and-order machinery that recalls a similar critique of political corruption in *Rang De Basanti*. Relatedly, the film sharply criticizes mass media journalism and networks in India. For instance, early brief cuts introduce us to how Indian television news channels pursue drama and viewership by disseminating a narrative about a dangerous monkey—called the black monkey (*Kaala Bandar*)—roaming the city and attacking people. Soon enough, multiple channels pick up this story and whip up public hysteria about this spectral figure. What then unravels is the fragile interethnic intimacy of Roshan and Dadi's community. As TV anchors and newscasters begin to ask provocative questions—is the monkey Hindu or Muslim?—others start fomenting ethnic hatred by arguing that the monkey is a conspiracy to attack and undermine the majority Hindu or minority Muslim (depending on the speaker) community. In this sequence, multiple jump cuts to different TV sets, playing different news channels, suggest the proliferating excess of media-fomented fear and anxiety. Thus, the film criticizes sensationalist media rhetoric that saturates contemporary Indian discourse and often generates violence. At the same time, the film's criticism of media is ambivalent: for example, the heroine Bittu is shown as an aspiring *Indian Idol* contestant, and the film celebrates this gutsy, aspirational self-fashioning of her youthful middle-class fantasy. This fantasy—its aspirational modernity—is celebrated as an alternative to the arranged marriage domesticity into which her father wants to force her.

In keeping with melodrama, an excess to the film mirrors the excesses it seeks to unveil. Through the visual idiom of different religions, the film calls for national secularity: for example, in the sequence depicting Mrs. Mehra and Roshan praying at the local Hindu temple's banyan tree, the background score presents a sufi song about "Allah," its audioscape thus overlaying and hybridizing the visualscape to produce a sensorial secular. Similarly, toward the end, as a surging crowd lifts the Hindu-Muslim male diasporic subject Roshan's nearly dead body toward the ambulance, the position of his body—lain flat, with his arms outstretched as he is carried forward—evokes the iconic Christian image of a suffering, crucified Jesus. These scenes, like others in the film, reinvent the performance of the secular in contemporary India. Indeed, I argue, they constitute a form, to engage Homi Bhabha's theorization, "of the writing of cultural difference in the midst of modernity that is inimical to binary boundaries: whether these be between past and present, inside and outside, subject and object, signifier and signified"—or, I suggest, Hindu and Muslim.[21]

From the start, *Delhi-6* tries to complicate simplistic ideas of home, nation, and community and stereotypical differences between Indians and Indian Americans. Sure, the grandmother's nostalgia for India (where she wishes to die in peace) smacks of the tired stereotypes of an exile's idealization of the lost homeland. However, the events at the end of the film give the lie to this idealization and nostalgia. There is no blissful reunion with one's country for men or women: there is only a contingent homeliness in the fragile, ever-moving secularity under crisis in globalized and mediatized India. *Delhi-6* depicts the relationship between the Indian nation and its diaspora as historically changing in response to evolving sociopolitical contexts, thus unsettling binaristic, sedimented ideas about India presented in earlier Hindi cinema. In this film, to use Purnima Mankekar's words from a different context, "diasporas and nationalisms re-create each other, and, in so doing, unsettle nation-bound constructs of subjectivity."[22] In the film's penultimate sequence, in which we see the monkey mask burning along with the effigy of Ravana as the camera fades out, Roshan's voiceover tells us, "As for me, I came back to my home." This statement leaves ambiguous where that home lies geographically; we are sure only that his various intimacies—with Bittu, with Uncle Baig, with Mandu—forged in the precarious secular of Old Delhi will survive. In complex ways, *Delhi-6* not only rejects the shrill voice and violence of ethnic extremism exacerbated by globalized media representations but also visually enacts the secular through the interplay of sight and sound. Dwyer observes that Hindi social films often reference mythological stories, "usually those of the two great epics, the *Mahabharata* and the *Ramayana*.... The melodrama of a film may be made more tragic by the evocation of the mythological story."[23] This extremely relevant feature factors in many Hindi films that bear a political message of cross-border and/or interethnic peace and secularism in the twenty-first century. Like Farah Khan's *Main Hoon Na* (2004), *Delhi-6* mobilizes the popular Hindu religious epic of the *Ramayana*, a story about the triumph of good over evil, as an allegorical layer in a story about enacting an ethical secular in the midst of difference in India.

Thomas Elsaesser argues that "melodrama, at its most accomplished, seems capable of reproducing more directly than other genres the patterns of domination and exploitation existing in a given society."[24] It is true that class consciousness and the discriminatory hierarchies of urban India, in which ethnic identity, caste, gender, and class oppression overlap, are unevenly addressed in *Delhi-6*. The film's feminist critique of the Dalit experience, represented by Jalebi's concurrent physical stigmatization and sexual exploitation by the men around her, remains muted and subaltern within the logic of the film. This is the limit of the political critique of *Delhi-6*. Mehra uses melodrama to interrogate India's contemporary politically dominant ethno-nationalist ideologies, inviting us to question how they mobilize religious identities to exploit and incite ordinary middle- and working-class Indians. In *Delhi-6*, even though Roshan is the victim hero, all the characters and communities involved are victims, ensnared in the mediatized anxious sensorium of fear fomented by extremism. Roshan is an insider and outsider in this community; in the film's multilayered emotional melodramatic representation of Roshan's hybrid, wounded masculinity, the near-sacrifice of his life brings together this divided community and restores the subaltern secular of Chandni Chowk. The film strives to unveil discrimination and inequality based on caste, religion, and gender in India, although its focus on India's crisis of secularism and Hindu-Muslim tension makes its critique of Dalit and gender discrimination limited and marginal. *Delhi-6* gestures to the inner potential of each human being and the collective potential of globalized media to succumb to, or generate, the capacity for violence. Its ending affirms hope for Indians' capacity to choose and perform the ethical secular in everyday life.[25]

Surviving Gendered Citizenship and Death in Shyam Benegal's *Mammo*

As discussed in the preceding chapters, in popular Hindi cinema as well as literature, the 1947 Partition is most directly invoked and addressed through its legacy of (1) the Kashmir conflict and/or (2) the vexed issue of equal rights for minority Muslim citizenship. Elsewhere, I track how recent mainstream Hindi films like *Gadar: Ek Prem Katha*, *Fanaa*, and *Sarfarosh* deploy the trope of heteronormative romance to represent normative Indian national citizenship.[26] To contextualize this trait: in the 1970s, Hindi films in India rarely depicted interethnic romance; their representations of secular intimacies largely appeared through the tropes of brotherhood and friendship between Hindu and Muslim characters rather than the more contentious representation of sexual intimacy. However, this trend changed in films made in the 1990s, which followed the political ascendancy of Hindu nationalism, the demolition of the ancient Babri Masjid in 1992, and the subsequent bomb blasts as well as riots between Hindus and Muslims that fanned across India. In a range of period films as well as contemporary social dramas, from *Gadar: Ek Prem Katha*, to *Bombay*, to *Veer-Zaara*, to *Dahek*, among others, we see Hindi cinema revisiting Partition violence, India-Pakistan relations, and contemporary Hindu-Muslim conflict through love stories about Hindu-Muslim couples, in which the men are Hindu and the women Muslim. These films turn to the heteronormative trope of interethnic marriage as secular resolution, thus recasting older ideological narratives of the family as symbolic of the nation. However, the patriarchal coding of these romantic intimacies leaves Hindu masculinity as hegemonic in these films. In these public fantasies about the nation, it is very rare to see Muslim male characters center stage as normative citizens and as spouses of Hindu women.[27] In this context, I turn to Benegal's award-winning 1994 film *Mammo*, an especially important representation of women's experiences of statelessness and citizenship after the 1947 Partition in South Asia. The story and script of *Mammo* were written by noted film critic and writer Khalid Mohamed, with Shama Zaidi credited for additional screenplay and Javed Siddiqui for dialogue. The film won the National Film Award for Best Feature Film in Hindi in 1995, and Farida Jalal (who plays Mammo) won the Filmfare Critics Award for Best Performance, among other accolades. The film is part of a trilogy made by Benegal, including *Sardari Begum* (1996) and *Zubeidaa* (2001). Across this feminist trilogy, Muslim women are protagonists, and their stories about the lived experience of ethnic citizenship in India offer a useful counterpoint to the Hindi films discussed above, in which men as normative citizens dominate the narration of the nation. This focus is especially interesting given that this shift from the iconic dominance of the woman as nation in popular nationalist discourse as well as in Hindi cinema in the 1940s and 1950s (recall Mehboob Khan's 1957 classic *Mother India*) to the male-centered action and social dramas of the 1990s itself parallels the rise of more muscular ethno-nationalism well chronicled by Anand Patwardhan's documentaries, including *In the Name of God* (1992), *Father, Son, and Holy War* (1994), and, most recently, *Reason* (2018).

Mammo's eponymous protagonist is a woman who migrates to Pakistan with her husband in 1947 and is happy living there until her husband passes away. Because she is childless, her relatives, in a bid to seize her late husband's property, cast her out of the family. Set in the 1980s, we see Mammo—short for Mehmooda Begum—returning to take refuge in India. She hopes to stay with her only remaining family settled in Bombay: her sister, Fayyazi (Surekha Sikri), and her grandson, Riyaz (Amit Phalke). As the film progresses, it illuminates Mammo's constant circulation in and out of minor refugee subjectivity in what Liisa Malkki calls "the national order of things."[28] As a Muslim woman, Mammo was initially displaced and went to Pakistan in 1947, as a refugee wife dutifully accompanying her husband, possibly fleeing for safety, and hoping for equal citizenship. Yet her nonreproductive femininity and widowhood are cited by her family in Pakistan as cause to dispossess her of her right to inherit her late husband's property. Mammo flees this familial-economic violence to seek refuge with her sister, Fayyazi, a middle-class Muslim citizen in Bombay, India.

Vasudevan notes that, conventionally, the form and themes of realist art cinema "invite the spectator to assume modern perceptual practices that can objectify and distance her from the 'traditional' and the 'feudal.'"[29] This observation partially resonates with Benegal's treatment of Mammo's story, insofar as we are invited to empathize with Mammo's oppression at the hands of "traditional" patriarchal family relationships that render her homeless. However, the film's realism is complicated insofar as it does not celebrate national modernity as an alternative to feudal or traditional society: instead, it criticizes the modern nation-state and its bureaucratic institutions, such as citizenship. Even as Mammo's nonreproductive femininity and widowhood turn her into a refugee in India, her subsequent struggles detail how she inhabits a precarious, peripheral subject position vis-à-vis nationality, as she is not officially a refugee. Initially on a visitor's visa, she is required to report to the local police station every month. She periodically extends her visa by bribing the local police officer, Inspector Apte. However, when Apte is transferred to another police station, his successor rounds up Mammo as an undocumented immigrant and deports her along with two other people. She is dragged out of her sister's home; with just the clothes on her back, she is forcibly deported on the Frontier Mail train to Pakistan. She loses touch with Fayyazi and Riyaz after this separation, and the film ends with a surprising denouement: fast-forwarding twenty years, a grown Riyaz, who has become a writer and has just finished writing a memoir about his aunt Mammo, opens his front door. We see Mammo at this door: indomitable, returned, and triumphant. Determined to stay in India, she enlists Riyaz's help and procures a fake death certificate, which they send to the immigration officer in the Bombay Police and the Pakistan High Commission. Thus, she officially stages her death. The film's last sequence concludes with Mammo, Riyaz, and Fayyazi sitting on a sofa in their living room, hugging and celebrating that she is now invisible: no one will be able to see her—or deport her. In her words, "I have turned into the djinn." Benegal thus unveils what Lauren Berlant calls the "slow death" attendant to disposable lives like that of Mammo[30] in the biopolitics of citizenship in postcolonial India, which culminates in her bureaucratic death—necessary to her physical survival. As Anuradha Dingwaney Needham notes, "Benegal's reticence about representing violence through and in all its excess and horror is of a piece with his 'realism' that, in opposition to the melodramatic mode embraced by popular Hindi cinema, relies on, indeed cultivates, low-key and understated images and sound for its effects."[31] Needham's analysis of Benegal's representation of Partition here, especially in relation to M. S. Sathyu's *Garm Hava* (1974), tracks how it is about the writer protagonist Riyaz's "recovery" and remembrance of his grandaunt Mammo as much as it is about the troubled history of repatriating women between India and Pakistan (well documented in Ritu Menon and Kamla Bhasin's *Borders and Boundaries*).

I am interested in this film for different reasons. Resonant with my discussion in Chapter 2 of Shauna Singh Baldwin's novel *What the Body Remembers*, I am struck by how multiple abandonments are strewn across the film's story about migration—for example, Mammo's abandonment by her in-laws, and Riyaz's abandonment by his father to be raised by his grandmother. In this shared marginality to normative structures and institutions of family, Mammo and Riyaz form an affective and ambivalent (from Riyaz's side) affiliation. The film's plot makes visible the affective economies of this peripheral existence eked out by its two widowed Muslim protagonists and a grandson/grandnephew, whose kinship cannot grant Mammo refuge or citizenship in her country of birth or in the land she considers her home. The sequence when she is deported is poignant: a female constable asks her, "Why are you crying? You are going to your own home." In a close-up shot of a sobbing Mammo, we see her reply, "My home is here; this is my earth. What would you lose if you gave me two measures of land?"

Although she eloquently rejects the structures of citizenship that forcibly construct the Pakistani nation as her home, her articulation of belonging reinforces her precarity: she is powerless within a system of nation-states structured by patriarchal relations of power. This exchange also reinforces one of the great ironies of modern migration, pointed out by Arendt: this impossibility of finding a new home is not about a lack of space but about political organization.

Further, the decisive ending is central to the film's critique of postcolonial national modernity, migration, and citizenship. This perspective is most evident when the national and patriarchal abandonments chronicled in the film are countered by Mammo's final act of resistance. In the end, Mammo stages her own death to stay in what she sees as her "home" with her divided family; in this way, Benegal exposes what Judith Butler calls, in a different context, "the social vulnerability of our bodies."[32] As Butler notes, "The body has its invariably public dimension. Constituted as a social phenomenon in the public sphere, my body is and is not mine."[33] Mammo seems to recognize this vulnerability; her decision to forge her structural death as a legal person claims the right to autonomy over her body, even as it becomes a grim indictment of Partition, the refugee experience, and secular citizenship in South Asia. It is emancipatory and annihilatory. What is also unique about this film is that it tells a story about the Partition migrations that takes place in Bombay (now called Mumbai), India. Given the predominant focus on northern India in the telling of Partition stories, which I discuss in greater detail in my last chapter, this decision to tell a Bombay story is significant; it also resonates with many of Saadat Hasan Manto's short stories from the early national period, which are set in Bombay. These stories invite us to consider how the city space of Bombay/Mumbai is constituted by multiple migrations, including those from 1947. Writing about Russian émigrés in exile and aesthetic practices, Svetlana Boym offers a compelling conception of diasporic intimacy: "Diasporic intimacy is possible only when one masters a certain imperfect aesthetics of survival and learns to inhabit exile."[34] Mammo's diasporic intimacy is about her canny survival of being exiled from the political modernity of the state and its institutions of citizenship and rights. This circumstance is, I argue, part of the failures of state secularism that Deepa Ollapally flags for us:[35] the intimate abandonments that shape Mammo's multiple exiles from normative national belongings, Indian and Pakistani, are shaped by family and country. They are reiterated in the political abandonments inflicted by the structures of nationality that cannot conceive of her multiple pasts and that refuse her right to return, because she is a Muslim who left during Partition.

Indo-Pak Intimacy and Border Crossings in Meghna Gulzar's *Raazi* and Kabir Khan's *Bajrangi Bhaijaan*

I would like to briefly turn to another, more recent representation of Indian Muslim female subjectivity, migration, and secular nationalism: Gulzar's Bollywood drama and thriller *Raazi* (Agree; 2018). *Raazi* is an adaptation of Harinder Sikka's novel *Calling Sehmat* (2008), which is based on the true story of an agent in the Indian Intelligence Agency Research and Analysis Wing (RAW) who marries into a Pakistani military family at her father's orders to spy for India before Bangladesh's 1971 War of Independence. The film revolves around a twenty-year-old Kashmiri student protagonist, Sehmat Khan (Alia Bhatt), who is asked by her deeply patriotic father, Hidayat Khan (Rajit Kapoor), to marry the younger son of Brigadier Syed (Shishir Sharma) in the Pakistani Army. Khan has been conducting espionage for India by spying on Syed. As Khan is dying of cancer, the impending geopolitical conflict between West and East Pakistan convinces him that Sehmat, if trained, could continue his espionage work for the Indian state. After Sehmat is trained, the marriage is arranged, and Sehmat settles into her new roles: performing as the dutiful daughter-in-law and coy wife in the household and spying. The plot eschews the tendency in Indian cinema to depict Pakistani Muslim men as aggressive and threatening. Resonating with recent films revolving around Indian, Pakistani protagonists' romantic coupledom, like *Veer-Zaara*, it traces a growing intimacy between an Indian and a Pakistani— Sehmat and her sensitive and caring husband, Iqbal Syed (Vicky Kaushal), a military officer in the Pakistani Army. Sehmat and Iqbal fall in love, and their growing intimacy is represented in melodramatic sequences shot with warm lighting and shallow focus close-ups to represent their mutual feelings. One day, when she successfully extracts and is conveying crucial intelligence about Pakistan's plan to attack the Indian aircraft carrier ship to RAW, she is discovered by the household's faithful domestic helper, Abdul. To protect herself, as he runs out of the house to find someone to alert about her truth, Sehmat runs over him twice in an army truck and kills him. Later, she murders her brother-in-law with ricin, because he is investigating Abdul's death and is suspicious of her. By the end, even Iqbal discovers her true identity as an Indian spy and feels betrayed by this new knowledge. While some of India's local collaborators and Iqbal are killed toward the end, Sehmat is successfully extracted by her bosses. The film ends with her return to and retirement in India.

The reference to the Partition migrations in this film appears through the subaltern figure of the Syed family's male servant, Abdul. Abdul is a silent, suspicious, brooding, and traumatized figure: at once a devoted and beloved member of the household, he is also cold and hostile toward Sehmat. We see him noiselessly circulating through the multistory house, appearing at uncanny moments, and keeping an eye on her. Abdul is suspicious of Sehmat, because she is Indian. We learn that he was once a Partition refugee, who, it is suggested, lost everyone in his family to Hindu-Muslim violence in 1947 in India. This trauma, the film suggests, endures in him: he rarely speaks and never physically leaves the safe space of the home to venture outside. This behavior suggests that Abdul is a survivor who lives with post-traumatic stress disorder (PTSD); along with his hostility toward Sehmat's Indian roots despite their shared Muslim identity, it embodies Abdul's traumatic memory of Partition. When Sehmat murders him to protect herself, Abdul is a traumatized refugee survivor, already bereft of family and community, who is sacrificed at the altar of Sehmat's Indian nationalism. In one of the earliest novels about Partition—Khushwant Singh's *Train to Pakistan*—the trope of heroic, suffering masculinity is central to the plot of its Partition migration story. The suffering masculinity of its Punjabi peasant protagonist, Jagga, who dies saving his Muslim beloved (who has become a refugee on the train to Pakistan), embodies the price paid by ordinary, secular Indians for national freedom at this time. In *Raazi*, the suffering masculinity of the Pakistani Partition survivor Abdul signals the sacrifice of the subaltern for the nationalist war project ultimately under critique. The cinematography of this sequence suggests that while this action keeps Sehmat alive, it is the first trauma that she experiences in the service of the nation. Close-up shots of Sehmat's face depict her determination, shock, and grief as she commits her first murder—a member of her household, and a Partition refugee survivor. It also foreshadows the recurring and more intensive traumas she experiences as the film progresses.

The film thus remembers and links multiple migration stories from 1947 and 1971 and raises questions about the sacrifices of male and female refugees and citizens because of the India-Pakistan conflict. As it unfolds, it dwells increasingly on the trauma of witnessing violence, enacting it, and experiencing loss in conflict. Eventually, disturbed by her role in these violent deaths and the grief she has caused in her marital family to people she recognizes as warm and kind, to people she loves, respects, and regards, Sehmat falls apart. She becomes the heroic and patriotic citizen subject who is traumatized by the labor demanded of her by the Indian nation-state. When she is discovered by Iqbal, he is shown as profoundly betrayed: in this sequence, the shock of discovering her double life is depicted through close-up scenes of Iqbal sobbing at his bathroom sink, tears streaming down his face. As he emerges from the bathroom, having regained some composure, he encounters Sehmat pointing a gun at him. In this sequence, close-up shots with point-of-view cuts of Iqbal's and Sehmat's heartbroken and teary-eyed faces register their mutual love, even as they verbally avow loyalty to their respective nation-states, over and above love. In this way, their international romantic intimacy embodies the tension between their mutual love and their patriotism for different countries. After Iqbal's violent death at the hands of RAW, a traumatized Sehmat asks her RAW supervisor to send her home to India. Thus, *Raazi*'s plot, as it unfolds, registers the traumas of patriotism for the Kashmiri Indian Muslim woman who travels across the Indo-Pakistan border in the service of the state.

Raazi was a box-office success upon its release and well reviewed by critics. Shah Faesal writes that *Raazi* is "about the disconcerting feeling of empathy for your enemy, in the Gandhian sense, rather than making you suffer the conventional triumphalism of India-Pakistan war movies, scripted to loathe, degrade, and dehumanize the other side." It is a film "where the slogans are missing, and the silences have been allowed to speak."[36] As many critics have noted, earlier Hindi films about Partition and the India-Pakistan conflict often depict Indians and Pakistanis in jingoistic and polarizing ways, dehumanizing and demonizing the Pakistani Muslim. In contrast, *Raazi* eschews this portrayal in favor of a representation that draws arcs of similarities between the two, primarily through the representation of familial love and patriotism. Thus, the film offers us a new, transformative recognition of the "other" as the same and, indeed, as beloved (for Sehmat and Iqbal). Both characters equally invite empathy as middle-class protagonists, performing patriotism for India and Pakistan as nationalisms demand and being undone by it. *Raazi* portrays Sehmat as a loyal Kashmiri, Muslim, and female citizen subject who is nonetheless traumatized by the labors of citizenship in the Indian nation-state. Toward the end, when she discovers that she is pregnant, she decides to raise her and Iqbal's child in India. The film concludes with a sequence depicting her son as a soldier in the Indian Navy and an unsmiling Sehmat sitting silently in a rocking chair and looking into the distance in a remote, unnamed rural area (indirectly suggesting that she has PTSD). As a silent brooding figure in the end, she replaces Abdul within the narrative's logic as a traumatized figure undone by border crossing, personal loss, and political violence. As in earlier films, such as *Fanaa*, *Raazi* poses futurity for the Indian Muslim citizen as a choice between national patriotism or heteronormative intimacy; however, the dissonance between the representation of Indian-Pakistani romantic love between Sehmat and Iqbal and the violent demands of statecraft creates a new space for looking askance at the system of nation-states and its endemic conflicts. Thus, the film creates a counterpublic engagement with war and peace in the system of nation-states. In *Raazi*, the nation-state and its institutions are mechanisms that traumatize the patriot citizen subject:

men and women, Pakistani and Indian. Even as the recognition of the shared humanity of Sehmat and Iqbal must be suppressed once their politics are revealed, the film invites us to mourn this act as a loss. Linking 1947 and 1971, *Raazi* presents traumatized refugees and citizen subjects without any easy reconciliation or justification for the war, conflict, and death enacted in the name of the nation. It is important to acknowledge that this public cultural representation of Sehmat as a Kashmiri Muslim woman who is the ideal patriot stands counter to the literary representation of Kashmiri Muslim women in Arundhati Roy's *The Ministry of Utmost Happiness*, discussed earlier. Roy's representation of Kashmiri Muslim women from the 1990s—as widows, as family members of murdered and disappeared men, as raped or dead subjects—indicts the Indian nation-state and its occupying army for brutality and violence. That representation resonates more with the depiction of Kashmir in Vishal Bhardwaj's *Haider* (2014), an adaptation of *Hamlet*, or Aamir Bashir's art film *Harud* (Autumn; 2010). In contrast, set in 1971, *Raazi* depicts an innocent and benign Indian nation-state and a Kashmiri Muslim woman who willingly serves, fights, and kills for India, until the trauma of doing so silences her.

This film draws upon two key themes that have preoccupied Bollywood cinema since 1947. The first is the suffering yet agentive woman (as wife, mother, or widow) who embodies the Indian nation, evident in such films as *Mother India* (1957), *Deewaar* (1975), and *Amar Akbar Anthony* (1977). Indeed, Nirupa Roy became the leading actress essaying this iconic role of the suffering mother in Hindi films of the 1970s and 1980s. In such films, the female subject's suffering (as wife and/or mother) represents the travails of the national community as a whole. Similarly, in *Raazi*, Sehmat is depicted as an agentive but increasingly traumatized and suffering woman—first, as a grief-stricken wife, when her husband, Iqbal, is killed by the Indian RAW official Khalid Mir, and later as a silent mother living in isolation. The second theme is that of the divided family, which, as Ganti observes, marks several films from the 1960s and 1970s, including *Amar Akbar Anthony* and *Seeta Aur Geeta* (1972). This theme is also engaged in *Raazi*, albeit in a new way. Ganti suggests that the resonance of the popular lost-and-found genre (in which family members are divided/separated) for Indian audiences lies in the fact that it invokes the Partition experience of millions of migrants and refugees, during which families were separated from their loved ones. In this genre, the family is typically separated by fate, natural calamity, religion, or the violence of criminal/evil characters. Usually, these films end happily, as the divided family members are reunited at the end. Ganti thoroughly enumerates the different features of this genre, which enforces the primacy of consanguineous relationships by depicting the "separation of an entire nuclear family, parent-child dyad, or siblings and their eventual reunification, usually twenty to twenty-five years later.... [I]n the lost and found films, the reasons for the family's separation are often the result of external forces, calamities, or agents beyond the control of the family, and the main moral disorder that needs to be resolved is the dispersal of the family."[37] Ganti also notes that "the interplay of the recognition, misrecognition, or the lack of recognition are important driving logics within the lost-and-found genre. Viewer pleasure (or frustration) derives from being aware of all the relationships in the film and waiting for the characters to discover them."[38] This theme is reiterated as well as recast in *Raazi* in a dystopian way: the Pakistani Syed family as well as household are increasingly divided and separated once Sehmat marries into them. First, Sehmat kills their loyal servant, Abdul, and then she murders her brother-in-law. In addition, the marriage and love that grow between Sehmat and Iqbal also end up divided, insofar as they are separated by their allegiance to different nations. In a pivotal scene toward the end of the film, when Iqbal has realized Sehmat's true identity as an Indian spy, their emotional exchange reveals their mutual love as well as its necessary sacrifice for their respective nations. Later, while pursuing Sehmat, who has fled to try to get extracted by her Indian team, Iqbal confronts a woman in a marketplace who is wearing Sehmat's burqa. Assuming that the woman is Sehmat and not wanting her to get caught by Pakistanis, RAW official Khalid Mir—who has come there to extract Sehmat and take her back to India—throws a grenade. The ensuing explosion kills Iqbal and the disguised Pakistani accomplice who had been working for India alongside Sehmat. Sehmat's love—her husband, Iqbal—is thus sacrificed for India. Unlike the typical lost-and-found film, the family is not reunited at the end; instead, this spy thriller ends on a note of death and trauma.

This is the second, little-examined, yet very important theme in Hindi cinema that is relevant to our analysis of *Raazi*: the choice between family, on the one hand, and the nation, on the other; between love, on the one hand, and patriotism, on the other. Year after year, decade after decade, Hindi cinema has produced such blockbusters as *Mother India* (1957), *Deewaar* (1977), *Shakti* (1982), *Border* (1997), *Dil Se* (1998), *Fanaa* (2006), *Rang De Basanti* (2006), and *Raazi* (2018), in which the protagonists face a choice between sons, husbands, friends, and lovers, on the one hand, and community or country, on the other. Each time, they must choose the country. Clearly, an anxiety about patriotism saturates Hindi cinema, if it must stage this choice over and over for its Indian audience. In *Mother India*, the mother, Radha (Nargis), kills her rebellious son, Birju (Sunil Dutt); in *Deewaar*, a mother, Sumitra Devi (Nirupa Roy), advises her son Ravi (Shashi Kapoor), a policeman, to kill his older brother Vijay (Amitabh Bachchan), a criminal who challenges the state's institutions; in *Fanaa*, a Kashmiri

Muslim, Zooni (Kajol), kills her husband, Rehan (Aamir Khan), when she discovers that he is a terrorist; and so on. In perhaps no other national cinema is the choice between family and country, between love and patriotism, staged so persistently for its citizens, for more than half a century.

In earlier films, this sacrifice is justified as one that preserves the community/nation/law, in the contest between law and justice (another popular theme, as noted by Ganti). However, in *Raazi*, the justification is, as Khalid Mir says, "war" and the nation. This reasoning introduces an ideological dissonance in the staging of the choice between family and country. While Iqbal is killed as the Indian nation-state demands, his death incites empathy in the viewer and invites us to mourn his death along with the multiple deaths in his family. Insofar as the film represents the Indian Muslim Sehmat as a loyal citizen and ideal patriot, it depoliticizes religion and subordinates it to nationality as orienting Indian identity in 1971. Further, in Sehmat's heroic femininity, the film challenges dominant discourses in Hindi cinema about heroic Indian masculinity constructed as normative patriotism. The film's ambivalent address of the nation is provocative: at the end, the plot has moved forward, and we see a sequence in which Sehmat and Iqbal's adult son Samar Syed (Sanjay Suri) is revealed to be a patriotic Navy officer aboard an Indian ship. Despite the film's anti-war message, and Sehmat's traumatized subjectivity, her son is assimilated into the service of the nation-state. Yet *Raazi* seeks to show, through Sehmat's border crossing and through her trauma, a recognition of precariousness shared by people on both sides, who labor and sacrifice for their respective nation-states. As I suggest above, it also, by the end, ambivalently questions this labor and sacrifice.

I turn now to *Bujrangi Bhaijaan* (2015), another recent film about border crossings, because it also stages encounters of Indian and Pakistani citizens that represent a new public fantasy about cross-border peace between both postcolonial nation-states, beyond war. In many post-1990 Bollywood films, we see the melodramatic representation of displacement and border crossing between India and Pakistan: these either revolve around Hindu-Muslim romance, like Yash Chopra's *Veer-Zaara* (2004) and Randhir Kapoor's *Henna* (1991), or war and terrorism, like Mani Ratnam's *Roja* (1992) and Gulzar's *Maachis* (1996). *Bajrangi Bhaijaan* is different. It revolves around the eponymous character Pawan Kumar Chaturvedi, whose nickname is Bajrangi (Salman Khan), a Hindu Brahmin vegetarian young man living in Delhi. Bajrangi is so named because he is a devout worshipper of the Hindu god Hanuman (one of whose many names is Bajrang Bali), a devout protector of Lord Ram. Bajrangi is depicted as a very simple, pious, and sincere young man. He meets a speech-impaired child, Shahida (Harshaali Malhotra), wandering alone in the city, hungry and silent. After seeing her nearly victimized by child traffickers, Bajrangi decides to protect and help her. He starts calling her Munni (a generic Hindi form of "little girl"). Eventually, he figures out what we, as the audience, already know from the opening sequences: that Munni is actually a nonvegetarian (she loves chicken), that she is from Pakistan (when she whoops it up for Pakistan while watching an India-Pakistan cricket match with Bajrangi), and that she has become separated from her family. The separation has occurred because Shahida's mother brought her to Delhi to visit a famous Sufi shrine, hoping that Munni's speech impairment would be cured. Bajrangi then resolves to reunite her with her family, and from this plan unfolds the film's exploration of what one critic calls "a border as a muse that opens up the world."[39]

On the one hand, this film plays loosely with elements of the popular lost-and-found genre in Hindi cinema, dating back to the 1940s. *Bajrangi Bhaijaan* successfully deploys elements of the lost-and-found melodrama to present a border-crossing narrative that, I suggest, advocates for India-Pakistan peace and an affective, if subaltern, secular. Unlike *Delhi-6*, this film was a big commercial success. It became the most watched Bollywood movie in the history of television when telecast in October 2015, and it won several awards, including the National Film Award for Best Popular Film Providing Wholesome Entertainment at the sixty-third National Film Awards. The film was nominated for Best Film and Best Actor Awards at the sixty-first Filmfare Awards, and it received the Filmfare Award for Best Story. It was also nominated for Best Foreign Film in China's sixth Douban Film Awards in 2015. (The popularity of Hindi cinema in China merits a separate discussion that is beyond the scope of this chapter.)

Two narratives interest me in the representation of Bajrangi's encounter with Munni. The first is how Bajrangi's limited worldview as a devout, vegetarian, Hindu encounters the difference of the Muslim "other" as embodied by Munni. The second—alternately comical and violent—is about the challenges he faces as he tries to get Munni across the border legally into Pakistan. He discovers that taking her back legally is nearly impossible; illegally, it is a cinch. Because she is speech-impaired, she does not have a passport, and Bajrangi does not know her legal name, Pakistani consular officials refuse to give them visas that would permit him to legally cross the border. He then meets human traffickers, who volunteer to drop them off at the border in the desert where they know a fence is vulnerable and where people routinely cross sides. Once he gets to this spot, however, he is caught by the Pakistani Army. When the army officers offer to look the other way so that he can enter Pakistan, Bajrangi, the honest hero, insists on being allowed to proceed to Pakistan legally. This comedic sequence draws attention to the absurdity of how state functionaries and border security operate.

It seems the border exists more to support the jobs of the people policing it, even as those people seem increasingly ambivalent about the valence of the barbed-wire walls separating the nation-states.

After a series of comical and tense adventures in which Shahida's precarity, Bajrangi's heroic masculinity and state violence are enmeshed in complex ways, Bajrangi successfully reunites the girl with her parents. Mission accomplished, the final sequences that show Bajrangi crossing the border and returning to India are interesting because they represent him as a transformed Indian citizen who has shed his naive Hindu ethnocentrism and is now claimed as a "brother" by Pakistanis. The ending sequence also shows him crossing the national border between India and Pakistan, which is, suggestively, a shallow watery stream with tall bamboo poles set up as a border fence. Slow-motion mid-shots of Bajrangi crossing the stream are crosscut with slow-motion, close-up shots of Munni's eager face as she tries get Bajrangi's attention through nonverbal gestures to say good-bye. In a final shot, an emotionally anguished Munni screams, "Maamu!" (Uncle!) and, in doing so, miraculously regains her speech. Of course, the loss and recovery of speech (or sight) is a common trope of Hindi cinema of the 1970s and its return here in a story about performing secular intimacies is significant. As a trope of reunion or the regaining of knowledge, it recalls and reinvents the fragile affective Indian-Pakistani, Hindu-Muslim bond that grows between Bajrangi and Munni. It is important to note that this is a differently imagined secular bond than is conventional in Hindi cinema: it does not hinge upon heteronormative romance, as in films like *Veer-Zaara* and *Bombay*, nor is it premised on the negation of the Pakistani as the evil "other," as in *Gadar*. Further, the actual romantic plot in the film, between Bajrangi and Rasika (Kareena Kapoor Khan), while present, is subordinated to the storyline of Bajrangi's effort to take Munni back home to her family.

This film's fantasy of India fashions a new public engagement with the geopolitical conflict between India and Pakistan. It posits the contact and cultural encounter generated by border crossing as the path to reinvent normative Hindu citizenship. This encounter reduces ignorance, forges secular cross-cultural relationships, and fantasizes about geopolitical peace that heals and restores. It does not challenge the sovereignty of both nation-states, although it critiques the bureaucracies of state institutions like the police, its politicians, the consulate, and the army. However, it also creates a new kind of subjectivity and a new kind of hero: Bajrangi is the truly faithful and empathetic, muscular, upper-caste, Hindu male citizen, whose ethical regard and empathy for the "other" is rooted in his very faith. By virtue of being true to his faith, Bajrangi helps a Muslim Pakistani and, indeed, forges an affective bond with her. Yes, crucial to this narrative is that the Pakistani who incites the transformation of Bajrangi's initial narrow, prejudiced worldview is a vulnerable female and nonverbal child. Like Bapsi Sidhwa's novel *Cracking India*, which narrates the nation from the perspective of the polio-stricken child Lenny, the film invites us to re-view the postcolonial nation-state from the vantage point of the migrant, the outsider, and the girl child. Further, it is new in that it reimagines India-Pakistan relations through the idiom of cross-cultural, secular precariousness. The film's title suggests that these bonds emerge when Bajrangi becomes, through the border crossing and encounters with Pakistanis, "Bajrangi Bhaijaan." This transformation of his name marks the mission of the film: the name of the Hindu god Hanuman is yoked to the Urdu word for brother, "Bhaijaan." As Urdu is often culturally associated with Muslims in India, this naming has symbolic significance. It creates a familial relationship between Bajrangi and the Pakistanis he meets; symbolically, it invokes the lost-and-found genre's roots in asserting consanguineous relationships between the two national communities.

In these varied ways, *Bajrangi Bhaijaan* invents a secular kinship that is simultaneously old and new and that recasts normative Hindu-Indian masculinity and Indian citizenship. On the one hand, this movie recalls the tropes of Hindu-Muslim brotherhood that films from the 1950s through the 1970s often deploy to represent India's secular community: Manmohan Desai's saga about three brothers separated at birth and raised in three different Indian faiths, *Amar Akbar Anthony* (1977), is the most vivid example.[40] However, in the context of the contemporary moment, Bajrangi's avuncular avatar displaces that tired trope. It can be argued that this film confirms what Vasudevan, in his essay on Ratnam's *Bombay*, refers to as the "necessity of assuming 'the masculine position' so that the link between the nation and the Hindu patriarchal hero is always maintained."[41] However, I suggest a different reading: this film stages a certain pleasure of the subaltern, affective secular that emerges through the Indian encounter with Pakistanis. From the friendship between Munni and Bajrangi to Bajrangi's various encounters with helpful Pakistanis, the film attempts to create a new space in public culture for the representation of Indo-Pakistani and Hindu-Muslim friendship and familial intimacy in India and in South Asia. (In this aim, it resonates with the border-crossing advertising I discuss in the next chapter.) This film also offers a new account of normative, upper-caste Hindu masculinity: as Anupama Chopra observes in her review of the film, "Bajrangi is interesting because he's not invincible. Of course you know that he will eventually make miracles happen, but he also bleeds and breaks."[42] Of course, unlike the trenchant critique of caste-based gendered violence presented in Anubhav Sinha's brave film *Article 15* (2019), *Bajrangi Bhaijaan* leaves unproblematized the violence of caste and Dalit experience. Its narrative focus is on the transformation and enlightenment of the upper-caste and initially chauvinistic Hindu Brahmin male citizen in ways that advocate for India-Pakistan peace and reimagine cross-border, secular communities.

In her keynote lecture at the University of Wisconsin's Annual South Asia Conference in 2017, historian Ayesha Jalal described the relation between India and Pakistan as a relationship between two brothers; she argued that India, as an elder brother, will have to decide whether it chooses relations of peace and amity or conflict with its younger brother, Pakistan. Resonating with this idea, the film deploys tropes about familial intimacies (shorn of their toxicity) to rethink the role of the citizen and secularism in the subcontinent. Like such recent films as *Rang De Basanti* and *Delhi-6*, the film also depicts journalists and media as potentially playing very powerful roles in mobilizing (or undermining) a national affect of secularism in both countries, toward geopolitical peace. This question of how technology and mass media reinvent discourses of the secular, migration, and geopolitical peace reappears in a different way in the next chapter, where I discuss the Google commercial "Reunion."

Pakistan, Political Violence, and Failed Intimacies in Sabiha Sumar's *Khamosh Pani*

Pakistani independent filmmaker Sumar's film *Khamosh Pani* (Silent Waters; 2003) is her first feature film. This India-Pakistan collaboration draws together actors and writers from both countries to take up the relation between the 1947 Partition and the 1979 Islamicization of the Pakistani state through the experience of a rural Punjabi woman in Pakistan. *Khamosh Pani* won critical acclaim at film festivals globally: between 2003 and 2005, it won several awards, including the prestigious Golden Leopard at the Locarno Film Festival, and the Indian Star of Germany award for Best Film at the Bollywood and Beyond Festival in Stuttgart. Originally planned as a documentary, Sumar believed that this type of film about women's experiences during Partition would reopen traumatic wounds. Further, she states in an interview, "I also thought it was very important that I somehow connect this violence with present-day violence, so that it's not as if it becomes a historical film that suggests that violence occurred and then it *ended* [italics original], but rather that it is a continuous process. I wanted to show the continuation of the violence against Ayesha [the protagonist]."[43]

Khamosh Pani tracks the political and cultural transformation of postcolonial Pakistan in 1979 through the experience of its protagonist, Ayesha (Kirron Kher). When President General Muhammad Zia-ul-Haq imposes martial law and turns Pakistan into a state governed by Islamic law, the life of this peasant woman living in the village of Charkhi is turned upside down. Ayesha's life revolves around her teenaged son, Saleem (Aamir Ali Malik), who is a tender, dreamy youth in love with the young and vibrant student Zubeida (Shilpa Shukla). Ayesha runs the house with the help of her dead husband's pension and by giving Quran lessons to young girls. The film depicts how ethno-religious politics transform everyday life and destroy her various intimacies of family, romance, and friendship. This transformation, quotidian and traumatic, intimately affects Ayesha and Zubeida as Saleem gets involved with ethno-religious nationalist politics.

The film subtly reveals the aggressive transformation of gender identities and belonging when two political activists, Rashid and Mazhar, arrive in the village. Offering a sense of purpose and social acceptance, they spread the ideology of a newly Islamized state and indoctrinate innocent, aimless rural young men with radical nationalist discourses. Looking for some work and meaning in his life, but with few prospects in sight, Saleem is pressured into joining these extremists. Slowly, he changes from a romantic, gentle youth into a hardened, young man who sees his radicalization as meaningful work for the Pakistani nation. As he tells Zubeida, "People listen to me [now]. I have become something." This radicalization is also effected through his rejection of intimacy and the demonization of femininity. He grows increasingly distant from both girlfriend and mother, sensing their disapproval. When Zubeida challenges his new nationalist ideas, he ends their romance; later, he castigates his mother when he discovers that she was a Sikh girl—a "kaffir"—who was abducted in 1947. The film gestures to how conservative religious groups capture the aimless, jobless youth of rural Pakistan and consolidate political power. For example, in one scene, Rashid leads a group of young men (including Saleem) in raising the walls of the local girls' school—ostensibly to protect "our women ... as Allah wishes." This sequence symbolically prefigures its suggestion that the surveillance and control of women's bodies grows in Pakistani sociopolitical life.

Khamosh Pani structurally connects this demonization and entrapment of femininity under the religious, state-sponsored orthodoxy in Zia's Pakistan to its traumatic prehistory: the ethnicized rape and abduction of women during the 1947 Partition. In this way, the film does memory work to retrieve the gendered violence that accompanied the 1947 migrations and present it as newly relevant in 1970s Pakistan. Using sepia-toned flashbacks to represent Ayesha's memories of the past in dream sequences, *Khamosh Pani* returns to the ethnic gendered violence she experienced during Partition, when she was a Sikh girl named Veero. Through cross-cutting, each flashback unveils Ayesha's return to her childhood memories of 1947; each flashback sequence's disembodied voiceover reveals more about her past and the intimate violence inflicted upon female subjects by Sikh and

Muslim men. We learn that Veero's Sikh father forced her mother and sister to commit suicide by jumping into the village well to avoid their potential rapes. In the second jump cut to a flashback, her voiceover calmly describes these events: "People started taking each other's wives. And cutting their own daughters. They said it was to save their honor. Some girls died. Some were saved.... Broken memories. Incomplete dreams." Here, like Lenny in *Cracking India* and Roop in *What the Body Remembers*, Ayesha's voice articulates the feminist critique of the rhetorics of honor invoked by men to sanction their dehumanizing violence against women. Jump cuts of sepia-toned shots of the local village well, followed by sepia-toned shots of a pair of running feet, repeatedly interrupt the narrative present each time that Ayesha's memories surface. The two images represent the choices that she faced in 1947: death by jumping into the well (like her mother and sister) as demanded by her father, to save his patriarchal "honor," or flight from that death. Thus, the violent memory of 1947 resurfaces; as the tension between her son and her grows, the memory sequences appear with increasing frequency, haunting the fraying fabric of her present. One sepia-toned sequence, shot in slow motion, dramatizes how Ayesha refuses to jump and instead runs away, only to be hunted down and gang-raped repeatedly by Muslim men. Yet she survives this traumatic violence; in the same sepia-toned sequence, when one of her rapists regrets his actions and feels sorry for her, he marries her. In this way, *Khamosh Pani* offers a feminist critique of Veero's/Ayesha's dual abjection at the hands of men from both Sikh and Muslim communities.

Khamosh Pani suggests that in this village, political leaders espousing a hard-line ethno-nationalism use Partition to justify the turn away from secular democracy and toward Islamic statehood. Simultaneously, the constant parallel between the scenes of Partition violence and family separation and the contemporary extremist violence connects those two seminal moments of political transformation in Pakistan's history. The juxtaposition links the revival of ethnic politics in the 1970s and its destruction of pluralism to the legacies of decolonization. In both contexts, through the use of religion, the female citizen subject is increasingly rendered subaltern as sexual object, patriarchal property, and undesired citizen. Ayesha performs a liberal, inclusive Islam, as she teaches the tolerance emphasized in the Quran to little girls in the village from within her home. She loses the battle with her son, who gets increasingly radicalized and represents state-sponsored politicized Islam. By the end, pushed into precarity, Ayesha is rendered an unwanted citizen like Mammo. An ethno-nationalist Muslim masculinity in Pakistan is thus depicted as emerging through the estranging and demonizing of female subjectivity as Sikh (in the case of Ayesha) and modern (in the case of Zubeida).

Sumar asserts, "It was very important for me to show the process of change in Pakistan, to show that we were once a liberal, secular society that underwent a completely insidious process of change. Pakistan did not have an Islamic revolution like Iran did, for example."[44] She explains that because there was no revolution, the incremental and everyday modes through which the political culture changed everyday life for Pakistani women and minorities in the 1970s were important to uncover. Sumar observes that the film's depiction of political change and the disappearance of liberal secularism is starkly evident in its portrayal of how Pakistani girls' and women's lives changed in minor ways: the walls around girls' schools became higher, fewer women were seen in public spaces in cities and using public transportation, women no longer wore short sleeves on outfits, and so forth. Sumar asserts that it was important for her to depict this ideological and political change in 1979 "so that I could look back at it and wonder what happened in these twenty years, how did we change from a liberal, secular society to a more conservative, religious people?"[45] Thus, *Khamosh Pani* offers a narrative that depicts this capture of the quotidian by the forces of ethno-nationalism. How this ethno-nationalist capture is engineered in the village through the fetishization of the female body—especially Ayesha's—is tracked and problematized by the film. The ideological conflicts within Pakistan over approaches to religion are staged at several different points, including a confrontation that Saleem has with Zubeida. When she challenges his dogmatic ideas, Saleem walks out after claiming that she has spoiled him: he says he now has to go pray. The film's political critique emerges at this point in the feminist subject Zubeida's voice: "Saleem, even I pray. But that does not mean I do not think."

The second key representation of Ayesha's precarious citizenship and her growing disenfranchisement appears when Sikh pilgrims arrive in Charkhi from India to visit a holy site: one of them is Ayesha's brother, Jaswant. Risking social ire, he asks around the village about the presence of any Sikh women who were left behind in 1947 and finally manages to meet her. Ayesha denies that she is Veero. Still, he urges her to return to India with him, because their dying father wants to see her. Ayesha's son witnesses this exchange and subsequently calls her a "kaffir" (nonbeliever). The public emergence of her once collectively suppressed past in the new extremist climate destroys her familial intimacies and friendships. In the following scene, Saleem, to appease his extremist friends, asks her to proclaim in the village public square for his sake: "I am a Muslim, and I have accepted Islam with my heart, truly." This sequence is shot mostly in darkness, with a single kerosene lantern illuminating a part of Saleem's figure. In the foreground, Ayesha's figure huddles in shadows as she works silently in the kitchen. This scene suggestively depicts Ayesha's increasing disenfranchisement and foreshadows her disappearance, as the dark forces of religious nationalism take over her home, her family, and her village. Her silence eloquently speaks her refusal to humiliate herself, even as her son's question, "Why are you killing me?" only ironically underscores her slow, social death and precarity in the face of these forces. The subsequent public acknowledgment of Ayesha's personal history in the village, in the face of the now-dominant extremist thinking, leads to her social ostracization by those who have been her closest, long-time friends—in spite of her embrace of Islam and her decades-long life as a devout Muslim. Bereft of the intimate patriarchal protection of husband and son in this changing sociopolitical context, Ayesha's painful, involuntary hybridity is expelled from national and social community.

Khamosh Pani is part of the archive of transnational films that we can name, following Naficy, "accented cinema." Accented cinema is exilic, diasporic, and ethnic; it is subject to the momentous national longing for form of the filmmaker's country: "They [accented filmmakers] cross many borders and engage in many deterritorializing and reterritorializing journeys, which take several forms, including home-seeking journeys, journeys of homelessness, and home-coming journeys."[46] Sumar's film, written by Indian writer Vohra and made possible by collaboration with French and German producers and Indian actors, offers a powerful psychological and political critique of ethnic nationalism articulated with state power that suggests, from a feminist perspective, that homecoming for the raped female Partition survivor is impossible. Through the liminal figure of Ayesha/Veero, the increasing subalternity of the female citizen in the postcolonial state is underscored and challenged. A sequence that stages the confrontation between Veero and her Sikh brother when she goes to the well enacts this feminist critique. When her brother again entreats her to return to India and meet their dying father, Ayesha refuses, questioning the selfish patriarchal violence of this request, given that he had wanted to kill her in 1947. The camera frames her in a close-up as she angrily expresses her pain:

> He wanted to kill me once for his own peace. Now what will happen if he sees me alive? Alive! And a Muslim! How will he go to the heaven for Sikhs? And what heaven is left for me? Sikh or Muslim? . . . Since so many years, you were happy having killed me. But I was alive. I made my life without you all. Now this is my life, and this is my house. Now go, and leave me alone to my fate. Now go—go back.

Asserting her agency and will, she chooses to stay in her home, as a Muslim woman, even as she underscores her in-betweenness to the rhetorics of ethnicity that try to suture her to patriarchal social relations.

The film thus creates a discursive space for the female subject to represent her pain and abjection by the violence of patriarchal ethnicities, which she equates structurally with that of male-dominated extremism in 1947 decolonized India and in 1979 Pakistan. Simultaneously, *Khamosh Pani* reveals the impossibility of being at home in the new Pakistani nation for the hybrid female subject like Ayesha, who is terrorized by the new forces of modern ethno-nationalism because of her traumatic past—especially when she lacks a husband's or son's patriarchal protection. This problem becomes apparent to her when the increasingly militant activists generate her social stigmatization in Charkhi, such that even her son expresses hatred toward her and her sisterly best friend requests that she avoid attending her daughter's wedding due to the uproar about her Sikh past. The dawning of this knowledge of her precarity and exile from belonging and equal citizenship follows the scenes of her discriminatory isolation, first by her son and then by her friend. These scenes show Ayesha increasingly in darkness, partially in shadow—poetically underscoring her recognition of her growing social and political erasure as a historical, political subject in Pakistan.[47]

Religion, nationalism, and performance become intricately enmeshed by the end, rendering gendered subjects as precarious citizens in different ways as the subaltern secular disappears from the fabric of social life in this village. The film ends by juxtaposing scenes of Saleem doing namaz at dawn in the public mosque while Ayesha does the same in her home's courtyard in private. Both perform the same prayer, to the same God, yet Ayesha—as female, convert, and widow—is now an undesired citizen subject. After her prayer, she wears the gold locket that her brother had snatched from her neck when she ran away from the killing well in 1947 and that he brought back to her on this pilgrimage. Although she had refused her brother, her privately wearing this locket suggests that she is embracing her earlier identity as Veero. Then, a long shot reveals her shalwar-clad figure jumping into the well that she had once rejected, thirty-two years earlier; the long shot emphasizes the insignificance of her death in the political landscape. She thus embraces the same death that she had resisted in 1947, as if signaling that the resistance has been pointless: "the subaltern cannot speak."[48] Ironically, while the film has been screened in theaters across the world, to much critical acclaim—including a three-month screening in India that played to packed houses—it has had limited distribution in Pakistan.

Khamosh Pani is an eloquent cinematic indictment of the continuity of patriarchal violence articulated with religion, across India and Pakistan, as triumphant: as the film unfolds, Ayesha's life as a citizen is rendered increasingly precarious. Butler suggests that precariousness is "a function of our social vulnerability and exposure that is always given some political form, and precarity [is] differentially distributed." Further, Butler argues, precaritization must be recognized as "an ongoing process": "Precaritization allows us to think about the slow death that happens to targeted or neglected populations over time and space."[49] Reminiscent of Benegal's neorealism, *Khamosh Pani* illuminates the precaritization of Ayesha and her son, albeit in different ways. In the changing political Islamicization of the Pakistani state in the late 1970s, the film shows the disappearance of the raped subaltern female as Partition migrant and survivor in Pakistan.

In Benegal's *Mammo*, discussed earlier, the Partition migrant survives her precaritization and lives by staging her bureaucratic death. On this continuum, tragically, Ayesha/Veero "chooses" death over her increasing dehumanization in postcolonial Pakistan at the hands of her own son, friends, and community. After her funeral, Saleem retrieves the locket and, strangely, gifts it to Zubeida. At this point, Zubeida's voiceover ambiguously says, "Today Veero is gone, and Ayesha is left behind. We did not wish that she should go." In Zubeida's voice, the film presents a feminist solidarity—not sentimentality—that notes the impossibility of Ayesha's position (recalling that of Mammo). As a secular feminist Pakistani citizen, by the end of the film, Zubeida is shown as alienated from Saleem's ethno-nationalism. Saleem becomes a political spokesperson for the new hard-line Islamic state. The last sequence shows Zubeida's back in the foreground, as she watches Saleem speaking on broadcast TV, explaining that it is only natural to make state laws Islamic: "After all, why did we create Pakistan? We created it for Islam." The last shot shows Zubeida walking away and out of the frame, suggesting her disagreement and allegorizing the disappearance of her liberal views from the public sphere. The camera poignantly remains on the street shop signs now visible because of her departure, and the sequence is accompanied by a mournful, elegiac background score. Like the novels by Sidhwa and Baldwin discussed thus far, *Khamosh Pani* is a transnational cultural text that marks a just memory, through its feminist perspective, of the differential legacies of precaritization for women's citizenship in South Asia. It represents national and political change through the perspective of the raped Partition survivor, Ayesha. Her experience of changing intimacies grimly bears witness to the precaritization wrought by decolonization as well as by the Pakistani state.

Conclusion: Performing the Secular, Inventing Peace

In tracking thus far, as my Introduction proffers, what has been created and what remains of the 1947 Partition migrations in public cultural archives of South Asia and the United States, I have sought to be attentive to the dangers of rhetoric about crisis that revolves around specific events, "given eventhood's propensity to function as, or be deployed as, a distraction from ordinary and ongoing violence."[50] My analysis of films in this chapter, across diverse aesthetic modes, shows how these films at once reference Partition as an event and go beyond it.[51] They gesture to and interrogate the ongoing, ordinary, and often state-sanctioned violence against the minority citizen, the migrant, and sexed subjects in post-Partition India and Pakistan. The films in this chapter's archive constitute new modes of public engagement and counterpublics that revisit migration and secularism in South Asia and abroad. The Bollywood melodramas I discuss reinvent popular genres to offer a public fantasy of mediatized, affective secularism that restories India-Pakistan border crossing, questions war and patriotism, and foregrounds the gendering of statelessness as well as citizenship. Differently, the feminist art and third cinema texts I analyze bear witness to the performance and erasures of the subaltern secular in women's lives—migrants as well as citizens—in India and Pakistan under regimes of hegemonic ethnic nationalism. "In the figure of the witness of a postcolonial modernity," Bhabha writes, "we have another wisdom: it comes from those who have seen the nightmare of racism and oppression in the banal daylight of the everyday."[52] *Mammo* and *Khamosh Pani* unveil the state-dominated oppressions rendered banal in post-Partition everyday life. These films invite us to recognize what Jasbir Puar eloquently describes in a different context as "the biopolitical production of precarity and (un)livability that runs across" particular gendered and ethnic identities in post-47 South Asia.[53]

Today, this precarity can also be seen in the systematic biopolitical expulsions of the ethnic Muslim Rohingya refugees from Myanmar, who, since August 2017, have been violently targeted by the Buddhist majority government as well as local mobs and forced to flee their homes in the northern province of Rakhine, despite having lived in the region for centuries. The Myanmar government denies citizenship to the ethnic minority Rohingya people (not the only ethnic minority group, but the only Muslim one in Myanmar), claiming they are illegal immigrants from Bangladesh. Reminding us of the transnational dimensions of the history of statelessness in post-45 Asia, Jayita Sarkar also describes how the current Rohingya refugee crisis has its roots in the mid-twentieth-century moment of decolonization and Partition.[54] Broadly speaking, in post-47 South Asia, this geopolitical displacement of the Rohingyas is adjacent to the forced migrations of Sri Lankan Tamils, the exile of Tibetans in India starting in the 1950s, and the internment of Chinese Indians in 1962. Elsewhere, I map the relationship between South Asian American representations of Partition and the cultural representation of the subaltern history of Chinese Indian statelessness.⁵⁵ By considering and creating new aesthetic archives that bear witness to and uncover the production of subaltern secular intimacies and precarity through expulsions in post-47 Asia, we, as critics and activists, can challenge how the postcolonial state perpetuates new global forms of displacement and forge new solidarities across national borders.

4

Transnational Asia, Testimony, and New Media

> The long shadow that Partition cast, touched not only those who lived through ... [or] died because of it, but also the generations that came after.... Perhaps the real moving on will come when we are able to work on these histories together across countries, across class, across caste and across gender.
>
> —Urvashi Butalia, *"Partition: The Long Shadow"*[1]

> Media and temporalizing processes are also closely implicated in how we remember and, equally significantly, forget aspects of the past, interpret and live in the present, and imagine the future.
>
> —Purnima Mankekar, *Unsettling India*[2]

Urvashi Butalia acknowledges that "the recovery of memory, the 'settling' (if that is ever possible) of questions of closure and justice, the sense that a history of trauma and loss, of guilt and culpability, can now be put behind, and people's lives can move on—clearly a period of nearly seven decades is in no way enough to deal with this."[3] In my analysis of statelessness, citizenship, and secularism through the transmediatic representation of Partition memories in the preceding chapters, I seek to uncover what Butalia foregrounds in the above epigraph: the intergenerational impact of the Partition migrations and the necessity for our reckoning with this history in intersectional ways that attend to the multiple axes of difference that shape subjectivity, agency, and power. Relatedly, and resonant with the epigraphs that open this book, Purnima Mankekar argues that "rather than conceptualize the past, present, or future as a priori or autonomous realms of experience, it makes sense for us to think of the ways in which transnational public cultures constitute the past, present, and future through, for instance, their mediation of memories of the past, experiences of contemporaneity, and discourses of futurity."[4] Shoshana Felman suggests that our era can precisely be defined as the age of testimony.[5] In this chapter, I draw upon this scholarship to show how Partition's migration stories in mass media and art, and the stories of border crossings that emerge in their shadows, unsettle nationalism to create new practices of the subaltern secular. They constitute migrants and refugees as the agents of history in postcolonial South Asia and use their migration stories to offer new political visions of fashioning subaltern secular solidarity under siege. I make this argument by tracking migration stories across new media representations, digital archives, and artistic practices of testimony about migration and conflict. As mentioned in earlier chapters, in India as well as in the South Asian American diaspora, there has been much recent public sphere discussion about the 1947 Partition—after many decades of neglect. This interest is evident in recent scholarship in the humanities, in the literary and film productions about Partition, in new media memory narratives, and in U.S.-based digital oral history archives, such as 1947Partition.org (which I founded in 2009) and 1947PartitionArchive.org (founded by Bay Area–based physicist Guneeta Singh Bhalla in 2011). One of my arguments in this book is that the texts and objects under consideration inhabit and invent postcolonial public and counterpublic spheres. Thus, in their circulation, their representations of migration and secularism create and contest dominant ideas about nationalism, citizenship, and the role of religion in public life in India as well as in Pakistan.

This archive of cultural texts then lies adjacent to the numerous public sphere initiatives—local as well as transnational—that tell Partition stories to work toward peace between the often-warring nation-states India and Pakistan. Smitu Kothari and Zia Mian have recently tracked the diverse initiatives for peace that have emerged from civil society between the two countries, across such spheres as education, film and theater productions, human rights activism, and others: they call these "the citizens' diplomacy movement."[6] As efforts to counter the debilitating effects of ongoing conflict and war, these civil society initiatives have emerged from different groups—journalists, women's groups, ex-military officers, filmmakers, lawyers, and activists. Included in these groups are such bodies as the Pakistan-India Peoples' Forum for Peace and Democracy (PIPFPD), "which started in 1994 as a group of 25 people from the two countries meeting in Lahore. Its joint convention, headed alternately in Pakistan and India, is now the largest regular gathering of citizens of the two countries." Other peace networks Kothari and Mian mention include "the Pakistan Peace Coalition (founded in 1999) and the Coalition for Nuclear Disarmament and Peace (2001)."[7] Apart from these initiatives based in the subcontinent, they point out the existence of transnational projects, such as South Asians for Human Rights (which includes Nobel Prize–winning economist Amartya Sen and, until her death in February 2017, lawyer Asma Jahangir, who served on Pakistan's Human Rights Commission), that work toward fostering social justice, gender equality, and bilateral cooperation instead of conflict between India and Pakistan. Offering other instances of nonstate initiatives, Kothari and Mian also point to "single-issue organizations," such as the South Asian Free Media Association, created by journalists from both countries, which "seeks the 'advancement of public good, peace and tranquility in the region,' while groups of retired military officers such as the India Pakistan Soldiers in Initiative for Peace, that include the former chief of Pakistan's Air Force and of India's navy, engage in dialogue with their counterparts across the border about national security."[8] These organizations' peace activism in the subcontinent thus is part of a wider public discourse that insists on rethinking the historical legacies of conflict to advocate for peace, dialogue, and cross-border collectivities. In this chapter, I discuss how Partition's migration stories are being mobilized and circulated in the contemporary public sphere in diverse modes that articulate technology, media, activism, and globalization. Considering different texts and objects, from new media advertising to digital humanities archives, to digital photo-based art installations, to oral histories, I trace how technology and new media forms are being deployed to map a just memory of the Partition migrations. Among my arguments is that many, if not all, articulate ethico-political solidarities that reveal new performances of the subaltern secular. In the process, they participate in a transnational dialogue about these transnational citizens' movements toward peace in South Asia.

Border-Crossing Advertising: Google and Secular Intimacies in the Commercial "Reunion" (2013)

In 2013, the American company Google decided to contribute to the wider rethinking of the 1947 Partition that was ongoing in the academy and in postcolonial public spheres. Google produced and uploaded to its video-streaming subsidiary, YouTube, a three-and-a-half-minute commercial called "Reunion." The commercial dwells on Partition's refugees, intergenerational memory, and traumatic histories—key issues in Partition Studies. It aims to promote Google's search engine in the Indian and Pakistani markets, which, at two billion people, is substantial. It revolves around the losses of Partition's migrants and the separation and reunion of long-lost friends. In considering this advertisement, I ask the following questions: How does this commercial memorialize a traumatic migration? What do the melodramatic aesthetics of the commercial—its sensual and emotional resonance—reveal about its politics in relation to nationalism, war, and globalization? What alternative modes of collective intimacy does it posit?

What is the place of this media production in contemporary conversations about Partition, secularism, and India-Pakistan relations?

The commercial's plot revolves around the losses of Partition's refugees through a story about the separation (and reunion) of two friends due to the Partition migrations: one Hindu, the other Muslim. The video depicts an elderly Hindu shopkeeper, Baldev Mehra (Vishwa Mohan Badola), a refugee now settled in Delhi, who describes to his granddaughter Suman (Auritra Ghosh) how he had to flee from the city of Lahore in 1947 due to ethnic violence. In two sequences—one set in his shop and the other on a park bench—he tells Suman that he counts among his losses his best friend, Yusuf (M. S. Sathyu); he reminisces about flying kites and stealing sweets called "jhajhariyas" with him in Lahore. Showing Suman a frayed, sepia-toned photograph of Yusuf and him together as children, which he has kept tucked away in a book, Baldev tells her with tears in his eyes, "I miss Yusuf a lot." Suman, being a tech-savvy young woman from Mumbai, uses Google's search engine to learn more about Baldev's past. She also successfully finds Yusuf in Lahore and calls him. Then, with the help of his grandson Ali (Syed Shabahat Ali), she secretly engineers a reunion of the two elderly friends on Baldev's birthday. What propels the narrative forward in the ad's diegetic space are the sequences depicting Google searches that the grandchildren, Suman and Ali, conduct on their laptops and smartphones in India and Pakistan. These sequences, in which each types specific terms on the search engine's page, constitute a layer of activity that interrupts the mood and yet allows the plot to move forward. These searches include Suman's quest for information like "what is jhajhariya" and the location and contact information of the sweet shop, called "Fazal Sweets," near Mochi Gate in Lahore that her grandfather mentions Yusuf's family owned. Later, she also searches for flight arrival information so that she can receive them at the airport. Her counterpart in Pakistan, Ali, is shown doing Google searches for information about visa applications, the weather in Delhi, and so on. Every search thus interrupts the story about the generational transmission of memory and loss *and* establishes its own centrality to the denouement, even while allowing Suman to learn more about her grandfather's past. The feel-good narrative closes with a sequence depicting Yusuf's arrival at Baldev's house. There, Yusuf wishes Baldev, "Happy birthday, my friend!" The two friends hug and then joyously sit on the floor in the house's inner courtyard together, drenched by a monsoon rain shower. Thus, two friends divided by a border are momentarily reunited, as Google imagines the redressal of migrants' trauma as well as the undoing of childhood loss. Further, in a nod to India-Pakistan cooperation and friendship, after the friends have hugged each other, the camera cuts to a sequence in which Suman expresses her nonverbal thanks to

Yusuf's grandson through her facial gestures, while the latter nonverbally acknowledges them. Throughout the commercial, close-up shots of both men's faces, with faraway looks and teary eyes, sentimentally emphasize their emotional pain.

Three issues bear examination in this commercial: its transnational reception, its aesthetic representation of intimacy and memory through what might properly be called "transnational sentimentality," and its relevance for the project of mourning and making legible Partition's losses. As I point out in the preceding chapters, unlike many other historical moments of division and conflict, the 1947 Partition, until 2017, had never been officially, institutionally memorialized by any of the countries involved—India, Pakistan, or Great Britain. In 2017, a nonprofit organization led by Lady Kishwar Desai and her daughter, Mallika Ahluwalia, started a Partition Museum in Amritsar. Thus, the return to accounting for Partition, to understand what happened, what the experience was like for its more than 12 million migrants, for the 150,000 women who were abducted and raped—all these conversations have been initiated in the public sphere by scholars, artists, journalists, and activists in places far apart—India, Pakistan, the United Kingdom, Europe, Canada, and the United States.

Given that the scholarly as well as collective remembering of Partition refugees' trauma has happened only belatedly (since the late 1990s, and over the last two decades) and through the work of (nonstate) citizen-led digital oral history projects like 1947PartitionArchive.org or scholarship, this commercial is interesting on multiple levels. For one, its mainstream and global circulation brings international attention to Partition's peripheral and subaltern history of migrations and its silenced refugees—if not to its accompanying gendered violence. Its reception also testifies to this new attention, although the commercial definitely fails the Bechdel test, and its critics have dismissed it as "fantasy," "unrealistic," "neoliberal," and exploitative.[9] Arguably, the commercial reproduces many of the gendered tropes of Indian secular nationalist discourse—of Hindu-Muslim brotherhood, Indo-Pak friendship, and so on. Indeed, Paul Woodward cautions, "Advertising trades in false connections." As he notes wryly, "Ironically, a real life connection that Google hopes its audience must have forgotten was evident in the Mumbai attacks themselves in which the terrorists used Google Earth to locate their targets."[10] Finally, it is important to acknowledge that this story is deeply gendered; it would not be as easy, perhaps, to show two female Partition survivors as reunited friends. For women during the Partition, as much scholarship reveals, the threat of rape intimately inhabits the memory of 1947 migrations. If remembered in the public sphere, that experience alone would considerably complicate this commercial's production of an affective, secular Indo-Pakistan relationship.

Nonetheless, I am interested in locating this commercial within the larger affective public culture it emerges from and in which it circulates. It can be understood, I argue, as a transmedia work that resonates with and participates in a new contemporary cultural discourse that memorializes this mid-twentieth-century migration. Further, I suggest, its memory work contributes to the activist politics of the works of literature, photography, film, and graphic narratives discussed earlier that seek to counter the border conflicts of the present day. Thus, like the films analyzed in the preceding chapter, the "Reunion" commercial employs a Bollywood aesthetic to create a new structure of feeling about India-Pakistan relationships. My approach draws upon Mankekar's seminal ethnographic work on affect, unsettlement, and temporality in the cultural production of the idea of "India." She examines "how the circulation of transnational media and public cultures compels us to rethink conceptions of cultural change and, thereby, conceive of culture as inherently unsettled."[11] Indeed, Mankekar's objective is to trace "the modalities through which India is simultaneously reified and reconfigured,"[12] and this method resonates for my approach here: I am interested in how oral histories as well as their digital and commercial representations may reify certain ideas about secularism and citizenship in the subcontinent as well as reinvent them. I approach this Google commercial, then, as a media object whose affective life invites us to understand subject and community formation by "taking into account movement, passage, and potentiality."[13] After all, as Mankekar argues, "ideological interpellation does not tell the whole story about how media move us."[14]

Created by Ogilvy and Mather India, within two months of its release on YouTube, "Reunion" (directed by Amit Sharma) had gone viral, tallying 1.8 million views. It was watched not only in India and Pakistan but also around the world before being broadcast on Indian TV in November 2013. The commercial is in Hindi, but subtitles have been translated into nine languages, including English, French, Malayalam, and Urdu. Today, it has racked up more than 15 million views, 8,700 positive comments, and 110,000 likes on YouTube; it has also been posted on other websites. Across the world, bloggers, writers, and activists have praised it—including Indians and Pakistanis in the subcontinent and diaspora, to be sure, but also other viewers across the globe, from Russia to Nigeria to New Zealand. One such champion of the commercial is Beena Sarwar, a journalist, graphic novelist, and human rights activist from Pakistan. She has established Aman Ki Asha (Hope for Peace), a nongovernmental organization (NGO) working for peace between India and Pakistan; through this NGO, she has also started the "Milne Do" (Let Us Meet) campaign, which advocates for the reduction of visa restrictions between India and Pakistan to facilitate travel and exchange. (In Chapter 1, I discuss her coauthored graphic narrative "Milne

Do" in Vishwajyoti Ghosh's anthology *This Side, That Side: Restorying Partition*.) In an essay on the central role women have played in peace-building initiatives in civil society, Sarwar also notes that increased visa restrictions for people to travel between India and Pakistan since the 1965 war have had debilitating effects on ordinary people and their connections across the border.[15] Hence, about this commercial, she comments, "If it doesn't move you, you've got a heart of stone. And oh, if it was that easy. For Pakistanis and Indians to get visas to visit each other's country is just short of impossible."[16] Indeed, as Pippa Virdee remarks, "The population exchange and territorial division cannot be undone, but the greater tragedy is the loss of homelands that people can no longer visit. Strict visa controls mean that the ordinary people still suffer the most because they are unable to visit the 'other' side."[17] The Urdu poet Gulzar offers a poem "If Possible . . ." that poignantly and ironically bears witness to this difficulty in crossing the India-Pakistan border. Its refugee speaker describes a dream of crossing the border to revisit the beloved home, fields, and land left behind. It concludes with the refugee acknowledging that this travel is impossible, because it is impossible to provide proof of one's dreams:

But all this is possible only in dreams
There are some political difficulties in going there now
It is still my motherland but it isn't my country anymore
To go there, I have to visit many offices of the two governments
Get my face stamped and provide proof of my dreams.[18]

These lines suggest that state bureaucracies in both countries deliberately render travel, encounter, and connection for ordinary citizens impossible. A similar ironic stance toward statecraft and Indo-Pak politics appears as a critique in some of the online comments on "Reunion." They indicate how it has elicited a positive response in a political climate of long-standing national animosities. For instance, Akshaya Aradhya comments on Google's Facebook page, "Google brought nations together in 3 minutes and 32 seconds. The politicians of both countries couldn't do this in 66 years."[19] Pakistani author and publisher Musharraf Ali Farooqi Tweets, "Google will go to Heaven because of this: http://t.co/JzyI2yqjPZ #Reunion."[20] Similarly, Muna Khan Tweets from Pakistan about how the commercial made her father nostalgic: "I showed the Reunion video to my dad who wants me to google the names of his school friends in India so he can have his own reunion. Uh oh." This transnational reception of the Google commercial, which mobilizes the provincial and the national in complex ways, suggests that this story resonates, at least in part, because it is the story of millions of migrants and refugees across Asia—whether in India and Pakistan, scarred by Partition; in North and South Korea, divided by war; or of the families divided by the oceanic borders between mainland China and Taiwan after 1949.

This commercial thus opens some new conversations, even as it forecloses others. Arguably, unlike the critique of the postcolonial state visualized in Ghosh's graphic narrative anthology *This Side, That Side*, the Google commercial participates in the contemporary conversation about Partition—but only to depoliticize it. It also glosses over the fact that it is very hard for Indians and Pakistanis to actually visit each other, unless one has high-level connections; getting a visa can take months. Further, when Pakistanis arrive in India, they are legally required to register themselves at the local police station as Pakistani citizens within twenty-four hours of arrival. So much is elided in the commercial, including the three wars that India and Pakistan have fought since Partition. The ad presents a globalized middle-class imaginary in which the bloody memory of Partition is erased, as is the ongoing tension between the two countries. Transnational sentimentality and Google unite the aspirational South Asian middle class across three generations and Partition's borders.

The commercial's representation of intimacy and memory, therefore, is worth exploring. The aesthetic of "Reunion" draws upon elements of Bollywood melodrama, including such techniques as a focus on emotional relationships, lush production values, the use of shallow focus, stylized gestures, and the extradiegetic Hindi song that heightens the moods being evoked (alternately happy and sad, then turning to joy at the end) in the visual unfolding of a story about migration and interethnic friendship. The focus on Baldev as a Partition refugee–turned-citizen constructs him as the central melodramatic subject; as in conventional melodrama, the personality is "the focus of its investments in the wake of modern social, political, and religious transformation."[21] Ravi Vasudevan points out that given its public, fictional form, there is a certain "excess and even visceral attraction in the way melodrama often braids domestic and public spaces to complicate and unsettle identity and disrupt the security (and oppression) of home, hearth, and lineage."[22] This intertwining of the domestic and the national public is center stage in the commercial: it foregrounds Baldev's traumatic memory of his migration during Partition, unsettling his identity as an Indian citizen. Evoking his refugee past, the ad anchors his affective life in a secular friendship with a Muslim Pakistani and historicizes his lineage beyond the nation. Gender and age function in interesting ways here: both men are not the authoritative and stereotypical patriarchs that litter some of the biggest hits of Bollywood cinema. Instead, both men are depicted as vulnerable and emotional subjects with excessive emotional attachments to each other. Conventional roles of caregiving are reversed in this plot, as both need the caregiving of their grandchildren to redress loss, and the modern Indian woman from Mumbai initiates their reunion.[23] Throughout the ad, close-up sequences in soft focus and warm lighting on Baldev's and Yusuf's faces highlight the faraway looks and teary eyes that emphasize their emotional pain.[24] The ad thus uses the metalanguage of cinematic Bollywood melodrama that is already familiar to its cinematic public to publicly situate technology as enabling reconciliation as well as the renewal of secular intimacies across India and Pakistan's border.

Writing in a different context, Judith Butler questions "the differential allocation of grief" in America and how the public recognition of minority lives as grievable can interrupt processes of state violence and war.[25] How does this commercial allocate refugees' grief? While the commercial does not return us to what Butler calls "a sense of ethical outrage," its melodramatic techniques renew attention to this mid-twentieth-century refugee history, establishing refugees' losses and lives as grievable. It invites us to empathize with migrants' trauma. This is contra the spectacular objectification and, often, dehumanization of refugees in mainstream news media in the contemporary moment. Like the childhood photograph that Baldev shows Suman when sharing his memories, to appropriate Graham Clarke's words, Google's "Reunion" ad "bears witness, in that it activates a circulation of a certain cultural memory, and exchange."[26] The commercial's sentimental visual narrative yokes together transnational cultures of consumption with the soft-focus tinge of memory. For aspirational middle-class South Asians, the emancipatory promise of technology and its speed also brings affective liberation from the intimate losses of decolonization and the refugee experience. In her evocative memoir essay about traveling to Pakistan, Kamla Bhasin writes:

> This is a story also about millions not accepting the "official" truths as truths, not accepting borders as borders, and millions first dreaming of and then reconnecting, reviving old bonds that refuse to perish; watering almost dry and dead roots of trees and seeing the miracle of green leaves sprouting. This is a story of love refusing to die in the face of manipulated hatred, friendship refusing to surrender to the madness of animosity.[27]

This sentiment about cross-border affiliations resonates with the visual aesthetic of "Reunion" and the affective registers it evokes: the scenes that depict Baldev's repeated remembrance of his friend Yusuf, first in the space of his shop and then in a park, instantiate the persistent memory of secular friendship untouched by state political ideology. Like the films discussed in Chapter 3, "Reunion" sidesteps the familiar Bollywood trope of Hindu-Muslim heteronormative coupledom as central to performing the secular properly. Instead, it unveils two generations of Indian and Pakistani citizens who reinvent and perform the secular intimacies shattered by the Partition migrations. We can note that Google does not challenge the fact of the two nation-states and their institutions of citizenship; remember that Ali does a Google search for "visa requirements." Further, the commercial does not create space for the representation of other affects toward the nation-state project, such as ambivalence, resentment, or anger. The ad maintains the integrity of national boundaries created by decolonization in 1947; it does not call for a reunion of the two partitioned nations. What it does do is point to the two nations' historical intimacy as coeval with their spatial intimacy. It invites us to recognize and honor a new transnational aesthetic of attachments that gathers in its fold refugees' subaltern secular attachments by moving forward and back. Thus, it marks diasporic intimacy—an intimacy that reflects collective memory formations but does not promise "a comforting return of identity through shared nostalgia for the lost home and homeland."[28] This diasporic intimacy is exilic. It makes legible one dimension of the refugee experience, bearing witness (like the photograph in the video) and placing value on the transmission of intergenerational memory of Partition's traumas. In this way, it recalibrates the relationship between the private and public spheres—a classic feature of melodrama.

If the commercial offers a Partition migration story in Hindi cinema's melodramatic cinematic mode, unveiling what remains and what has been created after Partition, its simultaneous function as a commercial for Google also suggests that technology, and specifically Google, is essential to undoing the melancholia of that migration and creating cross-border peace. The punctuation of the commercial's story world—with sequences that cut to the Google searches that Suman and Ali perform on their laptops and smartphones—is important. The search results allow Suman to contact Yusuf and, eventually, to engineer the cross-border reunion. The search sequences thus interrupt Baldev's story but also move it forward, suggesting that the class privilege and desire of middle-class, third-generation citizens might materialize Indo-Pakistan friendship and peace. This is not a nostalgic desire for the lost wholeness or unity of community; instead, it is an exilic intimacy. In staging the precarious intimacy of cross-ethnic and cross-national friendship, the commercial questions the closed borders in the current political situation. "Reunion" reanimates the memory of Partition migrations and the refugee experience, as a past that is very much, as Ghosh says, "still happening." It mobilizes refugees' memories of interethnic intimacies and invites us to recognize refugees' losses—not just of homes but also of intimate communities. On one register, it gestures to an affective, secular ethic—one that radically imagines a fluid border crossing that in reality is virtually impossible today. It sentimentally invokes the subcontinent's forgotten history of violent Partition migrations and invites us to respond with empathy to refugees' trauma.

Given that the commercial sutures the possibility for Indian-Pakistani secular intimacies to Google's search engine, it presents an American corporate giant as enabling reconciliation from the traumas of Partition engineered by the British. This emblematizes what Saskia Sassen calls the "overlap and interaction among the multiple spatialities and temporalities of the national and the global."[29] The expansion of the American multinational company—and, by extension, capital and its digital assemblages—appears through an intricate linkage of urban, global, and national in the narrative. Digital technology fuels the hypermobility of citizens across national borders and affirms transnational intimate communities. Viet Thanh Nguyen notes, "Both memory and forgetting are subject not only to the fabrications of art but also to the commodifications of memory."[30] This observation raises the question of whether this commodification of Partition memories is creative or destructive. I suggest that "Reunion" posits a future for secular, transnational intimacies in which nation-states exist, but their internecine wars are history. In this sense, it resonates with the fantasy of Indian-Pakistani peace presented in *Bajrangi Bhaijaan* (discussed in Chapter 3), even as it replaces devout Hindu masculinity with the urban Mumbai middle-class woman as an agent of border crossing and secular reunions.

Given that the Google commercial is strategically aimed at a two-billion-strong market, it participates in the contemporary conversation about Partition, such that the state and nationalism are curiously absent from its story. It addresses the cinematic public of South Asia, inviting an affective, precarious response to the shared pain and loss that continue to mark life for those divided by the 1947 migrations, like Yusuf and Baldev, and this message has resonated globally. Jim Chandler acknowledges that, following Max Horkheimer and Theodor Adorno, critics tend to view sentimentality in a pejorative sense; however, he suggests that we distinguish "the sentimental as a cultural form" from the casual dismissal of sentimentality.[31] In contrast, Lauren Berlant invites us to critique the production of mass national sentimentality. In distinguishing between sentimentality and solidarity, Berlant argues:

> There is nothing austere about sentimentality. This is why we politically motivated agents are so attached, sentimentally, to solidarity, because solidarity is organized by a recognition of a problem that does not require us to line up affectively in relation to each other or

to ourselves. Bound in the structure of solidarity, we need minimal affective likeness—we are free to be ambivalent about whole sets of things while attending to the transformation of the thing/scene/problem that has brought us together. For us to cultivate new kinds of affective collective ground we have to embrace the sheer formalism of solidarity, the affective freedom to be different but mutual amid the risk-taking of changing structure through practice.[32]

I suggest that although "Reunion" appears to fetishize sentimentality, in reality, multiple, new, affective intimacies that might constitute solidarity are being hinted at, staged, and reinvented. The relationship between the two friends, Baldev and Yusuf, is marked by transnational sentimentality—an aesthetic of India-Pakistan attachments that the commercial celebrates and holds up for view. Simultaneously, the relationship forged between the grandchildren, Suman and Ali, citizens of India and Pakistan, is one of potential solidarity. In its public fantasy of border crossing, and its release in the same year, it stands alongside but apart from the imagined and real border crossings of the subjects of many narratives in the graphic anthology *This Side, That Side: Restorying Partition*—albeit shorn of their poverty and, in many cases, their multigenerational abjection at the hands of the postcolonial state.

Ironically, Yusuf is played by one of India's most brilliant filmmakers, M. S. Sathyu, who directed the searing Hindu-Urdu film *Garm Hava* (Scorching Winds; 1973). Elsewhere, I analyze how *Garm Hava* powerfully criticizes Muslims' experience of discrimination, displacement, and minoritized citizenship in post-Partition India and offers a socialist critique of the failures of Indian secularism.[33] When Sathyu was asked how, after having made this landmark film, he could have participated in the making of this capitalist commercial for Google (which many have criticized as neoliberal), his response was "How could I have not?" He continued, "I don't work on a computer and I have no idea what Google is. But I am glad to be a part of what I thought was a very sentimental story."[34] The overwhelming success of this commercial led Google to create a series of related commercials that storied Yusuf and Baldev's time spent together in Delhi in the quotidian of everyday life. In these commercials, the plot turns on the two friends playing chess, cooking together, and attempting to nudge Suman and Ali toward heteronormative coupledom through diverse tactics—thus unfortunately repeating one of the classic tropes of Bollywood cinema.

The global popularity of "Reunion" can be misleading, for it is not unique. Before and after its release, a range of commercials in India and Pakistan that address India-Pakistan relationships through the representation of transnational border crossing as well as heteronormative India-Pakistan romantic coupledom constitute a subgenre that I call "border-crossing advertising." For instance, in 2010, the Pakistani spice company National Foods commissioned Page-33 Productions and Saatchi and Saatchi to create a commercial called "National Foods Eid" (directed by Saqib Malik), which has an aesthetic and theme similar to "Reunion."[35] "Eid" opens with a scene located in Delhi, India, in which a middle-aged woman turns on All India Radio. As an extradiegetic Urdu song fills the soundscape, she is shown writing a letter to her older sister "Apa" in Pakistan. The sequence cuts to a shot of Apa in Lahore holding a letter, while the voiceover reveals its contents: "Dear Apa: Eid Mubarak! On this Eid too, in Delhi, you and your delicious cooking will be missed." The commercial does not disclose how or why the two sisters are separated across India and Pakistan. As Apa reads the letter, she glances fondly at a frayed black-and-white photograph of two young girls (presumably of the two sisters) and looks into the distance with a half-smile. This gesture suggests that she is sentimentally reminiscing. As in "Reunion," the encounter with the frayed childhood photograph activates the past, memory, and exchange. In these scenes, close-ups emphasize individual remembrances and renew transnational affective investments. The camera then cuts to a shot of her son promising her: "Ami, we will celebrate this Eid in Delhi." Later, we see Apa in a kitchen cooking biryani and other foods with National Food spices, packing the food in a silver tiffin box, and riding in a train with her son from Lahore to Delhi with excitement and joy. As in "Reunion," an extradiegetic song creates an upbeat and nostalgic mood as the camera shows her and her son arriving in Delhi, her pointing out the monuments of Delhi to her son, and looking up with delight at old Delhi's crowded streets and monuments as they take a *tonga* (cycle carriage) to her sister's home. When Apa finally arrives as a surprise at her sister's doorstep, they share a tearful embrace and reunion; the commercial closes with a shot of the two of them surrounded by family, eating the food brought from Pakistan together inside the sister's home. As the song refrain fades, "Which guest has arrived today? Oh which guest?" the voiceover asserts, "National Recipe Masalas. Our foods, our festivals." Thus, like "Reunion," the commercial "Eid" presents an aspiration and a public fantasy beyond the present: it is an aspiration in which cross-border travel and reunion with beloved family members is easy and possible for Indians and Pakistanis, and the celebration of "our festivals" can be shared with those across the border. Its reception online has been similar to that of "Reunion," with more than five hundred thousand views, the comments it has elicited evoke sentimentality and an aspiration for India-Pakistan peace.

In the last decade, along with these commercials, many other ads for companies and products as diverse as Airtel, Fogg deodorants, Kohinoor basmati rice, Coca-Cola, and the online marketplace goto.com, have thematized border crossings and transnational intimacies between Indians and Pakistanis. These border-crossing commercials, like the Bollywood film *Bajrangi Bhaijaan* discussed in Chapter 3, eschew the more contentious theme of interethnic romantic intimacy. Instead, they present friendships and familial relationships that traverse the two countries. The border-crossing commercials instantiate the fact that these subaltern relationships exist, contra the hegemony of ethno-nationalist politics in both countries. They invite us to contemplate how diverse visions of secular as well as transnational affiliation and community might resonate with contemporary audiences in both countries as well as in the South Asian diaspora. I conclude by gesturing to the less popular activist commercial produced by the *Times of India* in January 2013, in collaboration with Pakistan's Jang Group, which uses a similar narrative style to promote cross-border connections: "TOI Aman Ki Asha Indo Pak Border." The commercial depicts groups of Indians and Pakistanis communicating across the national borders, through what looks like a game of dumb charades played at a distance, with Indians using binoculars to decipher what is being acted out through gestures by an elderly Pakistani man on the other side. It turns out that the group collaboration successfully yields a song request from the Pakistani villagers: they want the Indians to call All India Radio and request the cover song from the 1995 Bollywood hit *Dilwale Dulhania Le Jayenge*. The commercial ends with cross-cutting slow-motion scenes of joyful people dancing on both sides of the border, elated at their successful communication, with a background score whose lyrics suggest an ethic of transnational cohabitation and care. These commercials presented through new media channels constitute new archives of short representations that reimagine cross-border dialogue as well as travel, marked variously by humor, sentimentality, and secular aspiration.

Intergenerational Memories: Rebuilding Life and Reckoning with Loss in Mumbai, Pune, Hong Kong, and Washington, D.C.

> Instead of the register of the prophetic pronouncement, let me turn to the register of the everyday through which one may attempt to redeem life.
>
> —VEENA DAS, *Life and Words*[36]

Although India-based Partition oral historiography has thus far dwelt on northern India, as well as the areas of Punjab and Bengal that were Partitioned, my ongoing research on refugee stories from the 1947 migrations has occurred largely in the context of the city space of Bombay/Mumbai. This research began serendipitously. From 2008 to 2009, when I was on sabbatical in my hometown of Mumbai, relatives and friends would often ask me what my recently published book, *Violent Belongings*, was about. When I told them that it was about the 1947 Partition, to my surprise, more often than not, people would reveal that they, or their parents, or a neighbor, or a close friend, had come to India during Partition. As more and more stories began to be shared with me informally in the living rooms, parks, or markets of Mumbai, a new picture emerged for me—not only of my world of friends and family (which now also looked like one populated by many migrants and refugees of the Partition) but also of the city of Mumbai. As a literary critic, I was not sure what I was going to do with those stories, but it seemed important to me to hear them; they offered glimpses of the intimate, animated afterlife of the Partition migrations that was at once resonant with and different from the literary and film representations that normally populated my archive. I started recording them on my digital camcorder and created an online archive to share them. And so, my digital humanities project, 1947Partition.org—a history of migration and violence project—was born in 2009. In 2010, Bhalla, a Bay Area–based physicist, had a similar idea and started collecting Partition oral histories in a different location: California. Bhalla launched 1947PartitionArchive.org in 2011 (I discuss her scaled-up and innovative crowd sourcing of oral histories in the next section). Clearly, the desire to *visually* record refugees' and witnesses' accounts, to understand and honor the unrecorded stories of migrants' experiences, was gaining momentum. I do not mean to suggest that ours were the first initiatives: clearly, the path-breaking and brilliant historical work by Urvashi Butalia, Ritu Menon, and Kamla Bhasin had opened a new conversation that inspired scholars like me and grew in exciting ways with the work of Vazira Fazila-Yacoobali Zamindar, Yasmin Saikia, Sarmila Bose, Gyanendra Pandey, Sugata Bose, Ayesha Jalal, Neeti Nair, and others writing about South Asia. In 2007, Sharmeen Obaid-Chinoy had established the Citizens Archive of Pakistan (CAP) to recording Partition stories in that country. Further, as the work of Pippa Virdee, Rita Kothari, and others shows, the Partition migrations had a transnational impact: the refugees and migrants of 1947 not only crossed borders in Punjab and Bengal or ended up in northern cities, such as Delhi and Kolkata, but also ended up in Bombay Presidency (which was the fourth-largest recipient of migrants in the early national period); further, many eventually migrated to other places, including Great Britain, Hong Kong, East Africa, and North America.

For me, this labor of gathering stories has been important for two reasons. First, there had been no Truth and Reconciliation Commission, as in South Africa, or a large-scale, public, institutional memorialization to reckon with refugees' and minorities' experiences during 1947 in South Asia. As Virdee notes, although some small, little-known memorials exist (the Martyrs' Memorial in Chandigarh, India; the Bab-e-Pakistan Monument in Lahore, Pakistan; a small, private memorial on the Indian side of the Wagah-Attari border), "these initiatives barely receive widespread coverage and most of the public is unaware of their existence."[37] In my conversations with Bhalla, this lack of official recognition has proven important to her thinking as well. Second, the official narrative about the Partition's six to eight million refugees arriving in India has claimed that they were welcomed and easily assimilated into Indian national life and belonging. Yet the journalistic discourse I have tracked from the period as well as the oral accounts I have heard from women and men foreground the historical silencing of refugees under decolonization. Almost across the board, Partition's migrants (regardless of whether they identify as refugees) speak of a shared sentiment of neglect and invisibility. They describe their losses, suffering, and sacrifices as remaining unacknowledged and unhonored in the Indian nation. Virdee points to the shift in Partition Studies to a focus on "history from below" through oral histories, arguing that this focus has "democratized the discourse, with a greater diversity of voices emerging and being represented."[38] Later in this chapter, in my discussion of the 1947 Partition Archive, I revisit the role that technology can play in moving this epistemological border crossing toward a more peaceful political future.

Considerable historical and social scientific research has addressed the relationship between Partition refugees and the postcolonial nation-state in recent years. The remembered accounts, cultural representations, and scholarly analyses of Partition's migrants and refugees have reconstituted our knowledge about Indian history as well as decolonization and mid-twentieth-century displacement. For instance, Joya Chatterji illuminates how class difference has structured and shaped refugees' displacement in the state of Bengal. Drawing upon surveys and historical data, Chatterji shows how socioeconomic classes (middle class, peasant, or agricultural labor) dramatically shaped the timing of and reasons for Hindus' decision to migrate to Bengal in India from West Pakistan as well as their experiences with resettlement and citizenship in India. She notes, "Refugees, like economic migrants, went to places where they knew people who were ready to give them a helping hand until they found their feet, and to places where they judged they had the best chance of finding appropriate work."[39] Chatterji's work on Bengal also unveils that while the Indian nation-state allowed refugees to enter, its assistance was severely limited.[40] Chatterji analyzes not only the differences in the ways Jawaharlal Nehru's central government treated the Punjabi refugees and those in Bengal but also how the disavowal of the hapless refugees from Bengal became part of a disastrous state policy designed to marginalize rather than liquidate statelessness.[41] Similarly, Ranabir Samaddar identifies the complex discursive exchange among refugees, their organizations, and the Indian state, noting how the former claimed the state's assistance as their right, while the latter initially cast relief efforts as temporary assistance until people were able to return. Samaddar contends that it was not until the 1950s that the Indian state recognized that millions of refugees would not be able to return and instead would have to be incorporated into the national community.[42] Thus, this research on refugees' relationship to the new postcolonial state maps the shifting dynamics of institutional violence, recognition, and support, attending to Partition refugees' experiences of statelessness and precarious citizenship.

I am interested in oral migration stories as spaces where refugees' vulnerability is enunciated—about refugees becoming citizens (or not) and performing secularism, and about the hidden histories of how migration reinvented localities from Bombay to Hong Kong—a dimension I examine later in this chapter. Importantly, these stories vividly communicate the complex texture of everyday challenges, local obstacles, and ambivalent reception, such that what emerges from these details about everyday life, work, and sleep is a mix of feelings: anger and grief at migrants' experiences of forced displacement, to be sure, but also, often, pride in their ability to survive and rebuild their lives. While none of these stories has a unifying arc typical of other oral historical projects that delineate particular communities' experiences, like those of Punjabis, Sindhis, or Bengalis, they are linked spatially by the subjects' arrival in Bombay. Thus, I take the act of listening, gathering, and sharing these marginalized Bombay stories/refugee stories as a way "to carve out a public space" for them.[43] As Pandey suggests, "The agent and locus of history is hardly pre-designated. Rather, accounts of history, of shared experiences in the past, serve to constitute these, their extent, and their boundaries."[44]

In her analysis of state rehabilitation practices and the survivors of the 1984 violence against Sikhs, Veena Das writes, "When faced with the kind of trauma that violence visits on us, we have to be engaged in decisions that shape the way that we come to understand our place in the world."[45] For Das, it means embracing an ethic of responsibility, like Nguyen's "just memory," that is rooted in the everyday. My understanding of my place and role in the listening and sharing of refugees' stories is linked to these two articulations. I have been interested in hearing what the migrants remember of their lives before 1947, their decisions to finally migrate, how the border crossings were done, and how everyday lives were rebuilt: where they first arrived, where they stayed, whether assistance was received from the government or locals, how a home and work were found, and how refugees became citizens of postcolonial India, Hong Kong, or, eventually, the United States. The stories I have heard from migrants settled in Bombay/Mumbai have rarely discussed witnessing and enacting embodied violence. Instead, they are about the discrimination and loss entailed in becoming refugees. They are also about the material and discursive processes of everyday life through which migrants become citizens and, in the process, articulate an ethico-political position on just memory and secularism. In this mode, I have felt, as Das writes, that to appropriate "the very setting-into-process of public acknowledgement of hurt can allow new opportunities to be created for the resumption of everyday life."[46]

Unlike the scope of Bhalla's 1947 Partition Archive, the stories in my archive, for the most part, remain tied in some way to Bombay/Mumbai. And as I learned and trained myself to fulfill my ethical responsibilities as an oral historian as best as I could, and to ensure that my interviewees felt comfortable sharing their memories of the past and reflecting on them honestly and openly, I want to share two things that emerged from this experience. The first is the challenge of negotiating vulnerability—my subjects' as well as mine. Most of the subjects I interviewed were women; I am not sure why. Was it that they outlived the men, as most of the women I interviewed were already in their sixties or early seventies? Or was it that, given their social networks, most women connected me to other women to interview? What I learned, however, was that most of the people I met were eager to tell me about their experiences, in part because no one had asked them about them before. In fact, at the start of one interview in 2009, Maya Lalwani asked me, "Why are you interviewing us? No one has asked us about this for sixty years." I heard this sentiment over and over—it marked their vulnerability as silenced subjects, and it was a powerful indictment of the dominant erasure of the refugee experience in political life as well as in the public sphere. This invisibility, accompanied by anger and grief at their suffering, was important to hear articulated. For example, in a 2014 interview, one refugee, Sushila Kamlani, described where her family stayed for their first twelve years in a refugee camp after 1947, which had been the old army barracks in Bombay:

> It was a refugee camp, and a couple of [our] cousins used to visit us, like Billu and Beboo, and of course Indru, and the boys, and they all used to come. But it was pathetic, it was really pathetic, and you talk about bitterness—I am very bitter. . . . I'm bitter because I feel my parents lost a lot. My mother had to work very, very hard, and my father had to work very hard to educate us, to send us to good schools, good colleges, but they didn't enjoy life at all, and they came with nothing, like Ajit, they were also told we'll come back—everything was gone. And that's all that happened.

Similarly, my uncle Gul Mansukhani, who was seven years old when Partition happened, has described how difficult it was for his parents to secure his admission to a local school in Pune, India, in 1947, once it became clear that they would never go back to Pakistan; he recalls that he had come to Pune in the summer holidays of 1947 to see his cousins. He did not know that he would never see his home again and that the temporary holiday would become a permanent displacement. He notes that language was a big barrier to school admissions: he, like most Sindhis, did not know the requisite Hindi. But within six months, his parents had labored to make him fluent enough in Hindi to join the local school.

Thus, survival and rebuilding life in India came with the pressure to assimilate linguistically, and many of my Sindhi interviewees mourned this necessity, for it led to the diminishment and loss of the Sindhi language and its literary culture in subsequent generations.[47] Das observes, "Self-creation on the register of the everyday is a careful putting together of life—a concrete engagement with the tasks of remaking that is mindful of both terms of the compound expression: everyday and life. It points to the eventfulness of the everyday and the attempt to forge oneself into an ethical subject within this scene of the ordinary."[48] I am interested in this ethical subject formation, which emerges in these stories about refugee survival in the midst of re-creating the ordinary—an everyday life. These testimonies detail the business of living—and, indeed, of surviving—in the often-inhospitable geographies of refugee settlement in what was then called Bombay State.[49]

In Indian literary representations of secularism, as I map elsewhere, the figure of the suffering Partition refugee fleeing ethnic violence has often been idealized, presented as the ideal character who performs the secular in the face of communal violence being enacted by locals in the city or village. This literary idealization is in contradistinction to how refugees were represented in Indian newspapers and periodicals from 1946 to 1955. As discussed in the Introduction, journalistic discourses in the public sphere have often depicted refugees either as hapless objects of pity or as vengeful, violent subjects who hated members of the other ethnic community and told stories that caused slaughter.[50] I was curious, then, to see how refugees narrated their own displacement and its relationship to the secular. Did their experiences of becoming refugees due to a religious division make them more discriminatory against the religious "other," more ethno-nationalist, and less secular? Would the witness testimonies bear out the early national public sphere representations or contradict them?

In their reflections on their own migrations in 1947, the refugees I spoke to directly and indirectly addressed questions about secularism, survival, and citizenship. While Dipesh Chakrabarty discusses the figuration of the urban-rural relationship in Bengali oral narratives of the Partition in Kolkata, other scholars, including Urvashi Butalia, Ritu Menon, Kamla Bhasin, Yasmin Saikia, Pippa Virdee, Gyanendra Pandey, and Vazira Fazila-Yacoobali Zamindar, address the challenges of gathering oral histories of the intimate experience of violence—especially from women's perspectives—in Delhi, Karachi, and Dhaka. In this arena, the place of Bombay becomes interesting: perhaps because many migrants arriving in seaside Bombay came from the seaside city of Karachi, and often by ship, they came from the region of Sindh, which did not see as much violence as the partitioned states of Bengal and Punjab. They arrived in relative personal safety, and many did not witness or experience the horrific bodily violence that those interviewed by Butalia, Menon, and Bhasin did.[51] In addition, the refugees I spoke to in Mumbai and Pune were from different linguistic backgrounds—Sindhi, Gujarati, and Punjabi.[52] Their stories uncovered the constitutive role that the Partition migrations have played in the development of Bombay/Mumbai as a city. From inhabiting marshy, snake-infested barracks turned into refugee camps in then-remote spaces like Kalyan, Thane, Sion, Koliwada, and Ulhasnagar (which alone was home to more than one hundred thousand refugees), to eventually building cooperative societies; constructing colleges (like H. R. College and Jai Hind College, among many); and integrating into the food industry, the Bollywood film industry (G. P. Sippy, B. R. Chopra, Dalsukh Pancholi, and so forth), and other professional contexts, Partition's refugees have reinvented Bombay, and the marks of their enterprise and labor are scattered indelibly through its affluent neighborhoods in South Mumbai *and* its middle- and lower-middle-class suburbs.[53]

In the earlier chapters, I note how the feminist literary and film representations of Bapsi Sidhwa, Shauna Singh Baldwin, Shyam Benegal, and Sabiha Sumar present migration stories in which refugees perform an affective secular, even as they interrogate the ongoing discourses of nationality, governmentality, and citizenship that played a role in their displacement. As in these literary accounts that do memory work, in which the minor or refugee subject looks askance at the project of postcolonial nationalism, a majority of the survivors I spoke to affirmed their commitment to secularism while critiquing ethno-nationalist politics. Contra popular assumptions that the Hindu refugees' forced displacement would make them anti-Muslim, these very refugees disavowed discriminatory discourses as elite politics. They insistently affirmed a subaltern secular vision of community in their ethico-political reflections on their own experiences as refugees. For instance, Maya Lalwani, a Mumbai resident, described how her brothers-in-law returned to their hometown a few decades after Partition: "Even my brothers-in-law, they were here for the Sindhi forum, and they went to Pakistan. The warmth they were given by the local Muslims!

Sindhi Muslims! And local Muslims. The warmth they were given! But, [she shrugged] it's politics."

Similarly, one of my interviewees in Mumbai, Mr. Surendra Shah, was a Partition refugee from the Gujarati community that was originally settled in Karachi, Sindh. He recounted: "I was born on 30 September 1933. It has been sixty years since I left Karachi. Almost sixty years—maybe one month less. And my memories of that period are as sharp as if it has happened yesterday. I distinctly remember my house, people, airport, plane, our school, everything. So that part I can tell you as if it has happened yesterday." He reminisced about the school he attended, the fervor that embraced nationalist sentiment at his school, and even how, as late as August 1947, no one in their family seriously considered migrating to India: "I was in a school called Sharda Mandir; all my sisters, my brother, we were in the same school." Describing how swadeshi feeling loomed large in their school, such that even their uniforms were made of khadi, and recounting that they sang "Vande Mataram" in school every day, he also pointed out that it was only in late September 1947, when the situation had become so violent that the entire Gujarati community in Karachi, Sindh, started leaving for India, that his family made the reluctant and difficult decision to migrate: "All the trains were full, the steamers were full, there was no comfortable way of leaving." When they realized that they would have to flee their homeland, they embarked on their arduous journey across multiple modes of travel and the national borders. Eventually, they settled in Bombay/Mumbai. As he reflected on that refugee experience, his powerful assertion of secular memory struck me: "Even today, I can confidently say, no Sindhi Muslim is capable of, would lay a finger on, another Sindhi-Hindu or Muslim. It was the outsiders, the refugees, who started the trouble. But they had themselves lost everything and come there. So it was understandable. Everyone was caught up; it was all politics." The stories about migration and becoming Indian that these migrants told me thus resonated with Alok Bhalla's account, in which he argues, "It is apparent that most people did not choose to migrate before 1947 because they were confident that the civilization of which they were the inheritors together—a civilization carved out of a long duration of shared songs, stories, pilgrim routes, place-names, and rituals—was strong enough to sustain them through each of those disturbances that sometimes threaten the peace of every civil and political society."[54] This vision of a shared local culture structured the enunciation of the secular in the refugee stories I heard, over and over.

Of course, this trait was not uniform. I did meet a couple of interviewees who shared anti-Muslim sentiments, blaming Islam and Muslims for their suffering and losses. These moments were some of the most challenging for me as a scholar. I was heartened to hear the ethico-secular enunciation of just memory, one's own and others, in most of the testimonies, which recognized and affirmed the shared vulnerability of our bodies; the moments of discrimination and ethnic hatred caught me off-guard. I had to use these encounters to reflect on my labor honestly, on my own desires and motivations for preserving these stories: Did I really want to be recording and saving for posterity these testimonials in which these discriminatory feelings suddenly erupted, with violence and anger? Did I want to make visible to the world the ugly feeling of ethnic hatred? What would be the effect of making these testimonies available? Could they, would they, be misused? How would this testimony help us heal as a society and world? I did not have an easy answer for those questions; I still do not. I am simply reflexive and aware that those challenging moments have also appeared for others who have been gathering South Asian testimonies of division and displacement. In a recent interview, Saikia asserts:

> By engaging human voices, I understood the 1971 war not in the language of theoreticians and war history commentators, but in the experiences of the people of India, Pakistan, and Bangladesh. When we privilege military history as official history, we privilege male voices, men's experiences, and masculine violence. We need to find alternative voices for an inclusive, human understanding of who we are. Without searching for the human story, we will never learn the power of violence and its impact on our lives and what we are capable of doing to one another.[55]

In listening to and recording these migration stories and the stories gathered by the 1947 Partition Archive (discussed next), I have been curious to trace, as David Eng and David Kazanjian suggest, "what remains" and what has been created after 1947. I have been interested as much in the details about how the business of life, work, and living was slowly reinvented as in how belonging and citizenship were created anew. In this sense, my interests resonate with Das's observation that "the kind of work that needs to be done to maintain the everyday, and the ways in which the ordinary and the extraordinary are braided together in our ordinary lives are theoretically much more difficult to understand. Throughout very extraordinary moments, all kinds of ordinary things have to continue to be done."[56] To clarify, I do not claim for these migration stories any status as unmediated truth. As many scholars of trauma, testimony, and oral history note, narratives of memory are always already in part situated performances of storytelling that reconstruct and repurpose the past in the present. What I am trying to show is that these migration stories illuminate the refugees' creative survival and reinvention of life, even as they become performances that remember and reinvent an affective secular community. At times, they also offer counternarratives that challenge the elisions of hegemonic nationalisms and demand redress.

Virdee also notes how the Partition migrations generated subsequent global migrations, including post–World War II migrations to the United Kingdom from Punjab, given the labor shortages there.[57] Similarly, many Sindhis also emigrated to distant shores, as documented by Rita Kothari.[58] In 2010, I interviewed my then-student Chitra Panjabi's parents, Chandrabhan and Varsha Panjabi, who shared their fragmented recollection (for they were children) of their parents' accounts of migrating in 1947. They had come to Washington, D.C., to celebrate Chitra's graduation and generously agreed to an interview with me after the ceremony. We sat in my office as they recounted their memories of how hard life had been for them as children of Partition refugees. Chitra's mother recalled growing up in a refugee camp in Mumbai, with long lines for drawing water at communal taps and using communal bathrooms. She also described how their bold decision to subsequently emigrate to Hong Kong had finally led to financial security and material comfort. After speaking with them, I interviewed Chitra herself, who had been born and raised in Hong Kong. I was interested in hearing how she reflected upon her parents' experience. At this point, she recalled how in 2004, she had visited her extended family in India for the first time. She said, "I was shocked to see that my masi (my mother's cousin sister) still lived in the same barracks, the same refugee camp she grew up in." Unlike her cousin and brother-in-law who had emigrated to Hong Kong, after more than forty years, Chitra's aunt had not been able to achieve enough financial success to be able to move out of that first refugee dwelling, like many of those who continued to live in that Sindhi colony. And this realization of the financial dispossessions and familial dispersal that attended two refugee cousins' very different experiences of survival and rebuilding home was, for Chitra, a dramatic reminder of the price her family had paid in 1947. In the next section, I discuss the path-breaking transnational peace movement created on the ground, through memory work, by the digital oral history project of the 1947 Partition Archive.

New Art and Digital Archive Memory Projects: Testimony and Peace

In 2010, a physicist completing her postdoctoral research at the University of California, Berkeley (UC Berkeley), started recording oral histories of Partition witnesses on her video camera. The granddaughter of Punjabi refugees, Guneeta Singh Bhalla was born in Delhi and raised in India and in the United States. For her, a trip to Hiroshima inspired her to initiate an effort to memorialize Partition in a public, institutional way. In talks she has given across the United States, India, and Pakistan, citing Shoah.org and the Hiroshima memorial as her inspirations, Bhalla often poses this question: "If we didn't have the stories of people who lived through World War II or Hiroshima, how would we truly understand the magnitude of what happened then?" In 2011, Bhalla founded the 1947 Partition Archive, an online digital video archive that seeks to gather digital video oral histories of Partition witnesses.[59] Coming up against the limitations of time (when we were losing the generation to age), Bhalla created a new method of "crowd sourcing" oral histories. With support and training from UC Berkeley's oral history resources, Bhalla developed a process by which UC Berkeley undergraduates and community volunteers receive pro bono online training to become citizen historians. After the training, these citizen historians fan out and record stories of Partition witnesses in remote rural areas as well as urban centers. They submit their recordings, which are stored in a globally accessible digital cloud. Interviews are generally conducted in the language that the interviewee is most comfortable with, such as English, Urdu, Gujarati, Punjabi, Hindi, Bengali, Sindhi, Pashto, Kashmiri, and others. As Raj Aditya-Chaudhuri and Smitha Menon note, "The Archive has testimonies from people in 12 different countries . . . in 22 different languages including Hebrew, Spanish, Torwali (an endangered language from the North-West Frontier Province)[,] Urdu, Hindi, Punjabi, Bengali, Marathi, Sindhi, Kashmiri, Pashto among others."[60] This unique method of gathering oral histories is now successfully reproduced in India, Pakistan, and ten other countries. Each year, the archive also invites students and young scholars to apply to its popular oral history student internship program as well as its Story Scholar program. Both short-term programs range from three to six months; they give the selected scholars and interns an opportunity to contribute intensively to local oral history recordings, archive the stories received, and take a public role in the dissemination of these stories in their locality.

Funded by private donors and supported by different institutions across the world, ranging from Bikaner House in Delhi to the *Dawn* newspaper in Pakistan, to the Pakistani American Community Center in California, to California Humanities, and to Google for Nonprofits, this once-fledgling Archive has a presence in twelve countries, including the United States, the United Kingdom, India, Pakistan, Bangladesh, Israel, Canada, France, Australia, the United Arab Emirates, and others.[61] It holds more than nine thousand oral histories of people from diverse religious backgrounds—Hindu, Muslim, and Sikh—living in remote and rural areas in South Asia as well as in urban centers, including London, Los Angeles, and Mumbai. These Partition survivors' stories give us new, intimate glimpses into the lived refugee experiences born of decolonization. The Archive's mission statement asserts a commitment to "institutionalizing the people's history of Partition." Its materials emphasize its orientation as a civic platform to offer a multireligious, multidimensional view of the Partition migrations in transnational postcolonial public spheres.[62]

Besides constituting the first substantial, bipartisan, not-for-profit institution for recording and disseminating the oral histories of the Partition migrations from all the countries involved, the Archive also has a pedagogical dimension. It regularly works with universities, colleges, schools, and community centers to convene public dialogues about Partition with witnesses and scholars, and to create traveling multimedia installations and exhibits. In the Introduction, I discuss one of these events, Voices of Partition. These modes of instigating new conversations that link storytelling, art, and media educate local communities across urban centers in India and Pakistan, the United Kingdom, and the United States. The Archive's mission statement describes its aim to preserve this "people's history of Partition," by documenting and disseminating eyewitness accounts through its digital media platforms as well as through other media, including literature, film, public fora, and so forth.[63] In this aim, it resonates with the educational initiatives documented by activist and scholar Lalita Ramdas (who won the Ramon Magsaysay Award for her work on human rights) that are organized "with the objective of bringing to both Indians and Pakistanis alike a gradual understanding of a shared and composition cultural and historic heritage, which had little to do with narrow or bigoted perceptions of religion and any ideology of exclusion."[64]

The response to the Archive's digital humanities project and public outreach through multimedia exhibits, Voices of Partition events, and other activities (evident in the thousands of volunteers and witnesses who contribute to it) gestures to the resonant stakes of doing Partition's memory work in the contemporary moment. T. Lloyd Bens notes, "The 1947 Partition Archive, which invites those who experienced the mass relocations following division of India and Pakistan to share their stories, shows how the most intimate and local materials collected by such projects can provide scholars with information deeply rooted in ideas of geography and identity that cannot be attained by any other means."[65] The Archive's endeavors attend to many complex forms of social differentiation within South Asian communities, including gender: for instance, a photo exhibition being held at India Habitat Centre (IHC) in New Delhi on August 14–18, 2017, aimed "to bring out the social history of Partition through the eyes of women. . . . 'Through the very nature of the archival image, we learn about the circumstances of their migrations, we learn of family education, the plight of refugees, and most importantly the notion of hope,' the descriptor in the first photograph, introducing the series, states."⁶⁶ The Partition Archive has subsequently inspired many research projects and new initiatives to gather oral histories and memorialize Partition and shared its structure and methods with many of them. Among these is the Harvard South Asia Institute's initiative (started in 2017), which mimics the Archive's model of crowdsourcing oral histories through "citizen ambassadors" (similar to the Partition Archive's "citizen historians"). Such new initiatives and the growing conversation about Partition stories indicate the global impact of the Partition Archive and how these migration stories resonate anew for our times, given the crisis of secularism in South Asia. Bhalla's archive is relevant for our discussion because it is, in my understanding, the only one explicitly committed to gathering migration stories from all religious and national contexts. In this way, it enacts an ethical secular in the memorializing of this history of the migrant and refugee experience.

In October 2017, the Partition Archive announced a collaboration with Stanford University called "The 1947 Partition Archive: Survivors and Their Memories." Under the aegis of this joint initiative, Stanford University's library has made available four thousand video-based oral histories in the Archive. Recorded in more than three hundred cities from twelve countries and in twenty-two languages, these oral histories "attempt to uncover a complete life story shaped by Partition, highlighting pre-Partition life and culture, the Partition experience, and post-Partition transitions."⁶⁷ In one of the interviews that Stanford has made publicly available through this online archive, a Partition refugee, Baljit Dhillon Vikram Singh, shares her memories (recorded on January 1, 2016) of her migration as a child in 1947 and, subsequently, as an adult to the United States. The interview vividly exemplifies the transnational arcs of displacement and diaspora decolonization unleashed; it also reminds us of the contemporary stakes of instantiating a just memory of that displacement. Singh's interview concludes with her questioning ethno-nationalism on the basis of religious difference. She asserts, "It [religion] should be a cause for, what are we similar in, and how can we live in a harmonious way. . . . India is a secular state. We all lived in harmony." She then describes how she is troubled by contemporary anti-Muslim rhetoric she hears when she travels to India as a diasporic subject: "When I go back to India, and visit, and people say something about the Muslims, and I say, 'Where are you coming from?' . . . So, I struggle with that." Later she connects her own displacement with that of Syrian refugees in the present and says, "Religion should never divide us." Such subaltern enunciations of the secular from the subcontinent and the diaspora are especially critical to hear today: collectively, they constitute a project of redress and fashion secular solidarities across the differences that divide us. Digital humanities initiatives like the Partition Archive thus bridge the humanitarian goals of nonprofit organizations and institutions of higher education. They demonstrate the potential of storytelling and story gathering for transforming collective knowledge about the history of decolonization and nation formation.

Like Shoah.org, the Archive performs memory work. It aspires to contribute toward peace between India and Pakistan. Its witness testimonies become modes of performance and activism that challenge ethno-nationalist historiographic rhetorics in South Asia as well as in South Asian America. Many recent works in South Asian and Asian American literature invite us to provincialize the nation as a hegemonic form of imagining community and belonging. In its location and its labor originating in the diaspora, from the vantage point of the South Asian American immigrant experience, the Archive as an institution reconstitutes the local and the global in ways that provincialize the frame of the nation for understanding decolonization in the mid-twentieth century. The Archive's transnational work on refugees' and witnesses' stories radically recasts the narration of postcolonial nation formation, even as it mobilizes and performs a transnational secular affective memory of this experience. This mode of memory work and institution building has profound consequences for the contemporary crisis of secularism in India and South Asian America. It also shows, as Ghosh's anthology *This Side, That Side* does, the enduring legacies of those migrations for today's citizens, even as it creates new knowledge about contemporary ecological expulsions. For instance, from January to June 2018, story scholars recorded the migration stories of Partition refugees who were "resettled" by the Indian government in the inhospitable marshy, flood-prone landscape of the Sundarbans in 1947. Today, with the rising water levels, these refugees and their descendants, having rebuilt their precarious lives there, are about to become climate refugees.[68]

Alongside this diasporic initiative, and in dialogue with it, are the photo animations of Rhode Island–based Asian American artist Annu Palakunnathu Matthew in her series *Open Wound* (2012–present). Inspired by her photographic work with Holocaust survivors, Matthew has created photo animations that use refugee stories and their photographs to make visible this subaltern history. Matthew's refugee subjects for *Open Wound* were initially based in India; subsequently, with support from the URI Silvia Chandley Professorship for Peace and Non-Violence, she created more photo animations of stories from Pakistan and Bangladesh through contributions from immigrant communities in North America. In Matthew's words, "My aim is to collaborate with my subjects to create empathy and understanding for what the children of Partition had to go through. I do this using their family photographs. What happened to them should not be lost to history."[69]

Matthew's method of creating the photo animation is deliberate, creative, and performative, using technology to draw arcs of connection between refugees and citizens, between migration memories and the conventions of family portraiture in South Asian photographic practices. In some cases, the 1947 Partition Archive has helped Matthew find her subjects. In each photo animation displayed on an iPad, the viewer sees a pre-Partition portrait photo of the migrant merging into a recent photograph of the migrant taken by Matthew, often posed in a similar way. She first scans the earlier photograph—usually a family portrait in the subject's family album. Then she invites different generations to reenact the pose of the Partition migrant in the original photo. Using digital technology, she puts members of multiple generations back into the historical photo displayed on an iPad, which also shows an excerpt from her interview with the subject. Each photograph is overlaid with a line or two from that migrant's story about the experience of migration, as narrated to Matthew. The fragmented text gestures to the incompleteness of memory as well as to the traumatic rupture. The production of each photo animation involves locating refugee subjects who are willing to share their experiences as well as those who have a photograph or two that migrated with them. Above all, Matthew notes, "I had to find people who were children of Partition and were willing to trust me with their stories, and had two to three generations living nearby to take part in the collaborative project.... Creating the trust for the participants to take part took some time to develop."[70]

These photo animations have been exhibited in, and in some cases acquired by, a range of institutional and international locations, including the Royal Ontario Museum, the Ulrich Museum of Art (Wichita, Kansas), Bikaner House (New Delhi), San José Museum of Art, the University of Massachusetts (Dartmouth), the Kamloops Art Gallery (Kamloops, British Columbia), Lesley University (Cambridge, Massachusetts), the Dr. Bhau Daji Lad Mumbai City Museum (Mumbai, India), and sepiaEYE (New York City).[71] Matthew reported to me that the Bikaner House exhibition was the first to display Indian and Pakistani photo animation stories side by side. Repeatedly, she said, visitors declared to her, "These are the same stories!" Thus, this artistic production and its circulation enabled a border-crossing encounter with the other's precariousness, turning into "a resource for politics." It allowed the viewer to become part "of the slow process by which we develop a point of identification with suffering itself" and "be moved into a consideration of the vulnerability of others."[72] The subjects of *Open Wound* have been Hindu, Sikh, and Muslim, from India, Pakistan, and Bangladesh, traversing the subcontinent and the United States. This artistic practice creates a new space for the encounter with and an enunciation of a secular, affective relationship between self and other (as refugee, as migrant, as the person once "here" but now "there"). It historicizes contemporary South Asian citizenships as constituted by migrations.

Once we have a new force field of visual representations that allow us to encounter the other's history of displacement and loss, Butler suggests, "we might critically evaluate and oppose the conditions under which certain human lives are more vulnerable than others, and that certain human lives are more grievable than others. From where might a principle emerge by which we vow to protect others from the kinds of violence we have suffered, if not from an apprehension of a common human vulnerability?"[73] *Open Wound*, for me, becomes part of an artistic archive of memory work that makes visible this shared vulnerability. As such, it not only works toward peace between India and Pakistan but also invites us to rethink 1947 in order to understand contemporary statelessness differently. As Matthew explains on her website, in her narrative accompanying the photo animations of Pakistani families, "This album includes the stories of Pakistani families. The stories strongly parallel those that I collected in India and echo accounts of recent refugees from Syria and other countries in conflict."[74]

Discussing the photojournalistic archive of Margaret Bourke-White's photographs of the Partition migrations in relation to her photographic practice, Matthew notes that her own focus is on the genre of the family photograph. In this sense, while Bourke-White's photographs document the violence and mass migrations of Partition in the public sphere, and in such public spaces as the streets, fields, and refugee camps in the subcontinent, Matthew sees her work as giving a voice to the intimate family histories of people who became displaced by Partition. She says, "I think both can and should coexist."[75] Matthew is an artist who works with the medium of photography and technology in inventive ways as well as the former director of the Humanities Center at the University of Rhode Island.[76] Her oeuvre is preoccupied with questions about identity, race, and belonging in the United States, and it explores different conventions of photography—from the ethnographic to the familial—as they create and perform racial, ethnic, and gender differences. From *An Indian from India* to *To Majority Minority*, her provocative works illuminate racial performativity, minority experience, and dislocation.

Like Matthew's *Open Wound*, Mumbai-based Anusha Yadav's Indian Memory Project (est. 2010) also engages photography to revisit Indian history and the experience of displacement. The Indian Memory Project was the first visual- and narrative-based online archive interested in understanding history and identity in the Indian subcontinent "through images found in family and personal archives."[77] At the "Remembering Partition" event hosted by the Godrej India Culture Lab (Mumbai) in 2017, which I discuss in the Introduction, Yadav staged an installation that reproduced

Figure 4.1: Anusha Yadav's The Indian Memory Project at "Remembering Partition" event. Photo credit: Godrej India Culture Lab.

black-and-white portrait photographs from the 1930s and 1940s on eight-foot-tall stand-alone panels; beneath each photograph or set of photographs was a brief account that explained the family history of the photograph. The panels were arranged at angles, so that people could walk around and in between, in no fixed order, to encounter the varied image-text narratives (see Figure 4.1). The people represented in the photographs were from different ethnic, racial, and religious backgrounds, both British and South Asian. For instance, Mumbai-based author and editor Naresh Fernandes shares a photograph of his uncle Bunnu as a child, who, we learn through the account titled "The Mythical Uncle Bunnu," decided to stay in Karachi (Pakistan) after Partition even though the rest of his siblings and family left. Fernandes describes how his Goan Christian family, despite roots in Karachi that stretched back to four generations, decided to leave for India.

In another account, "The Only Valuable Thing," Rakesh Anand Bakshi shares a 1935 family portrait of his grandparents with their child—Rakesh's father, the prominent Bollywood lyricist Anand Bakshi. Rakesh describes how it was among the few things his grandfather grabbed as he fled Rawalpindi (Pakistan) overnight for Delhi on October 2, 1947. The photograph is especially significant because Anand lost his mother when he was only nine years old; as he explained to his Rakesh, "Pictures of her are all I have."

A third account, "My Grandfather's Secrets," presents a collage of photographs of a young British girl, Margurite Mumford, which the current owner, Jason Scott Tilley, discovered in his grandfather Bert Scott's archive of more than five thousand photographs and negatives. Scott's family had been in India since the seventeenth century; as a press photographer for the *Times of India*, Scott (b. 1915) worked until Partition became imminent. Subsequently, his family fled to the United Kingdom, and his romance with the Anglo Indian young woman, Margurite, remained a secret until Tilley found these wonderful photographs and, through them, tracked down a story about two young people that traversed India, the United Kingdom, the United States, and New Zealand. In juxtaposing the stillness of the pre-Partition portrait photograph—a posed for, and often, somber form—with textual descriptions full of sudden movement, displacement, and loss, Yadav's moving project skillfully yokes portraiture, photography, and the historical-familial memories of mid-twentieth-century displacement.

Another important part of this emergent, transnational, and historic public dialogue, "Remembering Partition," was a brief screening of portions of the award-winning Pakistani filmmaker and journalist Obaid-Chinoy's documentary *Home 1947*. (Obaid-Chinoy joined the dialogue at "Remembering Partition" by participating on a panel through Skype video, from London.) A vocal feminist artist, Obaid-Chinoy has won several Emmys and two Academy Awards; she is also the founder of Citizens' Archive of Pakistan (CAP), which has been collecting oral histories of the Partition in Pakistan since 2007. *Home 1947* was screened as part of an immersive installation that premiered at the Manchester International Festival in July 2017. Drawing upon her grandfather's account of his migration, Obaid-Chinoy's documentary is an evocative meditation that visually explores the psychic trauma for Partition's refugees of leaving home, across India and Pakistan. The documentary was screened in Lahore and as part of events related to the commemoration of seventy years of nation formation in August 2017. In unprecedented and powerful ways, the deliberate timing of its first screening in Lahore, like the Godrej-sponsored event "Remembering Partition," forces us to retell South Asia's history of postcolonial freedom and independence from British rule as bound up with the stories of millions of refugees who lost homes, lives, and communities in the process. For Obaid-Chinoy, the documentary is at once personal and political, about the past as well as the present: it is an ode to her grandparents and a film dedicated to exploring the experience and loss of becoming stateless for all refugees, be they from South Asia or Syria. As she notes, "This is personal. It's an ode to my grandparents' generation. How did it feel that, when you left your home, it not only stopped being your home, but became part of an enemy country?"[78] Anam Zakaria draws on Obaid-Chinoy's CAP for her novel narrative *The Footprints of Partition*. Part oral history and part travel narrative, this work explores the multigenerational legacy of the Partition migrations through a gathering of border-crossing narratives from Pakistan and India.[79] If border-crossing advertising encapsulates compressed fantasies of connection between Indians and Pakistanis, then a whole new genre of South Asian travel writing has emerged about traveling between India and Pakistan after 1947 that properly deserves recognition as "border-crossing travelogues." These narratives by Yoginder Sikand, Stephen Alter, Kamla Bhasin, and other writers describe the experience of travel and cross-cultural encounters in journeys across the border between India and Pakistan in ways that destabilize our dominant nationalist histories and contribute to a fresh understanding of what was created after the Partition migrations. While it is beyond the scope of this chapter to consider this unique archive, it merits future attention, especially as it constitutes an antiwar activist articulation of transnational political solidarity on the ground, toward peace in the subcontinent.

Conclusion

*Rethinking Mid-Twentieth-Century Asia
and the Present*

In the preceding chapters, I present a heterogenous cultural history of migration stories as well as the feminist counter-critique offered in the intimate literary, graphic, and visual representations of gendered statelessness, precarity, survival, and subaltern secularism. This multimedia archive, I suggest, urgently invites us to reimagine contemporary cultural formations of secular community and identity in ways that recast the relationship between nationalism and the mid-twentieth-century legacies of migration for South Asia and South Asian America. I conclude by juxtaposing the heterogeneous migration stories I have presented here with another story that gestures to how my analysis of what has been created after decolonization connects with the broader geopolitical shifts of mid-twentieth-century Asia as it lurched toward the Cold War. After one of my Regional Faculty Fellow research presentations at the University of Pennsylvania's Humanities Center, my colleague (and the director of that year's Penn Humanities Forum "Colors") Chi-ming Yang, who had heard the talk, approached me. An expert on the literary and visual culture of race and empire, she shared that she was profoundly moved—because it reminded her of her own father's pain when he was separated from his family in 1949 China. And from this sharing of stories, a new connection between mid-twentieth-century border crossings emerged for me: one that uncovered a story about a Chinese American Tibetan Studies scholar, Dr. Ho-chin Yang, whose migration stories linked Washington with the violent upheavals of the division of mainland China and Taiwan in 1949. Across the watery borders, as a wispy eleven-year-old boy, Dr. Yang had accompanied his father to Taiwan, fleeing the oncoming Communist regime. He left behind on the mainland his mother and three siblings. Like Partition's refugees, they thought this separation would last perhaps a year, maybe two or three; eventually, they thought, as in the past, the nationalists would return to power. But this separation proved to be a lasting trauma—he was not to see his mother and siblings again until after thirty painful years had passed, and he had built a new life on the west coast of America. During my 2015 video interview with him, it became evident to me that the pain of that separation and loss had stayed with him throughout his entire life. At one point in the interview, he showed me a letter his mother had written to him shortly after he had seen her again, in 1987. It was written in Mandarin, in red ink. It was one of many letters she had sent him over the years, discussing her daily life and her acknowledgment that his father had remarried and raised a new family in Taiwan. Everyone knew that the political circumstances prevented his parents from being together. Dr. Yang had long hoped to bring his parents to the United States, where they could at least meet once again in person, on neutral ground. But his father passed away before this reunion could happen, and Dr. Yang was never able to overcome his sorrow that he could not bring his parents back together. This story about 1949 sits adjacent to the archive of 1947 migration stories for me: both demand that we do memory work that bears witness to the intimate traumas of the mid-twentieth century that still live in the immigrants and refugees of Asia and Asian America. The linkages among the lost histories of the divisions across India, China, Vietnam, Korea, and other spaces in post-47 Asia are yet to be fully accounted for.

In a special issue of *Critical Inquiry*, Leela Gandhi and Deborah Nelson offer the frame "Around 1948" as a productive counterpoint and, I would argue, a more generative approach to studying the mid-twentieth century. They illuminate the heterogeneous, transnational transformations that the world witnessed across diverse geographies in the moment they call "around 1948." They assert, "Much of the political world in which we live took shape around 1948; for worse or for better, this shape might have been otherwise. Thinking organically about this new world has been hampered in several ways. While we conventionally understand disciplines to be constituted by their objects, we think less often and less well about how disciplines are constituted by their moments." Gandhi and Nelson alert us to the rhetorical and disciplinary strategies by which some moments (e.g., 1968, 1989) come into view while others recede, and some perspectives—such as those that privilege the frame of the nation for narrating history—dominate others.[1] In placing the above account of a (watery) partition and familial separation of a Chinese family in 1949 alongside the Partition stories of Indian residents in Hong Kong and Bombay in 1947, this Conclusion, I hope, participates in the project to provincialize the nation, so that we might better understand the dramatic and transnational transformations born of geopolitical conflict, migration, and statelessness in the mid-twentieth century.

A full, comparative accounting of these linked histories of mid-twentieth-century displacement in Asia and how they reshaped the intimacies of the community and the country has yet to be done. It is beyond the scope of this project to offer such an accounting; yet, what I chart in this book is how these mid-twentieth-century migrations offer a new vantage point from which we might trace the lost intimacies of four continents. I hope it is clear that what I am advocating for are not simply projects of recuperation and recovery, although those are certainly important and valuable, and they need to be done. Instead, what I gesture to is that the historical return to the past of Partition migrations—and, indeed, mid-twentieth-century migrations born of geopolitical division in Asia—can allow us to see the absence of those lost intimacies of migration as "an actively acknowledged loss within the present."[2] As Lisa Lowe explains, in a different context, "This is not a project of merely telling history differently, but one of returning to the past, its gaps, uncertainties, impasses, and elisions; ... It is an attempt to give an account of the existences of alternatives and possibilities that lay within, but were later foreclosed by, the determinations of the narratives, orders, and paradigms to which they gave rise."[3] That the possibilities within the articulations of subaltern secularism I identify across these different literary and media archives are at risk today is clear. As I write this, India, traditionally a welcoming and generous refuge for millions of refugees in Asia, is building detention centers to house undocumented people, from Assam in the northeast to Bengaluru, India's Silicon Valley, in the south; some activists who participated in the Shaheen Bagh protests against the Citizenship Amendment Act in early 2020 were arrested; Kashmir remains a tragic and dangerous flashpoint; and some political voices in India and Pakistan threaten each other with nuclear war and destruction. It is unclear how this crisis of secularism and its gendered as well as ethnic production of statelessness will unfold and whether it will be resolved to promote greater equality, inclusion, and social justice for all.

In the midst of these crises, it must be obvious then, that the stakes of this book for me, as for many of the writers and artists I discuss, are equally contemporary: they dwell on the crisis of secularism in contemporary South Asia and South Asian America in large measure, but they are also invested in speaking to the ongoing violence and loss experienced by millions of undocumented migrants and refugees from Syria, Afghanistan, Somalia, Tibet, Myanmar, Yemen, and other places. I advocate for conceptualizing the secular as a counterhegemonic practice—as a subaltern performance of just memory, as a practice based on the recognition of precariousness, and as a mode of planetary cohabitation that counters statelessness. Such an insurgent counterpractice, from the periphery, can, and indeed must, have consequences for the instruments of migration policy. As Homi Bhabha notes, "Understanding the despair of others is not merely an act of empathy; it is a risky business. It requires a mode of self-identification with 'alterity,' in the process of reversing the perspective of migration policy."[4] This invitation to understand the despair of others also appears in British Somali poet Warsan Shire's poem "Home."[5] In this poem, Shire urges the reader to enter into an empathetic understanding of refugees' despair; as such, the poem challenges discourses and policy approaches that center on constructions of migrant "choice." Today, the global proliferation of detention centers from China to Australia and the United States demands that we pay close attention to the linkages in how precarity unfolds through prisons, from racialized mass incarceration in the United States to the ethno-racial marking of migrant and minority detention around the world, as war and slow violence continue to generate expulsions. Historians will no doubt look back on today's millions of stateless people, as we now look back on 1947–1948, and mourn for the violence and grief wrought by geopolitical conflict and state-sponsored wars; we will grieve for the cruelty and dehumanization meted out to those who become stateless by the mechanisms of the modern nation-states on whose shores they arrive. My utopian hope is that in some small measure, our collective, historicizing modes of representation and storytelling—across different media and in different institutions—might help us work toward peaceful planetary cohabitation and create the end of statelessness.

Notes

INTRODUCTION

1. Paul Gilroy, *Postcolonial Melancholia* (New York: Columbia University Press, 2004), 3–4.
2. David Eng and David Kazanjian, eds., *Loss: The Politics of Mourning* (Berkeley: University of California Press, 2002), 2.
3. Bapsi Sidhwa, *Cracking India: A Novel* (Milwaukee: Milkweed Editions, 1991), 169.
4. I present a brief overview of the Partition experience as well as a discussion of historiographical and cultural accounts of this moment in my essay "Partition," *Blackwell Encyclopedia of Postcolonial Studies*, eds. Sangeeta Ray and Henry Schwarz (London: Wiley-Blackwell, 2016), 1278–1286.
5. Urvashi Butalia, ed., "Partition: The Long Shadow: An Introduction," in *Partition: The Long Shadow* (New Delhi: Zubaan Books, 2015), ix.
6. Vishwajyoti Ghosh, ed., *This Side, That Side: Restorying Partition* (Delhi: Yoda Press, 2013).
7. Yến Lê Espiritu, *Body Counts: The Vietnam War and Militarized Refugees* (Berkeley: University of California Press, 2014), 3.
8. Ibid., 21.
9. Viet Thanh Nguyen, *Nothing Ever Dies: Vietnam and the Memory of War* (Cambridge, MA: Harvard University Press, 2016), 12.
10. For a compelling analysis of this crisis of secularism as it has unfolded across the world in the contemporary moment, see Andrew Copson, *Secularism: Politics, Religion, and Freedom* (Oxford: Oxford University Press, 2017).
11. Iftikhar Dadi and Hamad Nasar, eds., *Lines of Control: Partition as a Productive Space* (London: Green Cardamom and Herbert F. Johnson Museum of Art, 2012). See also Karin Zitzewitz's thoughtful exploration of the indirect idiom of the secular in Indian modernist art: *The Art of Secularism: The Cultural Politics of Modernist Art in Contemporary India* (New York: Oxford University Press, 2014).
12. Robert J. Young, "Postcolonial Remains," *New Literary History* 43, no. 1 (2012): 21.

13. Arie M. Dubnov and Laura Robson, eds., "Introduction: Drawing the Line, Writing beyond It: Toward a Transnational History of Partitions," in *Partitions: A Transnational History of Twentieth-Century Territorial Separatism* (Stanford, CA: Stanford University Press, 2019), 27.

14. Deepika Bahri, *Native Intelligence: Aesthetics, Politics, and Postcolonial Literature* (Minneapolis: University of Minnesota Press, 2003), 119.

15. Talal Asad, *Secular Translations: Nation State, Modern Self, and Calculative Reason* (New York: Columbia University Press, 2018), 49.

16. Dipesh Chakrabarty, *Provincializing Europe: Postcolonial Thought and Historical Difference* (Princeton, NJ: Princeton University Press, 2000).

17. To name a few: Sarah Ansari (2005); Urvashi Butalia (1998, 2015); Dipesh Chakrabarty (1995); Joya Chatterji (2007); Jill Didur (2006); Patrick French (1997); Sukeshi Kamra (2002); Ritu Menon and Kamla Bhasin (1998); Gyanendra Pandey (2001); Bhaskar Sarkar (2009); Vazira Zamindar (2007); Neeti Nair (2011); Nandita Bhavnani (2014); Amritjit Singh, Nalini Iyer, and Rahula K. Gairola (2016); Yasmin Khan (2008); Pippa Virdee (2017); Deepti Misri (2014); Aanchal Malhotra (2017); Jisha Menon (2012); Anam Zakaria (2015).

18. See Rita Kothari, *The Burden of Refuge: The Sindhi Hindus of Gujarat* (New Delhi: Orient Longman, 2007); Nandita Bhavnani, *The Making of Exile: Sindhi Hindus and the Partition of India* (Chennai: Tranquebar Press, 2014); Joya Chatterji, *The Spoils of Partition: Bengal and India, 1947–1967* (New York: Cambridge University Press, 2007); and Joya Chatterji, *Bengal Divided: Hindu Communalism and Partition, 1932–1947* (Cambridge: Cambridge University Press, 1994), among others.

19. See also Jasodhara Bagchi, *The Trauma and the Triumph: Gender and Partition in Eastern India* (Kolkata: Stree Books, 2003); Nisid Hajari, *Midnight's Furies: The Deadly Legacy of India's Partition* (New York: Houghton Mifflin Harcourt, 2015); and Ayesha Jalal, *The Pity of Partition: Manto's Life, Times, and Work across the India-Pakistan Divide* (Princeton, NJ: Princeton University Press, 2013), among others.

20. Nguyen, *Nothing Ever Dies*, 16.

21. Yasmin Saikia, *Women, War, and the Making of Bangladesh* (Durham, NC: Duke University Press, 2011), 9.

22. Dipesh Chakrabarty, "Modernity and Ethnicity in India: A History for the Present," *Economic and Political Weekly* 30, no. 52 (December 30, 1995): 3373–3380.

23. "Kartarpur Corridor: India Pilgrims in Historic Visit to Pakistan Temple," *BBC*, November 9, 2019, accessed on November 20, 2019, available at https://www.bbc.com/news/world-asia-india-50342319.

24. Shabnum Tejani, *Indian Secularism: A Social and Intellectual History, 1890–1950* (Bloomington: Indiana University Press, 2008).

25. Wendy Brown, *Walled States, Waning Sovereignty* (Brooklyn: Zone Books, 2014), 62.

26. Anuradha Dingwaney Needham and Rajeswari Sunder Rajan, eds., *The Crisis of Secularism in India* (Durham, NC: Duke University Press, 2007).

27. Ibid., 31.

28. See, for instance, the essays in Angana P. Chatterji, Thomas Blom Hansen, and Christophe Jaffrelot, eds., *Majoritarian State: How Hindu Nationalism Is Changing India* (New Delhi: HarperCollins, 2019). Other works that study the changing face of secularism in India include Achin Vanaik, *The Rise of Hindu Authoritarianism: Secular Claims, Communal Realities* (London: Verso, 2017); and Sumantra Bose, *Secular States, Religious Politics: India, Turkey, and the Future of Secularism* (Cambridge: Cambridge University Press, 2018).

29. I discuss this in greater depth in my first book, *Violent Belongings: Partition, Gender, and National Culture in Postcolonial India* (Philadelphia: Temple University Press, [2008] 2011); see also, Lopamudra Basu, *Ayad Akhtar, the American Nation, and Its Others after 9/11: Homeland Insecurity* (Lanham, MD: Lexington Books, 2018).

30. Such scholars as Arvind Rajagopal, Vijay Prashad, and Biju Mathew have well documented the rise of Hindu nationalism in the diaspora. See, for example, Biju Mathew and Vijay Prashad, "The Protean Forms of Yankee Hindutva," *Ethnic and Racial Studies* 23, no. 3 (2000): 516–534. Of course, as many South Asianists delineate, South Asian immigration has a long history, which has varied in its address of communalism or politicized religion, depending on the historical moment, ranging from the 1920s to the post-Partition generation, and later, in the professional, educated immigrant classes of the 1960s and 1970s. Vijay Prashad's *The Karma of Brown Folk* and, more recently, Anupama Jain's *How to Be South Asian in America* illuminate some of the contours of this multilayered history. However, I am most interested in the formation of "Hindu American" in the post-9/11 moment, where the intersection of hate crimes against those of South Asian and Middle Eastern descent, Islamophobia, and overseas Hindu nationalist organizations has drawn South Asian Americans (and British Asians) into imagined communities and political identities rooted in religion that, I believe, need to be reflected upon in a historical way.

31. Priya Kumar, *Limiting Secularism: The Ethics of Coexistence in Indian Literature and Film* (Minneapolis: University of Minnesota Press, 2008), 45.

32. Lloyd Rudolph and Susanne Rudolph, *In Pursuit of Lakshmi: The Political Economy of the Indian State* (Chicago: University of Chicago Press, 1987), 38.

33. Ibid.

34. Anshuman Mondal, "The Limits of Secularism and the Construction of Composite National Identity in India," in *Alternative Indias: Writing, Nation, and Communalism*, ed. Peter Morey and Alex Tickell (Amsterdam: Editions Rodopi, 2005), 8.

35. Saba Mahmood, *Religious Difference in a Secular Age: A Minority Report* (Princeton, NJ: Princeton University Press, 2015), 21. See also Saba Mahmood, "Secularism, Sovereignty, and Religious Difference: A Global Genealogy?" *Society and Space* 35, no. 2 (2017): 197–209.

36. Young, "Postcolonial Remains," 31.

37. Mushirul Hasan, *Moderate or Militant: Images of India's Muslims* (Delhi: Oxford University Press, 2008), 55.

38. Asad, *Secular Translations*, 22.

39. Deepa M. Ollapally, *The Politics of Extremism in South Asia* (New York: Cambridge University Press, 2008), 140.

40. See Judith Butler, "Is Judaism Zionism?" in *The Power of Religion in the Public Sphere*, ed. Eduardo Mendieta and Jonathan Vanantwerpen (New York: Social Science Research Council and Columbia University Press, 2011), 70–91.

41. Talal Asad, *Formations of the Secular: Christianity, Islam, Modernity* (Stanford, CA: Stanford University Press, 2003).

42. Ibid., 25.

43. Ibid., 26.

44. Ibid., 25.

45. Edward Said, quoted in Michael Sprinker, *Edward W. Said: A Critical Reader* (London: Blackwell, 1992), 232–233.

46. Charles Beitz, *The Idea of Human Rights* (New York: Oxford University Press, 2009), xii.

47. Ashis Nandy, *The Intimate Enemy: Loss and Recovery of Self under Colonialism* (Oxford: Oxford University Press, 2010).

48. See Manav Ratti, *The Postsecular Imagination: Postcolonialism, Religion, and Literature* (Abingdon, UK: Routledge, 2013); and Kumar, *Limiting Secularism*.

49. Neha Vora, *Impossible Citizens: Dubai's Indian Diaspora* (Durham, NC: Duke University Press, 2013), 29.

50. Butler, "Is Judaism Zionism?" 88.

51. Ibid., 72.

52. See Kumkum Sangari and Sudesh Vaid, eds., *Recasting Women: Essays in Colonial History* (New Delhi: Kali for Women, 1989); Rajeswari Sunder Rajan, *Real and Imagined Women: Gender, Culture, and Postcolonialism* (New York: Routledge, 1993); Asha Nadkarni, *Eugenic Feminism: Reproductive Nationalism in the United States and India* (Minneapolis: University of Minnesota Press, 2014); and Gita Rajan and Jigna Desai, *Transnational Feminism and Global Advocacy in South Asia* (New York: Routledge, 2013).

53. Ritu Menon and Kamla Bhasin, *Borders and Boundaries: Women in India's Partition* (New Brunswick: Rutgers University Press, 1998).

54. Cathy J. Schlund-Vials, *War, Genocide, and Justice: Cambodian American Memory Work* (Minneapolis: University of Minnesota Press, 2012), 186–187.

55. Walter Benjamin, "The Storyteller," in *Illuminations: Essays and Reflections*, ed. Hannah Arendt (New York: Schocken Books, 1988), 96.

56. Espiritu, *Body Counts*, 107–108.

57. "About," Twelve Gates Art, available at http://www.twelvegatesarts.org/about1.

58. Cathy Caruth, ed., "Trauma and Experience: Introduction," in *Trauma: Explorations in Memory* (Baltimore: Johns Hopkins University Press, 1995), 11.

59. Schlund-Vials, *War, Genocide, and Justice*, 4.

60. Nguyen, *Nothing Ever Dies*.

61. Svetlana Boym, *The Future of Nostalgia* (New York: Basic Books, 2001), 251.

62. Ibid.

63. Lisa Yoneyama, *Cold War Ruins: Transpacific Critique of American Justice and Japanese War Crimes* (Durham, NC: Duke University Press, 2016), 36.

64. Shoshana Felman, "Education and Crisis, or the Vicissitudes of Teaching," in *Trauma: Explorations in Memory*, ed. Cathy Caruth (Baltimore: Johns Hopkins University Press, 1995), 17.

65. To mention a few, Satya Rai (1965), Ranabir Samaddar (1999), Robert Corrucini and Samvit S. Kaul (1990), and Lubna Saif (2010).

66. Liisa Malkki, *Purity and Exile: Violence, Memory, and National Cosmology among Hutu Refugees in Tanzania* (Chicago: Chicago University Press, 1995), 9–11.

67. Ibid., 13–15.

68. Saskia Sassen, *Guests and Aliens* (New York: New Press, 1999), 6.

69. Rajini Srikanth, *Constructing the Enemy: Empathy/Antipathy in U.S. Literature and Law* (Philadelphia: Temple University Press, 2012), 171.

70. Gulzar, Govind Nihalani, and Saibal Chatterjee, eds., *Encyclopaedia of Hindi Cinema* (Mumbai: Prakashan, 2003), 70.

71. Giorgio Agamben, *Homo Sacer: Sovereign Power and Bare Life* (Stanford, CA: Stanford University Press, 1998), 11.

72. Yến Lê Espiritu, "Toward a Critical Refugee Study: The Vietnamese Refugee Subject in US Scholarship," *Journal of Vietnamese Studies* 1, no. 1–2 (February/August 2006): 410–433.

73. "Refugee and Migrant Health," World Health Organization, available at https://www.who.int/migrants/en/.

74. Mimi Thi Nguyen, *The Gift of Freedom: War, Debt, and Other Refugee Passages* (Durham, NC: Duke University Press, 2012), 25.

75. Rod Norland, "A Mass Migration Crisis, and It May Yet Get Worse," *New York Times*, October 31, 2015, available at https://www.nytimes.com/2015/11/01/world/europe/a-mass-migration-crisis-and-it-may-yet-get-worse.html.

76. Ibid.

77. Safak Timur and Rod Nordland, "Erdogan Threatens to Let Migrant Flood into Europe Resume," *New York Times*, November 25, 2016, available at https://www.nytimes.com/2016/11/25/world/europe/turkey-recep-tayyip-erdoganmigrants-european-union.html.

78. "As Europe Battles over Border Policy, Migrants Flood to Spain," *PBS Newshour*, accessed January 15, 2019, available at https://www.thirteen.org/programs/pbs-newshour/desperate-journey-1539989195/.

79. Sassen, *Guests and Aliens*, xii. Similarly, as Ato Quayson argues, "It is a profound irony that despite the moral panic often expressed in many parts of Europe and North America today at the prospect of immigrants and asylum seekers on their borders, the period of extensive migrations from Europe itself in the seventeenth century and after was marked by the same forces that have underpinned the desperate movement of populations from the global South to the global North from the latter part of the twentieth: spasmodic nation-states, famine and natural disasters, inter-ethnic conflicts and religious persecutions." Ato Quayson, ed., "Introduction," in *The Cambridge History of Postcolonial Literature* (Cambridge: Cambridge University Press, 2011), 9.

80. Hannah Arendt, *The Origins of Totalitarianism* (New York: Harcourt, Brace and World, 1968), 276.

81. Ibid.

82. I owe this insight to Cathy J. Schlund-Vials's suggestion to draw upon Arendt's moving essay. Hannah Arendt, "We Refugees," in *The Jewish Writings*, ed. Jerome Kohn and Ron H. Feldman (New York: Schocken Books, 2007), 264, available at https://www.jus.uio.no/smr/om/aktuelt/arrangementer/2015/arendt-we-refugees.pdf.

83. Ibid., 265.

84. Hannah Arendt, *The Origins of Totalitarianism* (New York: Harcourt, 1968), 276.

85. Ibid.

86. Ibid., 173.

87. Ibid., 173–174.

88. Judith Butler, *Frames of War: When Is Life Grievable?* (London: Verso, 2009).

89. Extending this critique to the limits of the human rights regime, Randall Williams tracks the persistence of neocolonialism in current human rights rhetoric and politics as well as the potential for resistance through the language of human rights. Randall Williams, *The Divided World: Human Rights and Its Violence* (Minneapolis: University of Minnesota Press, 2010). See also Crystal Parikh, *Writing Human Rights: The Political Imaginaries of Color* (Minneapolis: University of Minnesota Press, 2017).

90. Saskia Sassen, *Expulsions: Brutality and Complexity in the Global Economy* (Cambridge, MA: Belknap-Harvard University Press, 2014); Schlund-Vials, *War, Genocide, and Justice*; Upamanyu Pablo Mukherjee, *Postcolonial Environments: Nature, Culture, and the Contemporary Indian Novel in English* (New York: Palgrave MacMillan, 2010); Rob Nixon, *Slow Violence and the Environmentalism of the Poor* (Cambridge,

MA: Harvard University Press, 2011); and Sunil Amrith, *Crossing the Bay of Bengal: The Furies of Nature and the Fates of Migrants* (Cambridge, MA: Harvard University Press, 2015).

91. K. Muthukumar, "Godrej Group—Enterprise, Ethics: The Two Pillars of an Empire," *Hindu Business Line*, August 17, 2016, updated March 10, 2018, available at https://www.thehindubusinessline.com/specials/godrej-group-enterprise-ethics-the-two-pillars-of-an-empire/article21689683.ece1.

92. The Godrej India Culture Lab is a new public cultural space in Mumbai that fosters challenging dialogues year-round through speaker events, art exhibits, films, and media engagements on a range of politically resonant and social justice issues, from LGBTQ rights to poverty, to migration, to trans inclusion, to urban development, to environmentalism, and so forth.

93. Parmesh Shahani, email message to author, December 5, 2019.

94. Parmesh Shahani, email message to author, December 6, 2019.

95. Pheng Cheah, *What Is a World? On Postcolonial Literature as World Literature* (Durham, NC: Duke University Press, 2016).

96. Jennifer Green-Lewis, *Victorian Photography, Literature, and the Invention of Modern Memory: Already the Past* (New York: Bloomsbury, 2017), 143.

97. Eric Tang, *Unsettled: Cambodian Refugees in the New York City Hyperghetto* (Philadelphia: Temple University Press, 2015), 5.

98. Parikh, *Writing Human Rights*, 2.

99. Lauren Berlant, *The Female Complaint: The Unfinished Business of Sentimentality in American Culture* (Durham: Duke University Press, 2008), 147.

100. Daiya, *Violent Belongings*.

101. Leela Gandhi and Deborah L. Nelson, "Editors' Introduction," *Critical Inquiry* 40, no. 4 (Summer 2014): 285–297.

102. Vazira Fazila-Yacoobali Zamindar, *The Long Partition and the Making of Modern South Asia* (New York: Columbia University Press, 2007), 239.

CHAPTER 1

1. Judith Butler, *Frames of War: When Is Life Grievable?* (London: Verso, 2009), 135.

2. Upamanyu Pablo Mukherjee, *Postcolonial Environments: Nature, Culture, and the Contemporary Indian Novel in English* (New York: Palgrave Macmillan, 2010), 13.

3. Susan Buck-Morss, *The Dialectics of Seeing: Walter Benjamin and the Arcades Project* (Cambridge: Massachusetts Institute of Technology Press, 1991), 340.

4. Christopher Pinney, "Introduction: How the Other Half . . . ," in *Photography's Other Histories*, ed. Christopher Pinney and Nicolas Peterson (Durham, NC: Duke University Press, 2003), 8.

5. Ibid.

6. Christopher Pinney, *"Photos of the Gods": The Printed Image and Political Struggle in India* (London: Reaktion, 2004), 144.

7. Ibid., 204.

8. Ibid.

9. Ibid., 205. Others, including Sumathi Ramaswamy and Martin Jay, have subsequently also produced work on thinking through the historical relationship between nationalism and popular visual production. Sumathi Ramaswamy and Martin Jay, eds., *Empires of Vision: A Reader* (Durham, NC: Duke University Press, 2014).

10. Kajri Jain, *Gods in the Bazaar: The Economies of Indian Calendar Art* (Durham, NC: Duke University Press, 2007), 174.

11. Sumathi Ramaswamy, "Artful Mapping in Bazaar India," *Tasveer Ghar*, available at http://www.tasveergharindia.net/cmsdesk/essay/116/index_3.html. Ramaswamy's book *The Goddess and the Nation: Mapping Mother India* (Durham, NC: Duke University Press, 2010) offers an exhaustive catalog of Indian print culture about nationalist cartography that articulates this dual mapping of the nation and the female goddess as "Mother India."

12. Strangely, or perhaps not, in the post-Partition prints that have survived, this densely embodied gendered and religious diversity is largely absent; usually between one and four male political figures inhabit the post-1947 pictorial representations of the Indian map. See examples in Ramaswamy, "Artful Mapping in Bazaar India."

13. Pinney, "*Photos of the Gods*," 135.

14. Theodor Adorno, quoted in Buck-Morss, *The Dialectics of Seeing*, 43.

15. Andrea Immel, "Frederick Lock's Scrapbook: Patterns in the Pictures and Writing in the Margins," *The Lion and the Unicorn* 29, no. 1 (2005): 66–67.

16. Ibid., 70.

17. Benedict Anderson, *Imagined Communities: Reflections on the Origin and Spread of Nationalism* (London: Verso, 1982).

18. Nandini Chandra, *The Classic Popular: Amar Chitra Katha, 1967–2007* (New Delhi: Yoda Press, 2008), 9.

19. Ben Vinson III, *Before Mestizaje: The Frontiers of Race and Caste in Colonial Mexico* (New York: Cambridge University Press, 2017).

20. Chandra, *The Classic Popular*, 10.

21. I discuss David's work in "Gender, Sexuality and the Family in South-Asian Fiction," in *Oxford History of the Novel in English (Volume 10). The Novel in South and South-East Asia*, ed. Alex Tickell (Oxford: Oxford University Press, 2018), 44–57.

22. Chandra, *The Classic Popular*, 10.

23. I thank Mika Natif for making this observation when I presented this research at GW's Sigur Center for Asian Studies in 2017.

24. Saskia Sassen, *Expulsions: Brutality and Complexity in the Global Economy* (Cambridge, MA: Belknap-Harvard University Press, 2014), 211.

25. Ibid., 215.

26. Pallavi Pundir, "Stories from the Other Side," *India Express*, August 30, 2013, available at http://indianexpress.com/article/cities/chandigarh/stories-from-the-other-side-2/#sthash.YXYTMm1H.dpuf.

27. Kim Arora, "Vishwajyoti Ghosh: Partition Is Marked by Memories, Speculation—and Curiosity," *Times of India*, August 28, 2013, accessed on December 4, 2014, available at http://timesofindia.indiatimes.com/interviews/Vishwajyoti-Ghosh-Partition-is-marked-by-memories-speculation-and-curiosity/articleshow/22101779.cms.

28. Bharath Murthy offers a fine overview of graphic narratives in India in "An Art without a Tradition: A Survey of Indian Comics," *Marg Magazine* 61, no. 2 (December 2009): 38–53.

29. See especially Karline McLain, *India's Immortal Comic Books: Gods, Kings, and Other Heroes* (Bloomington: Indiana University Press, 2009); and Chandra, *The Classic Popular*, for an insider's look at the production of *ACK* titles. See also the essays in Lawrence A. Babb and Susan S. Wadley, eds., *Media and the Transformation of Religion in South Asia* (Delhi: Motilal Banarsidass, 1998).

30. Chandra, *The Classic Popular*, 5.
31. Kavita Daiya, ed., "Introduction: South Asia in Graphic Narratives," in *Graphic Narratives about South Asia and South Asian America: Aesthetics and Politics* (London: Routledge, 2019), 3–10.
32. Vishwajyoti Ghosh, "Inverted Calm: An Interview with Vishwajyoti Ghosh," by Ryan Holmberg, *The Comics Journal*, October 23, 2013, available at http://www.tcj.com/inverted-calm-an-interview-with-vishwajyoti-ghosh/.
33. Daiya, "Introduction."
34. Monica Chiu, *Drawing New Color Lines: Transnational Asian American Graphic Narratives* (Hong Kong: Hong Kong University Press, 2015), 10–11.
35. Hillary Chute, *Graphic Women: Life Narratives and Contemporary Comics* (New York: Columbia University Press, 2010), 193.
36. Ibid., 136.
37. Hillary Chute, *Disaster Drawn: Visual Witness, Comics, and Documentary Form* (Cambridge, MA: Belknap Press of Harvard University Press, 2016), 161.
38. Martha J. Cutter and Cathy J. Schlund-Vials, eds., "Introduction," in *Redrawing the Historical Past: History, Memory, and Multiethnic Graphic Novels* (Athens: University of Georgia Press, 2018), 2.
39. Pramod K. Nayar, *The Indian Graphic Novel: Nation, History, and Critique* (New York: Routledge, 2016), 8.
40. Vishwajyoti Ghosh, ed., "A Good Education," in *This Side, That Side: Restorying Partition* (Delhi: Yoda Press, 2013), 151.
41. For a thorough account of the historical formation and working of this project, see Debjani Sengupta, "From Dandakaranya to Marichjhapi: Rehabilitation, Representation and the Partition of Bengal (1947)," *Social Semiotics* 21, no. 1 (2011): 101–123.
42. Ghosh, "A Good Education," 152.
43. Ibid., 153.
44. Ibid.
45. Radha Kumar, *The History of Doing: An Illustrated Account of Movements for Women's Rights and Feminism in India 1800–1990* (New Delhi: Zubaan Books, 1997); Sangeeta Ray, *En-Gendering India: Woman and Nation in Colonial and Postcolonial Narratives* (Durham, NC: Duke University Press, 2000); Kumari Jayawardena and Malathi de Alwis, eds., *Embodied Violence: Communalising Women's Sexuality in South Asia* (London: Zed Books, 1996); and Ania Loomba and Ritty A. Lukose, eds., *South Asian Feminisms: Contemporary Interventions* (Durham, NC: Duke University Press, 2012).
46. Aditi Gupta and Rajat Mittal, "The Taboo," in *This Side, That Side: Restorying Partition*, ed. Vishwajyoti Ghosh (New Delhi: Yoda Press, 2013), 238.
47. Ibid., 240.
48. Ibid., 239.
49. Sonya Fatah and Archana Sreenivasan, "Karachi Delhi Katha," in *This Side, That Side: Restorying Partition*, ed. Vishwajyoti Ghosh (New Delhi: Yoda Press, 2013), 196.
50. Ibid.
51. Ibid., 197.
52. Ibid.
53. Ibid., 201.
54. Ibid.
55. Chute, *Disaster Drawn*, 178.
56. Maria M. Litwa, "Welcome to Geneva Camp," in *This Side, That Side: Restorying Partition*, ed. Vishwajyoti Ghosh (New Delhi: Yoda Press, 2013), 253.

57. Ibid., 254.

58. Mahruba Mowtushi, "The Urban Experience of Displacement: Re-Viewing Dhaka through Street Art and Graphic Narrative," in *Graphic Narratives about South Asia and South Asian America: Aesthetics and Politics*, edited by Kavita Daiya (London: Routledge, 2019), 234.

59. Litwa, "Welcome to Geneva Camp," 256.

60. Cutter and Schlund-Vials, "Introduction," 4.

61. Mowtushi, "The Urban Experience of Displacement," 234.

62. Suvadip Sinha and Amit R. Baishya, eds., "Introduction: Postcolonial Animalities," in *Postcolonial Animalities* (New York: Routledge, 2019), 3–4. For a compelling new approach to how postcolonial literature turns to the representation of human and nonhuman bonds in the conflict zone, see Sreyoshi Sarkar, "Conflict Ecologies: Gender, Genre, and Environment in Narratives of Violent Conflict in Postcolonial India" (Ph.D. diss., George Washington University, 2017).

63. Talal Asad, *Formations of the Secular: Christianity, Islam, Modernity* (Stanford, CA: Stanford University Press, 2003), 178–179.

64. Syeda Farhana and Nitesh Mohanty, "Little Women," in *This Side, That Side: Restorying Partition*, ed. Vishwajyoti Ghosh (New Delhi: Yoda Press, 2013), 260.

65. Ibid.

66. Ibid.

67. Ibid., 263.

68. Ibid., 266.

69. Jain, *Gods in the Bazaar*, 26.

70. Ravish Kumar, Ikroop Sandhu, and Shveta Sarda, "Which Side?" in *This Side, That Side: Restorying Partition*, ed. Vishwajyoti Ghosh (New Delhi: Yoda Press, 2013), 56.

71. Farhana and Mohanty, "Little Women," 266.

72. Stella Oh, "Movement and Mobility: Representing Trauma through Graphic Narratives," *Asian American Literature: Discourses and Pedagogies* 7 (2016): 66–67.

73. Jennifer James, "Ecomelancholia: Slavery, War, and Black Ecological Imaginings," in *Environmental Criticism for the Twenty-First Century*, edited by Stephanie LeMenager, Teresa Shrewry, and Ken Hiltner (New York: Routledge, 2011), 166.

74. Ibid., 167.

75. Arundhati Ghosh and Appupen, "Water Stories," in *This Side, That Side: Restorying Partition*, ed. Vishwajyoti Ghosh (New Delhi: Yoda Press, 2013), 130.

76. Ibid., 134.

77. M. Hasan and Sukanya Ghosh, "Making of a Poet," in *This Side, That Side: Restorying Partition*, ed. Vishwajyoti Ghosh (New Delhi: Yoda Press, 2013), 138.

78. Ibid., 140.

79. Ibid., 142.

80. Ibid., 144.

81. Beena Sarwar and Prasanna Dhandharphale, "Milne Do," in *This Side, That Side: Restorying Partition*, ed. Vishwajyoti Ghosh (New Delhi: Yoda Press, 2013), 312.

82. Ahmad Rafay Alam and Martand Khosla, "90 Upper Mall or 1 Bawa Park," in *This Side, That Side: Restorying Partition*, ed. Vishwajyoti Ghosh (New Delhi: Yoda Press, 2013), 189.

83. Ibid., 189.

84. Nina Sabnani, "Know Directions Home?" in *This Side, That Side: Restorying Partition*, ed. Vishwajyoti Ghosh (New Delhi: Yoda Press, 2013), 111.

85. Hillary Chute, *Why Comics? From Underground to Everywhere* (New York: HarperCollins, 2017), 173.
86. Hillary Chute and Patrick Jagoda, eds., "Special Issue: Comics and Media," *Critical Inquiry* 40, no. 3 (Spring 2014): 1–10.
87. Bani Abidi, "The News," in *This Side, That Side: Restorying Partition*, ed. Vishwajyoti Ghosh (New Delhi: Yoda Press, 2013), 163.
88. Ibid., 164.
89. Ibid., 167.
90. See Sreyoshi Sarkar, "The Art of Postcolonial Resistance and Multispecies Storytelling in Malik Sajad's Graphic Novel 'Munnu: A Boy from Kashmir,'" in *Graphic Narratives about South Asia and South Asian America: Aesthetics and Politics*, ed. Kavita Daiya (London: Routledge, 2019), 104–124; and Amit R. Baishya, "Endangered (and Endangering) Species: Exploring the Animacy Hierarchy in Malik Sajad's *Munnu*," in *Graphic Narratives about South Asia and South Asian America: Aesthetics and Politics*, ed. Kavita Daiya (London: Routledge, 2019), 50–69. See also Andrew Hock Soon, "Nationalism and the Intangible Effects of Violence in Malik Sajad's 'Munnu: A Boy from Kashmir,'" in *Graphic Narratives about South Asia and South Asian America: Aesthetics and Politics*, ed. Kavita Daiya (London: Routledge, 2019), 159–174.
91. Urvashi Butalia, *The Other Side of Silence: Voices from the Partition of India* (New Delhi: Viking, 1998), 3.
92. Susan Sontag, *Regarding the Pain of Others* (New York: Picador, 2003), 115.
93. Asma Naeem, "Partition and the Mobilities of Margaret Bourke-White and Zarina," *American Art* 31, no. 2 (Summer 2017): 81–88.
94. Ibid., 81–82. Thus, Naeem concludes, despite their different cultural origins, their transcultural mobilities link them, through the Partition: "Just as Zarina's time in the United States relocated subjectivities previously tethered to India, Bourke-White's time in India unfixed patriotic sentiments formerly attached to her native country." Ibid., 87.
95. Jennifer Green-Lewis, *Framing the Victorians: Photography and the Culture of Realism* (Ithaca, NY: Cornell University Press, 1996), 31.
96. "As inheritors of what I have called the shadow archive, we do not have a single body image to call our own, but live for others and ourselves in relation to a concatenation of such images that more or less approaches and avoids shadowy prototypes that rarely if ever reveal themselves for what they are, even in our dreams." Nancy Armstrong, *Fiction in the Age of Photography: The Legacy of British Realism* (Cambridge, MA: Harvard University Press, 1999), 31.
97. He also writes, "In the postcolonial era the dead or dying body has become in itself the visual sign of the human reality in the Third World." David Spurr, *The Rhetoric of Empire: Colonial Discourse in Journalism, Travel Writing, and Imperial Administration* (Durham, NC: Duke University Press, 1993), 25.
98. Armstrong, *Fiction in the Age of Photography*, 29.
99. Christopher Wright, "Supple Bodies: The Papua New Guinea Photographs of Captain Francis R. Barton, 1899–1907," in *Photography's Other Histories*, ed. Christopher Pinney and Nicolas Peterson (Durham, NC: Duke University Press, 2003), 166.
100. Butler, *Frames of War*, 97.
101. Naeem, "Partition and the Mobilities of Margaret Bourke-White and Zarina," 84. See also C. M. Naim's reflections on Partition memories from the vantage point of the diaspora in his book *Ambiguities of Heritage: Fictions and Polemics* (Karachi: City Press, 1999).
102. Butler, *Frames of War*, 62.

103. Ibid., 64.

104. Cathy J. Schlund-Vials, *War, Genocide, and Justice: Cambodian American Memory Work* (Minneapolis: University of Minnesota Press, 2012).

105. For Butler, "The photograph is linked through its 'tense' to the grievability of a life, anticipating and performing that grievability. In this way we can be haunted in advance by the suffering or deaths of others." Butler, *Frames of War*, 98.

106. Images from the exhibit are available at http://www.unhcr.org/en-us/news/stories/2016/6/5702c1594/where-the-children-sleep.html.

107. Butler, *Frames of War*, 96.

108. Ibid., 144.

109. For one example among many, see Hannah Ellis-Petersen and Manoj Chaurasia, "India Racked by Greatest Exodus since Partition due to Coronavirus," *Guardian*, March 30, 2020, available at https://www.theguardian.com/world/2020/mar/30/india-wracked-by-greatest-exodus-since-partition-due-to-coronavirus.

110. Butler, *Frames of War*, 62.

111. Dionne Bunsha and Homai Vyarawalla, "History in Black and White," *Frontline* 22, no. 17 (2005), available at https://frontline.thehindu.com/other/article30205888.ece.

CHAPTER 2

1. Ranjana Khanna, "Ethical Ambiguities and Specters of Colonialism," in *Feminist Consequences: Theory for the New Century* (New York: Columbia University Press, 2001), 121.

2. Pheng Cheah, *What Is a World? On Postcolonial Literature as World Literature* (Durham, NC: Duke University Press, 2016), 194.

3. Khanna, "Ethical Ambiguities and Specters of Colonialism," 121.

4. Crystal Parikh, *Writing Human Rights: The Political Imaginaries of Writers of Color* (Minneapolis: University of Minnesota Press, 2017), 6. Parikh's compelling account of the role of literature in rethinking human rights is relevant here.

5. Cheah, *What Is a World?*, 5.

6. Neha Vora, *Impossible Citizens: Dubai's Indian Diaspora* (Durham, NC: Duke University Press, 2013), 28.

7. I discuss this diasporic investment in emergent postcolonial national politics in my essay "The 1947 Partition, War, and Internment: Hidden Histories of Migration and Displacement in Transnational Asia," in *Volume II: Asian American Literature in Transition (1930–1965)*, eds. Victor Bascara and Josephine Nock-Hee Park (New York: Cambridge University Press, forthcoming).

8. My discussion of worlding is influenced by Sreyoshi Sarkar's research on how global Anglophone fiction represents gender and environment in narratives about conflict zones. See Sreyoshi Sarkar, "Conflict Ecologies: Gender, Genre, and Environment in Narratives of Violent Conflict in Postcolonial India," (Ph.D. diss., George Washington University, 2017).

9. Ankhi Mukherjee, *What Is a Classic? Postcolonial Rewriting and Invention of the Canon* (Palo Alto, CA: Stanford University Press, 2014), 161.

10. Lisa Lowe, *The Intimacies of Four Continents* (Durham, NC: Duke University Press, 2015), 40.

11. Cathy J. Schlund-Vials, *War, Genocide, and Justice: Cambodian American Memory Work* (Minneapolis: University of Minnesota Press, 2012), 17.

12. Ibid., 118.

13. Parikh, *Writing Human Rights*, 2.

14. Ulka Anjaria, *Realism in the Twentieth-Century Indian Novel: Colonial Difference and Literary Form* (New York: Cambridge University Press, 2012), 1.

15. Ibid., 127.

16. Bapsi Sidhwa, *Cracking India: A Novel* (Milwaukee: Milkweed Editions, 1991), 23.

17. Anupama Jain, *How to Be South Asian in America: Narratives of Ambivalence and Belonging* (Philadelphia: Temple University Press, 2011).

18. Sidhwa, *Cracking India*, 11.

19. Sangeeta Ray, *En-Gendering India: Woman and Nation in Colonial and Postcolonial Narratives* (Durham, NC: Duke University Press, 2000), 131–132.

20. Kavita Daiya, *Violent Belongings: Partition, Gender, and National Culture in Postcolonial India* (Philadelphia: Temple University Press, [2008] 2011), 54–86.

21. See Partha Chatterjee, *The Nation and Its Fragments: Colonial and Postcolonial Histories* (Princeton, NJ: Princeton University Press, 1993).

22. Rashna B. Singh thoroughly explores the representation of Parsis in relation to nationalism in this novel in her article "Traversing Diacritical Space: Negotiating and Narrating Parsi Nationness," *Journal of Commonwealth Literature* 43, no. 2 (June 2008): 29–47.

23. Sidhwa, *Cracking India*, 29.

24. See Kavita Daiya, "Refugees, Gender and Secularism in South Asian Literature and Cinema," in *Representations of War, Migration and Refugeehood: Interdisciplinary Perspectives*, ed. Daniel Rellstab and Christiane Schlote (New York: Routledge, 2014), 263–280.

25. Sidhwa, *Cracking India*, 20.

26. Ibid., 15.

27. Ibid., 24.

28. Ibid., 249.

29. Thanks to Sreyoshi Sarkar for this astute reminder about how age and class location crucially sustain Lenny's view on able-bodiedness.

30. Sidhwa, *Cracking India*, 224.

31. Ibid., 226.

32. Bapsi Sidhwa, "Grief and Survival in *Ice-Candy Man*: In conversation with Bapsi Sidhwa," in *Partition Dialogues: Memories of a Lost Home*, ed. Alok Bhalla (New York: Oxford University Press, 2006), 234–235.

33. Sidhwa, *Cracking India*, 224.

34. Ibid., 224.

35. Ibid., 227.

36. Lauren Berlant and Michael Warner, "Sex in Public," in *Intimacy*, ed. Lauren Berlant (Chicago: University of Chicago Press, 2000), 322. An earlier version of parts of this argument appears in my analysis of public sphere representations of refugee experiences in Daiya, "Refugees, Gender and Secularism in South Asian Literature and Cinema."

37. Sidhwa, "Grief and Survival in *Ice-Candy Man*," 237.

38. Ritu Menon and Kamla Bhasin, *Borders and Boundaries: Women in India's Partition* (New Brunswick: Rutgers University Press, 1998), 57.

39. Of course, this is not unique; the modernist short stories of Urdu writer Saadat Hasan Manto offer a similar critique of gendered violence during Partition (I analyze some of Manto's stories in my first book, *Violent Belongings*). The neorealist Partition films of Ritwik Ghatak and some Bollywood films, like Chandraprakash Dwivedi's

Pinjar (2003), which is based on a Punjabi novel, *Pinjar*, by Amrita Pritam, also address these historical roots of violence against women.

40. Deepti Misri, *Beyond Partition: Gender, Violence, and Representation in Postcolonial India* (Urbana: University of Illinois Press, 2014), 72.

41. Shauna Singh Baldwin, *What the Body Remembers: A Novel* (New York: Doubleday, 1999), 465–466.

42. Ibid., 466.

43. Ibid., 467.

44. Judith Butler, *Frames of War: When Is Life Grievable?* (London: Verso, 2009), 14.

45. Ibid.

46. Anjaria, *Realism in the Twentieth-Century Indian Novel*, 26.

47. Baldwin, *What the Body Remembers*, 46.

48. Ibid., 455.

49. Ibid., 455–456.

50. Butler, *Frames of War*, 62.

51. Menon and Bhasin, *Borders and Boundaries*, 18.

52. Baldwin, *What the Body Remembers*, 411.

53. Mimi Thi Nguyen, *The Gift of Freedom: War, Debt, and Other Refugee Passages* (Durham, NC: Duke University Press, 2012), 185.

54. Another beautiful novel that offers a similar critique is Karan Mahajan's *The Association of Small Bombs* (New York: Penguin Books, 2016).

55. Charmi Harikrishnan, "Fiction Not Being Real Undermines Fiction: Arundhati Roy," *Economic Times*, June 2, 2017.

56. Arundhati Roy, *The Ministry of Utmost Happiness* (New York: Knopf, 2017), 13.

57. Ibid., 45.

58. Ibid.

59. Ibid., 42.

60. Ibid. 167.

61. Ibid., 168.

62. Ibid., 342–343.

63. Taslima Nasrin, *Lajja: Shame* (New Delhi: Penguin India, 2014).

64. Jennifer Harford Vargas, *Forms of Dictatorship: Power, Narrative, and Authoritarianism in the Latina/o Novel* (New York: Oxford University Press, 2017), 190.

65. Ulka Anjaria, quoted in Filippo Menozzi, "'Too Much Blood for Good Literature': Arundhati Roy's *The Ministry of Utmost Happiness* and the Question of Realism," *Journal of Postcolonial Writing* 55, no. 1 (2018), 21.

66. Ibid., 31.

67. Ibid., 32.

68. Chatterjee, *The Nation and Its Fragments*.

69. Roy, *The Ministry of Utmost Happiness*, 319.

70. Harikrishnan, "Fiction Not Being Real Undermines Fiction."

71. Kavita Daiya, "The World after Empire; or, Whither Postcoloniality?" *PMLA* 132, no. 1 (May 2017): 150.

72. Arundhati Roy, *Power Politics* (Cambridge, MA: South End Press, 2001), 140.

73. Peeyush Khandelwal, "Muzaffarnagar Riots: News of Death Shadows Fleeing Refugees," *Hindustan Times*, September 13, 2013, available at https://www.hindustantimes.com/india/muzaffarnagar-riots-news-of-death-shadows-fleeing-refugees/story-aWg7Twze3eRqkHHFh5sRQM.html.

74. "State of Fear from Kashmir to Kanyakumari: Jamiat Ulama-I-Hind Demands Law Against Lynching," *Outlook Web Bureau*, November 6, 2019, available at https://www.outlookindia.com/website/story/india-news-state-of-fear-from-kashmir-to-kanyakumari-jamiat-ulama-i-hind-demands-law-against-lynching/341820.

75. "Pakistani Hindu Refugees Get Respite, MEA Extends Their Visa," *India Today Online*, April 9, 2013, available at http://indiatoday.intoday.in/story/pakistani-hindu-refugees-get-respite-mea-extends-their-visa/1/261429.html.

76. "Over 30,000 Refugee Families Struggling in Jammu," *Governance Now*, September 26, 2011, available at http://www.governancenow.com/news/regular-story/over-30000-refugee-families-struggling-jammu.

77. Basharat Peer, "Epilogue," in *Curfewed Night* (New Delhi: Random House, 2008), 241.

78. Suvir Kaul, *Of Gardens and Graves: Kashmir, Poetry, Politics* (Durham, NC: Duke University Press, 2017); and Misri, *Beyond Partition*. See also Mona Bhan, *Counterinsurgency, Democracy, and the Politics of Identity in India: From Warfare to Welfare?* (New York: Routledge, 2014); Arundhati Roy et al., *Kashmir: The Case for Freedom* (New York: Verso, 2011); and Ather Zia, *Resisting Disappearance: Military Occupation and Women's Activism in Kashmir* (Seattle: University of Washington Press, 2019).

79. Kaul, *Of Gardens and Graves*, xvi. Misri similarly argues that, along with Partition, "equally urgent today are other histories, forms, and enactments of violence that may be shaped not only by Partition and the communal sentiment that is its legacy but also by other aspects such as caste and class structures, gender asymmetries, globalization, and development foisted upon the poor, and pervasive militarization among state and non-state actors." Misri, *Beyond Partition*, 8.

80. Srishtee Sethi, "Tribes at the Borderland: Locating 'Pakistani Hindu Bhils' in Jodhpur," *Journal of Adivasi and Indigenous Studies* 8, no. 2 (August 2018): 51–62.

81. Sheikh Zaffar Iqbal, "Race to Take Credit as Refugees in Jammu and Kashmir Get Settlement Funds," NDTV, November 11, 2017, available at https://www.ndtv.com/india-news/race-to-take-credit-as-refugees-in-jammu-and-kashmir-get-settlement-funds-1774257.

82. Rakesh Mohan Chaturvedi, "Jammu's West Pakistan Refugees to Hold a Rally to Thank Govt," *Economic Times*, August 31, 2019, available at https://economictimes.indiatimes.com/news/politics-and-nation/jammus-west-pak-refugees-to-hold-a-rally-to-thank-govt/articleshow/70918574.cms?from=mdr.

CHAPTER 3

1. Linda Williams, "Melodrama Revised," in *Refiguring American Film Genres: Theory and History*, ed. Nick Browne (Berkeley: University of California Press, 1998), 50.

2. Wendy Brown, *Walled States, Waning Sovereignty* (Brooklyn: Zone Books, 2014), 24.

3. Wendy Brown, "Reclaiming Democracy: An Interview with Wendy Brown on Occupy, Sovereignty, and Secularism," by Robin Celikates and Yolande Jansen, *Critical Legal Thinking*, January 30, 2013, available at http://criticallegalthinking.com/2013/01/30/reclaiming-democracy-an-interview-with-wendy-brown-on-occupy-sovereignty-and-secularism/.

4. Tejaswini Ganti, *Bollywood: A Guidebook to Contemporary Cinema* (New York: Routledge, 2013), 21.

5. She notes, "The Hindi film industry prides itself on being secular, and it is secular in the sense of 'equal respect' being given to each religion. The diversity of the industry goes back to its earliest days, at least in Bombay, where Bengali Hindus worked alongside Germans (New Theater), while in other companies many Muslim stars worked alongside Hindus, Jews and Parsis." Rachel Dwyer, *Filming the Gods: Religion and Indian Cinema* (London: Routledge, 2006), 134.

6. Ibid., 166.

7. Ravi Vasudevan, *The Melodramatic Public: Film Form and Spectatorship in India* (New York: Palgrave Macmillan, 2011), 402.

8. Priya Joshi, *Bollywood's India: A Public Fantasy* (New York: Columbia University Press, 2015), 15.

9. Ibid., 131.

10. Dwyer, *Filming the Gods*, 133.

11. Kavita Daiya, *Violent Belongings: Partition, Gender, and National Culture in Postcolonial India* (Philadelphia: Temple University Press, [2008] 2011).

12. Vasudevan, *The Melodramatic Public*, 366, 367.

13. Ibid., 367.

14. Rachel Saltz, "Indian Soul," review of *Delhi-6*, directed by Rakeysh Omprakash Mehra, *New York Times*, February 9, 2007.

15. Anupama Chopra, "Delhi-6," review of *Delhi-6*, directed by Rakeysh Omprakash Mehra, NDTV Movies, March 7, 2014, available at http://movies.ndtv.com/movie-reviews/delhi-6-379.

16. Rajeev Masand, "*Delhi-6*, a Film with Heart," *news18.com*, February 21, 2009, available at https://www.news18.com/videos/india/now-showing-54-309381.html.

17. Achin Vanaik, "Hindutva's Forward March," *Jacobin*, September 19, 2017, available at https://www.jacobinmag.com/2017/09/india-modi-bjp-cow-vigilantism-judiciary-corruption.

18. Vijay Mishra, *Bollywood Cinema: Temples of Desire* (New York: Routledge, 2002), 266.

19. Ibid., 267.

20. Bhaskar Sarkar, "The Melodramas of Globalization," *Cultural Dynamics* 20, no. 1 (2008): 43.

21. Homi Bhabha, *The Location of Culture* (New York: Routledge, 1994), 251.

22. Purnima Mankekar, *Unsettling India: Affect, Temporality, Transnationality* (Durham, NC: Duke University Press, 2015), 66.

23. Dwyer, *Filming the Gods*, 147.

24. Thomas Elsaesser, "Tales of Sound and Fury: Observations on the Family Melodrama," in *Imitations of Life: A Reader on Film and Television Melodrama*, ed. Marcia Langly (Detroit: Wayne State University Press, 1991), 86.

25. A more extensive analysis might draw upon Baishya's analysis of postcolonial animalities to consider the representation of human-animal boundaries in this film and the colorism inherent in the particular juxtaposition of the mythical "black monkey" and Hanuman of the *Ramayana*, which is invoked at the beginning and the end of the film. It is also interesting to note that Mehra originally wanted the film to have a different ending: he wanted Roshan to die at the end, but the producers pressured him to change the script. The assumption was that it would not succeed at the box office unless there was a happy ending. After the film was a commercial flop, a year later, Mehra reshot the beginning and the ending scenes. In the new version, Mehra

returns to the original story, and Roshan dies. This version of the film was accepted and screened at the Venice Film Festival in 2010.

26. See Kavita Daiya, "Visual Culture and Violence: Inventing Intimacy and Citizenship in Recent South Asian Cinema," *South Asian History and Culture* 2, no. 4 (2011): 589–604.

27. Rajkumar Hirani's film *PK* (2014) is a welcome break from this trend: it establishes romantic and sexual intimacy between a Muslim Pakistani man and a Hindu Indian woman who meet as students in Europe very early in the film; albeit heteronormative, it is also one of the few films that reunites them and actually allows both characters to live at the end of the film.

28. Liisa Malkki, *Purity and Exile: Violence, Memory, and National Cosmology among Hutu Refugees in Tanzania* (Chicago: Chicago University Press, 1995), 253.

29. Vasudevan, *Melodramatic Public*, 167.

30. Lauren Berlant, "Slow Death (Sovereignty, Obesity, Lateral Agency)," *Critical Inquiry* 33, no. 4 (2007): 754–780.

31. Anuradha Dinwaney Needham, *New Indian Cinema in Post-independence India: The Cultural Work of Shyam Benegal's Films* (New York: Routledge, 2013), 97.

32. Judith Butler, *Precarious Life: The Powers of Mourning and Violence* (London: Verso, 2004), 20.

33. Ibid., 26.

34. Svetlana Boym, "On Diasporic Intimacy: Ilya Kabokov's Installations and Immigrant Homes," in *Intimacy*, ed. Lauren Berlant (Chicago: University of Chicago Press, 2000), 252.

35. See Deepa Mary Ollapally, *The Politics of Extremism in South Asia* (New York: Cambridge University Press, 2008), 140.

36. Shah Faesal, "What a Spy Thriller Teaches Us about Patriotism and Empathy," *Times of India*, May 27, 2018, available at https://timesofindia.indiatimes.com/home/sunday-times/all-that-matters/what-a-spy-thriller-teaches-us-about-patriotism-and-empathy/articleshow/64335499.cms.

37. Ganti, *Bollywood*, 148–149.

38. Ibid., 148.

39. Srijana Mitra Das, "Bajrangi Bhaijaan Movie Review," review of *Bajrangi Bhairaan*, directed by Kabir Khan, *Times of India*, July 17, 2015.

40. See a compelling analysis of the representation of Indian secularism in this film in William Elison, Christian Lee Novetzke, and Andy Rotman, *Amar Akbar Anthony: Bollywood, Brotherhood, and the Nation* (Cambridge, MA: Harvard University Press, 2016).

41. Ibid., 232.

42. Anupama Chopra, "Tears, Cheers," review of *Bajrangi Bhaijaan*, directed by Kabir Khan, *Hindustan Times*, September 22, 2015.

43. Sabiha Sumar, "Interview with Sabiha Sumar," by Nermeen Shaikh, *Asia Society*, April 8, 2005, available at https://asiasociety.org/interview-sabiha-sumar.

44. Ibid.

45. Ibid.

46. Hamid Naficy, *An Accented Cinema: Exilic and Diasporic Filmmaking* (Princeton, NJ: Princeton University Press, 2001), 6.

47. Pavitra Sundar suggestively argues that the film uses "distantiated sound" to represent Ayesha's traumatic experience in visceral ways. See Pavitra Sundar, "Silence and the Uncanny: Partition in the Soundtrack of *Khamosh Pani*," *South Asian Popular Culture* 8, no. 3 (2010): 277–290.

48. Gayatri Chakravorty Spivak, "Can the Subaltern Speak?" in *Marxism and the Interpretation of Culture*, eds. Cary Nelson and Lawrence Grossberg (Urbana-Champaign: University of Illinois Press, 1988), 308.

49. Judith Butler, "Precarity Talk," *TDR: The Drama Review* 56, no. 4 (2012): 169.

50. Lauren Berlant and Jordan Greenwald, "Affect in the End Times: A Conversation with Lauren Berlant," *Qui Parle* 20, no. 2 (2012): 83.

51. Deepti Misri makes a similar argument in her book *Beyond Partition: Gender, Violence, and Representation in Postcolonial India* (Urbana: University of Illinois Press, 2014).

52. Bhabha, *The Location of Culture*, 254.

53. Jasbir K. Puar, *Right to Maim: Debility, Capacity, Disability* (Durham, NC: Duke University Press, 2017), xxiv.

54. "In postwar British Burma, the colonial rulers conferred on the Rohingyas significant administrative posts in Arakan as reward for their wartime participation in the British military efforts against the Japanese. The Rohingya leaders used their newly found positions of leverage to seek administrative autonomy, but in vain. As the Partition of British India loomed large, the Rohingyas hoped to join the future Muslim-majority province of East Pakistan. In May 1946, they sent a group of leaders to meet with Muhammad Ali Jinnah, the soon-to-be founding president of Pakistan, requesting that the two Muslim-majority townships of Buthidaung and Maungdaw be incorporated into the new Muslim country." While Jinnah declined, eventually, "after Burmese independence in 1948, the mistreatment of Rohingyas by the Burmese military led to admonition by neighboring Pakistan. Many Rohingyas were fleeing to what was then East Pakistan, where they found a population not only receptive to their plight but also responsive through economic and military support for the persecuted. . . . Until the 1971 war leading to the creation of Bangladesh, the cause of the Rohingyas oppressed by the Buddhist majority of Burma was not dissimilar to the struggles of the Bengali Muslims repressed by Urdu-speaking Pakistan. Operation Nagamin of 1978 and the 1982 Citizenship Act by the Ne Win government completed the political and legal otherization of the Rohingyas as we understand today. The former was a Burmese military-led ethnic cleansing leading to over 200,000 fleeing to newly independent Bangladesh using similar routes as those of the refugees in the current conflict. The latter made it impossible for Rohingyas to establish their citizenship in Myanmar till this day." Jayita Sarkar, "Rohingyas and the Unfinished Business of Partition," *Diplomat*, January 16, 2018, accessed on May 5, 2018, Available at https://thediplomat.com/2018/01/rohingyas-and-the-unfinished-business-of-partition/.

55. Kavita Daiya, "The 1947 Partition, War, and Internment: Hidden Histories of Migration and Displacement in Transnational Asia," in *Volume II: Asian American Literature in Transition (1930–1965)*, eds. Victor Bascara and Josephine Nock-Hee Park (New York: Cambridge University Press, forthcoming).

CHAPTER 4

1. Urvashi Butalia, ed., "Partition: The Long Shadow: An Introduction," in *Partition: The Long Shadow* (New Delhi: Zubaan Books, 2015), xviii.

2. Purnima Mankekar, *Unsettling India: Affect, Temporality, Transnationality* (Durham, NC: Duke University Press, 2015), 20.

3. Butalia, "Partition."

4. Mankekar, *Unsettling India*, 20.

5. Shoshana Felman, "Education and Crisis, or the Vicissitudes of Teaching," in *Trauma: Explorations in Memory*, ed. Cathy Caruth (Baltimore: Johns Hopkins University, 1995), 13–60.

6. Smitu Kothari and Zia Mian, eds., "Introduction," in *Bridging Partition: People's Initiatives for Peace between India and Pakistan* (New Delhi: Orient Black Swan, 2010), 6.

7. Ibid., 3.

8. Ibid., 5.

9. Rahul Gairola, "Migrations in Absentia: Multinational Digital Advertising and Manipulation of Partition Trauma," in *Revisiting India's Partition: New Essays on Memory, Culture, and Politics*, ed. Amritjit Singh, Nalini Iyer, and Rahul K. Gairola (Lanham, MD: Lexington Books, 2016), 54.

10. Paul Woodward, "Google's Bold and Deceptive Partition Ad Campaign," *War in Context*, November 17, 2013, available at http://warincontext.org/2013/11/17/googles-bold-and-deceptive-partition-ad-campaign/.

11. Mankekar, *Unsettling India*, 241.

12. Ibid., 228.

13. Ibid., 17.

14. Ibid.

15. "Visa and travel restrictions imposed since the 1965 war (until then, the Karachi Bombay serebii and Lahore Amritsar Road were used freely by Indians and Pakistanis crossing over for weekend shopping trips, to visit relatives and watch films) were much more stringent during the early 1980s. Till early 2007 there was only one visa-issuing authority in all of India for Pakistan and vice versa, although the reopening of their respective consulates in Karachi and Mumbai has been approved in principle. For those not resident in Islamabad or New Delhi, where the embassies are located, the entire process is particularly time-consuming and expensive in terms of transport, and, unless they have relatives in the capital, board and lodging. To compound matters, intelligence agency personnel often harass those appearing at either embassy to apply for visas. These factors are all particularly a problem for women." Beena Sarwar, "Women's Role in Building Peace," in *Bridging Partition: People's Initiatives for Peace between India and Pakistan*, ed. Smitu Kothari and Zia Mian (New Delhi: Orient Black Swan, 2010), 177–178.

16. Beena Sarwar, "Google's Tearjerker 'Reunion' Ad, and the 'Milne Do' Campaign," *Journeys to Democracy*, November 14, 2013, available at https://beenasarwar.com/2013/11/14/googles-tearjerker-reunion-ad-and-the-milne-do-campaign/.

17. Pippa Virdee, *From the Ashes of 1947: Reimagining Punjab* (New York: Cambridge University Press, 2017), xvi.

18. Reproduced with permission from Gulzar's *Footprints on Zero Line: Writings on the Partition of India*, trans. Rakhshanda Jalil (Noida: Harper Perennial, 2018), 23.

19. Akshaya Aradhya, quoted in Palash Ghosh, "'Reunion': Google's Ad Evoking Partition Separation a Big Hit in India and Pakistan," *International Business Times*, November 19, 2013, available at https://www.ibtimes.com/reunion-googles-nasdaq-goog-ad-evoking-partition-separation-big-hit-india-pakistan-video-1477042.

20. https://twitter.com/microMAF/status/400879025498767360.

21. Ravi Vasudevan, *The Melodramatic Public: Film Form and Spectatorship in India* (New York: Palgrave Macmillan, 2011), 42.

22. Ibid., 402.

23. I thank Donna Scarboro for this insight into considering how gender and male friendship work here.

24. Vasudevan maps how "melodrama's maneuvering amongst the intimate and the social realm is relayed through a sensationalized, heightened form of narration. Its methods involve a dizzying density of plot shifts and reversals, emotional peripeteia and a mode of address scaled up in presentation of body, gesture, and speech." Vasudevan, *The Melodramatic Public*, 403.

25. Judith Butler, *Precarious Life: The Powers of Mourning and Violence* (London: Verso, 2004), 37.

26. Graham Clarke, quoted in Gerhard Richter, "Between Translation and Invention: The Photograph in Deconstruction," in *Copy, Archive, Signature: A Conversation on Photography*, ed. Jacques Derrida (Stanford, CA: Stanford University Press, 2010), xxiii.

27. Kamla Bhasin, "A Quarter Century of Building Bridges," in *Bridging Partition: People's Initiatives for Peace between India and Pakistan*, eds. Smitu Kothari and Zia Mian (New Delhi: Orient Black Swan, 2010), 152.

28. Svetlana Boym, *The Off-Modern* (New York: Bloomsbury Publishing, 2017), 81.

29. Saskia Sassen, *Territory, Rights, Assemblages: From Medieval to Global Assemblages* (Princeton, NJ: Princeton University Press, 2008), 390.

30. Viet Thanh Nguyen, *Nothing Ever Dies: Vietnam and the Memory of War* (Cambridge, MA: Harvard University Press, 2016), 13.

31. James Chandler, *An Archaeology of Sympathy: The Sentimental Mode in Literature and Cinema* (Chicago: University of Chicago Press, 2013), 35.

32. Lauren Berlant and Jordan Greenwald, "Affect in the End Times: A Conversation with Lauren Berlant," *Qui Parle* 20, no. 2 (2012): 87.

33. Kavita Daiya, *Violent Belongings: Partition, Gender, and National Culture in Postcolonial India* (Philadelphia: Temple University Press, [2008] 2011).

34. M. S. Sathyu, quoted in Woodward, "Google's Bold and Deceptive Partition Ad Campaign."

35. I thank my student Aqsa Khan for alerting me to this NFL commercial.

36. Veena Das, *Life and Words: Violence and the Descent into the Ordinary* (Berkeley: University of California Press, 2007), 215.

37. Virdee, *From the Ashes of 1947*, 221.

38. Ibid., xxi.

39. Joya Chatterji, *The Spoils of Partition: Bengal and India, 1947–1967* (New York: Cambridge University Press, 2007), 122.

40. "In November 1948, the problems of destitute refugees who sought shelter in camps became more urgent after the government of West Bengal ruled that no able-bodied male refugee could receive 'doles' either for himself or for his dependents for more than seven days after he arrived in West Bengal." Ibid., 122.

41. As she writes, "After this, government and the refugees moved on to a collision course. The ministry came to see the refugees as political undesirables and hardened its stance. Finally in 1964, when scores of new refugees flooded into West Bengal after the Hazratbal incident, the government decided upon its final tactic: henceforth it would not permit any more refugees to settle in West Bengal and it would offer assistance only to those who agreed to go to designated places outside the province. Of the million or more refugees who arrived in India from East Bengal between 1964 and March 1971, most were packed off to colonies or camps in other provinces, hastily constructed by reclaiming wastelands or forest tracts." Ibid., 135. Chatterji's fascinating history remains a landmark account of the experience of refugees in Bengal, one that neatly parses how class and occupation dynamics and rural and urban locations shaped refugee migrations, state policies on refugee rehabilitation, and, ultimately, the sociopolitical outcomes of

Bengali Hindu refugees' resettlement and integration into Indian life. Beyond the scope of this book, a similar historical account of the complex politics and dynamics of refugee experience in the Bombay Presidency is yet to be written.

42. Ranabir Samaddar, ed., *Refugees and the State: Practices of Asylum and Care in India, 1947–2000* (Thousand Oaks, CA: Sage Publications, 2003).

43. Das, *Life and Words*, 220.

44. Gyanendra Pandey, *Remembering Partition: Violence, Nationalism, and History in India* (Cambridge: Cambridge University Press, 2001), 4.

45. Das, *Life and Words*, 210.

46. Ibid., 218.

47. Rita Kothari and other scholars note this ecomelancholic relationship between the loss of land and language for the Sindhi community. See, for instance, Rita Kothari, *The Burden of Refuge: The Sindhi Hindus of Gujarat* (New Delhi: Orient Longman, 2007).

48. Das, *Life and Words*, 218.

49. The Bombay State (previously called the Bombay Presidency and the Bombay Province under British rule, and one of the seventeen main administrative units of British India) was a large section of western India that, in its heyday, included regions that spanned from Sind (until 1935) to Aden (in present-day Yemen) and portions of Karnataka. After 1947, when the Sindh Province became part of Pakistan, the Bombay Province became part of India and, in 1950, was reorganized into the Bombay State. Until its partition in 1960 to create the two states of Maharashtra and Gujarat, the Bombay State included several communities and princely states that acceded to India after 1947, including parts of Gujarat, Konkan, and Karnataka, with its capital being Bombay City.

50. Kavita Daiya, *Violent Belongings: Partition, Gender, and National Culture in Postcolonial India*, 111.

51. See Urvashi Butalia, *The Other Side of Silence: Voices from the Partition of India* (New Delhi: Viking, 1998); and Yasmin Saikia, *Women, War, and the Making of Bangladesh* (Durham, NC: Duke University Press, 2011).

52. Nandita Bhavnani well describes the specific history of the experience of Hindu Sindhis in 1947 and their relatively delayed emigration to India following the Karachi pogroms of 1948. See Bhavnani, *The Making of Exile: Sindhi Hindus and the Partition of India* (Chennai: Tranquebar Press, 2014). See also Rita Kothari's complex account of the experience of Sindhi refugees in post-47 Gujarat: *The Burden of Refuge: The Sindhi Hindus of Gujarat* (New Delhi: Orient Longman, 2007). Also relevant, from the perspective of Karachi, Bombay's "twin" city by the sea in Pakistan, is Sarah Ansari's account of the changing relations between Sindhis and Partition migrations: *Life after Partition: Migration, Community and Strife in Sindh, 1947–1962* (Karachi: Oxford University Press, 2005).

53. In addition to Bhavnani's work, new writing in the news media has recently captured the intimate, local urban history of Mumbai through the settling of Partition migrants. See, for instance, Saaz Aggarwaal, "After Partition, Sindhis Turned Displacement into Determination and Enterprise," *The Wire*, August 11, 2017, available at https://thewire.in/166634/after-partition-displacement-of-sindhis-turned-into-determination-and-enterprise/. See also Chandrima Pal's "Colaba's Sindhi Connection," *Mumbai Mirror*, November 19, 2017, available at https://mumbaimirror.indiatimes.com/others/leisure/colabas-sindhi-connection/articleshow/61706962.cms.

54. Alok Bhalla, *Partition Dialogues: Memories of a Lost Home* (New York: Oxford University Press, 2006), 14.

55. Yasmin Saikia, "Interview," *The Free Library*, 2014, accessed on April 8, 2018, available at https://www.thefreelibrary.com/INTERVIEW.-a0286561779.

56. Veena Das, "Listening to Voices: An Interview with Veena Das," by Kim Turcot DiFruscia, *Altérités* 7, no. 1 (2010): 137.

57. Virdee, *From the Ashes of 1947*, 230.

58. Kothari, *The Burden of Refuge*.

59. Matthew Artz, "Partition Violence Still Haunts South Asians," *East Bay Times*, August 12, 2011, available at https://www.eastbaytimes.com/2011/08/12/partition-violence-still-haunts-south-asians/. See also http://bayareadesi.com/article/spotlight-1947-partition-archive-npo-ded. More press articles since 2011 can be found at the archive's own media page, available at http://www.1947partitionarchive.org/?q=in_the_news.

60. Raj Aditya-Chaudhuri and Smitha Menon, "The People of Partition Are Now a Click Away," *Conde Nast Traveller*, August 14, 2017, available at http://www.cntraveller.in/story/people-partition-now-click-away/#s-cust0/.

61. "Explore the Personal Stories of Partition," 1947 Partition Archive, Stanford University Libraries, available at https://exhibits.stanford.edu/1947-partition.

62. "We are concerned global citizens committed to preserving this chapter of our collective history. We come from diverse cultural and religious backgrounds, nationalities, and professions. It is our view that a strong foundation in history will pave the way for a more enlightened future for the subcontinent and hence the world. At the moment our team consists of 100% volunteer based staff, interns, advisers and experts who are passionate about preserving the people's history of Partition." See https://www.1947partitionarchive.org/about.

63. "1.) Documenting, preserving and sharing eye witness accounts from *all* ethnic, religious, and economic communities affected by the Partition of British India in 1947. *To do this, we have created a digital platform for anyone anywhere in the world to collect, archive, and display oral histories that document not only Partition, but pre-Partition life and culture as well as post-Partition migrations and life changes.*

"2.) Collecting, preserving, and sharing personal items and artifacts associated with the people's memory of the 1947 Partition.

"3.) Bringing knowledge of Partition into widespread public consciousness through i.) creative and scholarly expression including but not limited to literature, film, theater, visual arts, other creative medium, and academic research; ii.) proactive worldwide primary education curricula; iii.) traveling exhibits as well as physical 'Centers for Learning' designed to memorialize the people's history of Partition and serve the public for research and educational purposes. *Presently, a portion of our collected works are being made available in limited capacity via our online Story Map* [italics original]." See https://www.1947partitionarchive.org/mission.

64. Lalita Ramdas, "Dismantling Prejudice: The Challenges for Education," in *Bridging Partition: People's Initiatives for Peace between India and Pakistan*, ed. Smitu Kothari and Zia Mian (New Delhi: Orient Black Swan, 2010), 217.

65. T. Lloyd Bens, "Geohistory Crowdsourcing and Democratizing the Landscape of Battle," *Journal of the Civil War Era* 2, no. 4 (2012): 587–588.

66. Ashwaq Masoodi, "Partition through the Eyes of Women," *Livemint*, August 15, 2017, available at http://www.livemint.com/Politics/OobQ0j4Sj7eBjsLopbemHM/Partition-through-the-eyes-of-women.html/.

67. "This Collection," The 1947 Partition Archive, Stanford University Libraries, available at https://exhibits.stanford.edu/1947-partition/about/this-collection.

68. Guneeta Singh Bhalla, "Inside Sundarbans: Wildlife and Climate Displacements Haunt Partition Refugees," *Economic Times*, August 24, 2018.

69. Annu Palakunnuthu Matthew, email message to author, March 4, 2018.
70. Ibid.
71. The photo animations can also be seen at http://www.annumatthew.com.
72. Butler, *Precarious Life*, 30.
73. Ibid.
74. "Open Wound—Stories of Partition—Pakistan," Annu Palakunnathu Matthew, available at http://www.annumatthew.com/gallery/open-wound-pakistan/.
75. Matthew, email message.
76. As Holland Cotter recently wrote in the *New York Times*, "The mostly album-size photographs in this compact but far-ranging gallery survey are about the intensities and confusions of a cultural mixing that makes the artist, psychologically, both a global citizen and an outsider, at home and in transit, wherever she is. And it's about photography as document and fiction: souvenir, re-enactment and imaginative projection. A beautiful show that could too easily slip away." See "Museum and Gallery Listings for Dec. 25–31," available at https://www.nytimes.com/2015/12/25/arts/design/museum-amp-gallery-listings-for-dec-25-31.html.
77. "About the Founder," *The Memory Company Presents Indian Memory Project*, The Indian Memory Project, available at http://www.indianmemoryproject.com/about-the-founder/.
78. Homa Khaleeli, "Sharmeen Obaid-Chinoy: 'I Know There Will Be an Attempt to Silence Me,'" *Guardian*, June 27, 2017.
79. Anam Zakaria, *The Footprints of Partition: Narratives of Four Generations of Pakistanis and Indians* (New Delhi: HarperCollins, 2015).

CONCLUSION

1. Leela Gandhi and Deborah L. Nelson, "Editors' Introduction," *Critical Inquiry* 40, no. 4 (Summer 2014): 287.
2. Lisa Lowe, *The Intimacies of Four Continents* (Durham, NC: Duke University Press, 2015), 207.
3. Ibid., 175.
4. Homi Bhabha, "Migration, Rights, and Survival: The Importance of the Humanities Today," *European South* 3 (2018): 11.
5. Warsan Shire, "Home," *Facing History and Ourselves*, accessed on December 9, 2019, available at https://www.facinghistory.org/standing-up-hatred-intolerance/warsan-shire-home.

Bibliography

"About the Founder." *The Memory Company Presents Indian Memory Project*. The Indian Memory Project. Available at http://www.indianmemoryproject.com/about-the-founder/.

Aditya-Chaudhuri, Raj, and Smitha Menon. "The People of Partition Are Now a Click Away." *Conde Nast Traveller*, August 14, 2017. Available at www.cntraveller.in/story/people-partition-now-click-away/#s-cust0/.

Agamben, Giorgio. *Homo Sacer: Sovereign Power and Bare Life*. Stanford: Stanford University Press, 1998.

Aggarwaal, Saaz. "After Partition, Sindhis Turned Displacement into Determination and Enterprise." *The Wire*, August 11, 2017. Available at https://thewire.in/166634/after-partition-displacement-of-sindhis-turned-into-determination-and-enterprise/.

Alam, Ahmad Rafay, and Martand Khosla, "90 Upper Mall or 1 Bawa Park." In *This Side, That Side: Restorying Partition*, edited by Vishwajyoti Ghosh, 177–189. New Delhi: Yoda Press, 2013.

Amrith, Sunil. *Crossing the Bay of Bengal: The Furies of Nature and the Fates of Migrants*. Cambridge, MA: Harvard University Press, 2015.

Anam, Tahmima. *A Golden Age*. New York: HarperCollins, 2007.

Anderson, Benedict. *Imagined Communities: Reflections on the Origin and Spread of Nationalism*. London: Verso, 1982.

Anjaria, Ulka. *Realism in the Twentieth-Century Indian Novel: Colonial Difference and Literary Form*. New York: Cambridge University Press, 2012.

Ansari, Sarah F.D. *Life after Partition: Migration, Community and Strife in Sindh, 1947–1962*. Karachi, Pakistan: Oxford University Press, 2005.

Arendt, Hannah. *Imperialism*. New York: Harcourt, Brace and World, 1968.

———. *The Origins of Totalitarianism*. New York: Harcourt, Brace and World, 1968.

———. "We Refugees." In *The Jewish Writings*, edited by Jerome Kohn and Ron H. Feldman, 264–274. New York: Schocken Books, 2007. Available at https://www.jus.uio.no/smr/om/aktuelt/arrangementer/2015/arendt-we-refugees.pdf.

Armstrong, Nancy. *Fiction in the Age of Photography: The Legacy of British Realism.* Cambridge, MA: Harvard University Press, 1999.

Arora, Kim. "Vishwajyoti Ghosh: Partition Is Marked by Memories, Speculation—and Curiosity." *Times of India,* August 28, 2013. Available at http://timesofindia.indiatimes.com/interviews/Vishwajyoti-Ghosh-Partition-is-marked-by-memories-speculation-and-curiosity/articleshow/22101779.cms.

Artz, Matthew. "Partition Violence Still Haunts South Asians." *East Bay Times,* August 12, 2011. Available at https://www.eastbaytimes.com/2011/08/12/partition-violence-still-haunts-south-asians/.

Asad, Talal. *Formations of the Secular: Christianity, Islam, Modernity.* Stanford, CA: Stanford University Press, 2003.

———. *Secular Translations: Nation State, Modern Self, and Calculative Reason.* New York: Columbia University Press, 2018.

"As Europe Battles over Border Policy, Migrants Flood to Spain." *PBS Newshour.* Available at https://www.thirteen.org/programs/pbs-newshour/desperate-journey-1539989195/.

Babb, Lawrence A., and Susan S. Wadley, eds. *Media and the Transformation of Religion in South Asia.* Delhi: Motlal Banarsidass, 1998.

Baetens, Jan, and Hugo Frey. *The Graphic Novel: An Introduction.* Cambridge: Cambridge University Press, 2014.

Bagchi, Jasodhara. *The Trauma and the Triumph: Gender and Partition in Eastern India.* Kolkata: Stree Books, 2003.

Bahri, Deepika. *Native Intelligence: Aesthetics, Politics, and Postcolonial Literature.* Minneapolis: University of Minnesota Press, 2003.

Baishya, Amit R. "Endangered (and Endangering) Species: Exploring the Animacy Hierarchy in Malik Sajad's *Munnu.*" In *Graphic Narratives about South Asia and South Asian America: Aesthetics and Politics,* edited by Kavita Daiya, 50–69. London: Routledge, 2019.

Baldwin, Shauna Singh. *What the Body Remembers: A Novel.* New York: Doubleday, 1999.

Basu, Lopamudra. *Ayad Akhtar, the American Nation, and Its Others after 9/11: Homeland Insecurity.* Lanham, MD: Lexington Books, 2018.

Beitz, Charles. *The Idea of Human Rights.* New York: Oxford University Press, 2009.

Benegal, Shyam, dir. *Mammo.* DVD. Delhi: Sky, 1995.

Benjamin, Walter. "The Storyteller." In *Illuminations: Essays and Reflections,* edited by Hannah Arendt, 83–110. New York: Schocken Books, 1988.

Bens, T. Lloyd. "Geohistory Crowdsourcing and Democratizing the Landscape of Battle." *Journal of the Civil War Era* 2, no. 4 (2012): 586–597.

Berlant, Lauren. "Intimacy: A Special Issue." *Critical Inquiry* 24, no. 2 (1998): 281–288.

———. "Slow Death (Sovereignty, Obesity, Lateral Agency)." *Critical Inquiry* 33, no. 4 (2007): 754–780.

Berlant, Lauren, and Jordan Greenwald. "Affect in the End Times: A Conversation with Lauren Berlant." *Qui Parle* 20, no. 2 (2012): 71–89.

Berlant, Lauren, and Michael Warner. "Sex in Public." *Intimacy,* edited by Lauren Berlant, 311–330. Chicago: University of Chicago Press, 2000.

Bhabha, Homi. *The Location of Culture.* New York: Routledge, 1994.

———. "Migration, Rights, and Survival: The Importance of the Humanities Today." *From the European South* 3 (2018): 7–12.

Bhalla, Alok. *Partition Dialogues: Memories of a Lost Home.* New York: Oxford University Press, 2006.

Bhalla, Guneeta Singh. "Inside Sundarbans: Wildlife and Climate Displacements Haunt Partition Refugees." *Economic Times*, August 24, 2018.
Bhan, Mona. *Counterinsurgency, Democracy, and the Politics of Identity in India: From Warfare to Welfare?* New York: Routledge, 2014.
Bhargava, Rajeev. *Secularism and Its Critics (Themes in Politics)*. Delhi: Oxford University Press, 2005.
Bhasin, Kamla. "A Quarter Century of Building Bridges." In *Bridging Partition: People's Initiatives for Peace between India and Pakistan*, edited by Smithu Kotari and Zia Mian, 151–168. New Delhi: Orient Black Swan, 2010.
Bhavnani, Nandita. *The Making of Exile: Sindhi Hindus and the Partition of India*. Chennai: Tranquebar Press, 2014.
Bose, Sarmila. *Dead Reckoning: Memories of the 1971 Bangladesh War*. London: Hurst, 2011.
Bose, Sumantra. *Secular States, Religious Politics: India, Turkey, and the Future of Secularism*. Cambridge: Cambridge University Press, 2018.
Boym, Svetlana. *The Future of Nostalgia*. New York: Basic Books, 2001.
———. *The Off-Modern*. New York: Bloomsbury Publishing, 2017.
———. "On Diasporic Intimacy: Ilya Kabokov's Installations and Immigrant Homes." In *Intimacy*, edited by Lauren Berlant, 226–252. Chicago: University of Chicago Press, 2000.
Brown, Wendy. "Reclaiming Democracy: An Interview with Wendy Brown on Occupy, Sovereignty, and Secularism." By Robin Celikates and Yolande Jansen. *Critical Legal Thinking*, January 30, 2013. Available at http://criticallegalthinking.com/2013/01/30/reclaiming-democracy-an-interview-with-wendy-brown-on-occupy-sovereignty-and-secularism/.
———. *Walled States, Waning Sovereignty*. Brooklyn: Zone Books, 2014.
Buck-Morss, Susan. "Aesthetics and Anaesthetics: Walter Benjamin's Artwork Essay Reconsidered." *October* 62 (Autumn 1992): 3–41.
———. *The Dialectics of Seeing: Walter Benjamin and the Arcades Project*. Cambridge: Massachusetts Institute of Technology Press, 1991.
Bunsha, Dionne, and Homai Vyarawalla. "History in Black and White." *Frontline* 22, no. 17 (2005). Available at https://frontline.thehindu.com/other/article30205888.ece.
Butalia, Urvashi. *The Other Side of Silence: Voices from the Partition of India*. New Delhi: Viking, 1998.
———, ed. "Partition: The Long Shadow: An Introduction." In *Partition: The Long Shadow*, vii–xviii. New Delhi: Zubaan Books, 2015.
Butler, Judith. *Frames of War: When Is Life Grievable?* London: Verso, 2009.
———. "Is Judaism Zionism?" In *The Power of Religion in the Public Sphere*, edited by Eduardo Mendieta and Jonathan Vanantwerpen, 70–91. New York: Social Science Research Council and Columbia University Press, 2011.
———. *Precarious Life: The Powers of Mourning and Violence*. London: Verso, 2004.
———. "Precarity Talk." *TDR: The Drama Review* 56, no. 4 (2012): 163–177.
Caruth, Cathy, ed. "Trauma and Experience: Introduction." In *Trauma: Explorations in Memory*, 3–12. Baltimore: Johns Hopkins University Press, 1995.
Chakrabarty, Dipesh. "Modernity and Ethnicity in India: A History for the Present." *Economic and Political Weekly* 30, no. 52 (December 30, 1995): 3373–3380.
———. *Provincializing Europe: Postcolonial Thought and Historical Difference*. Princeton, NJ: Princeton University Press, 2000.

———. "Remembered Villages: Representations of Hindu-Bengali Memories in the Aftermath of the Partition." *Economic and Political Weekly* 31 (1996): 1221–1125.

Chandler, James. *An Archaeology of Sympathy: The Sentimental Mode in Literature and Cinema.* Chicago: University of Chicago Press, 2013.

Chandra, Nandini. *The Classic Popular: Amar Chitra Katha, 1967–2007.* New Delhi: Yoda Press, 2008.

Chatterjee, Partha. *The Nation and Its Fragments: Colonial and Postcolonial Histories.* Princeton, NJ: Princeton University Press, 1993.

Chatterji, Angana P., Thomas Blom Hansen, and Christophe Jaffrelot, ed. *Majoritarian State: How Hindu Nationalism Is Changing India.* New Delhi: HarperCollins, 2019.

Chatterji, Joya. *Bengal Divided: Hindu Communalism and Partition, 1932–1947.* Cambridge: Cambridge University Press, 1994.

———. *The Spoils of Partition: Bengal and India, 1947–1967.* New York: Cambridge University Press, 2007.

Chaturvedi, Rakesh Mohan. "Jammu's West Pakistan Refugees to Hold a Rally to Thank Govt." *Economic Times,* August 31, 2019. Available at https://economictimes.indiatimes.com/news/politics-and-nation/jammus-west-pak-refugees-to-hold-a-rally-to-thank-govt/articleshow/70918574.cms?from=mdr.

Cheah, Pheng. *What Is a World? On Postcolonial Literature as World Literature.* Durham, NC: Duke University Press, 2016.

Chiu, Monica. *Drawing New Color Lines: Transnational Asian American Graphic Narratives.* Hong Kong: Hong Kong University Press, 2015.

Chopra, Anupama. "Delhi-6." Review of *Delhi-6,* directed by Rakeysh Omprakash Mehra. NDTV Movies, March 7, 2014. Available at http://movies.ndtv.com/movie-reviews/delhi-6-379.

———. "Tears, Cheers." Review of *Bajrangi Bhaijaan,* directed by Kabir Khan. *Hindustan Times,* September 22, 2015.

Chute, Hillary. *Disaster Drawn: Visual Witness, Comics, and Documentary Form.* Cambridge, MA: Belknap Press of Harvard University Press, 2016.

———. *Graphic Women: Life Narratives and Contemporary Comics.* New York: Columbia University Press, 2010.

———. *Why Comics? From Underground to Everywhere.* New York: HarperCollins, 2017.

Chute, Hillary, and Patrick Jagoda, eds. "Special Issue: Comics and Media" *Critical Inquiry* 40, no. 3 (Spring 2014): 1–10.

Copson, Andrew. *Secularism: Politics, Religion, and Freedom.* Oxford: Oxford University Press, 2017.

Corruccini, Robert S., and Samvit S. Kaul. *Halla: Demographic Consequences of the Partition of the Punjab, 1947.* Lanham, MD: University Press of America, 1990.

Cotter, Holland. "Museum and Gallery Listings for Dec. 25-31." *New York Times,* December 24, 2015. Available at https://www.nytimes.com/2015/12/25/arts/design/museum-amp-gallery-listings-for-dec-25-31.html.

Cutter, Martha J., and Cathy J. Schlund-Vials, eds. "Introduction." In *Redrawing the Historical Past: History, Memory, and Multiethnic Graphic Novels,* 1–17. Athens: University of Georgia Press, 2018.

Dadi, Iftikhar, and Hamad Nasar, eds. *Lines of Control: Partition as a Productive Space.* London: Green Cardamom and Herbert F. Johnson Museum of Art, 2012.

Daiya, Kavita. "Gender, Sexuality and the Family in South-Asian Fiction." In *Oxford History of the Novel in English (Volume 10). The Novel in South and South-East Asia,* edited by Alex Tickell, 44–57. Oxford: Oxford University Press, 2018.

———, ed. "Introduction: South Asia in Graphic Narratives." In *Graphic Narratives about South Asia and South Asian America: Aesthetics and Politics*, 3–10. London: Routledge, 2019.

———. "The 1947 Partition, War, and Internment: Hidden Histories of Migration and Displacement in Transnational Asia." In *Volume II: Asian American Literature in Transition (1930–1965)*, edited by Victor Bascara and Josephine Hock-Nee Park. New York: Cambridge University Press, forthcoming.

———. "Partition." In *Blackwell Encyclopedia of Postcolonial Studies*, edited by Sangeeta Ray and Henry Schwarz, 1278–1286. London: Wiley-Blackwell, 2016.

———. "Provincializing America: Engaging Postcolonial Critique and Asian American Studies in a Transnational Mode." *South Asian Review* 26, no. 2 (December 2005): 265–275.

———. "Refugees, Gender and Secularism in South Asian Literature and Cinema." In *Representations of War, Migration and Refugeehood: Interdisciplinary Perspectives*, edited by Daniel Rellstab and Christiane Schlote, 263–280. New York: Routledge, 2014.

———. *Violent Belongings: Partition, Gender, and National Culture in Postcolonial India*. Philadelphia: Temple University Press, 2008, 2011.

———. "Visual Culture and Violence: Inventing Intimacy and Citizenship in Recent South Asian Cinema." *South Asian History and Culture* 2, no. 4 (2011): 589–604.

———. "The World after Empire; or, Whither Postcoloniality?" *PMLA* 132, no. 1 (May 2017): 149–155.

Das, Srijana Mitra. "Bajrangi Bhaijaan Movie Review." Review of *Bajrangi Bhaijaan*, directed by Kabir Khan. *Times of India*, July 17, 2015.

Das, Veena. *Life and Words: Violence and the Descent into the Ordinary*. Berkeley: University of California Press, 2007.

———. "Listening to Voices: An Interview with Veena Das." By Kim Turcot DiFruscia. *Altérités* 7, no. 1 (2010): 136–145.

Didur, Jill. *Unsettling Partition: Literature, Gender, Memory*. Toronto: University of Toronto Press, 2006.

Dubnov, Arie M., and Robson, Laura, eds. "Introduction: Drawing the Line, Writing beyond It: Toward a Transnational History of Partitions." In *Partitions: A Transnational History of Twentieth-Century Territorial Separatism*, 1–30. Stanford, CA: Stanford University Press, 2019.

Dwyer, Rachel. *Filming the Gods: Religion and Indian Cinema*. London: Routledge, 2006.

Eisner, Will. *Comics and Sequential Comics and Sequential Art*. New York: Poorhouse Press, 1985.

Elison, William, Christian Lee Novetzke, and Andy Rotman. *Amar Akbar Anthony: Bollywood, Brotherhood, and the Nation*. Cambridge, MA: Harvard University Press, 2016.

Ellis-Petersen, Hannah, and Manoj Chaurasia. "India Racked by Greatest Exodus since Partition due to Coronavirus." *Guardian*, March 30, 2020. Available at https://www.theguardian.com/world/2020/mar/30/india-wracked-by-greatest-exodus-since-partition-due-to-coronavirus.

Elsaesser, Thomas. "Tales of Sound and Fury: Observations on the Family Melodrama." In *Imitations of Life: A Reader on Film and Television Melodrama*, edited by Marcia Langly, 68–91. Detroit: Wayne State University Press, 1991.

Eng, David, and David Kanzanjian, eds. *Loss: The Politics of Mourning*. Berkeley: University of California Press, 2002.

Espiritu, Yến Lê. *Body Counts: The Vietnam War and Militarized Refugees.* Berkeley: University of California Press, 2014.

———. "Toward a Critical Refugee Study: The Vietnamese Refugee Subject in US Scholarship." *Journal of Vietnamese Studies* 1, no. 1–2 (February/August 2006): 410–433.

"Explore the Personal Stories of Partition." 1947 Partition Archive, Stanford University Libraries. Available at https://exhibits.stanford.edu/1947-partition.

Faesal, Shah. "What a Spy Thriller Teaches Us about Patriotism and Empathy." *Times of India*, May 27, 2018. Available at https://timesofindia.indiatimes.com/home/sunday-times/all-that-matters/what-a-spy-thriller-teaches-us-about-patriotism-and-empathy/articleshow/64335499.cms.

Farhana, Syeda, and Nitesh Mohanty. "Little Women." In *This Side, That Side: Restorying Partition*, edited by Vishwajyoti Ghosh, 259–273. New Delhi: Yoda Press, 2013.

Fatah, Sonya, and Archana Sreenivasan, "Karachi Delhi Katha." In *This Side, That Side: Restorying Partition*, edited by Vishwajyoti Ghosh, 191–205. New Delhi: Yoda Press, 2013.

Felman, Shoshana. "Education and Crisis, or the Vicissitudes of Teaching." In *Trauma: Explorations in Memory*, edited by Cathy Caruth, 13–60 Baltimore: Johns Hopkins University Press, 1995.

French, Patrick. *Liberty or Death: India's Journey to Independence and Division.* London: HarperCollins, 1997.

Gairola, Rahul. "Migrations in Absentia: Multinational Digital Advertising and Manipulation of Partition Trauma." In *Revisiting India's Partition: New Essays on Memory, Culture, and Politics*, edited by Amritjit Singh, Nalini Iyer, and Rahul K. Gairola, 53–70. Lanham, MD: Lexington Books, 2016.

Gandhi, Leela, and Deborah L. Nelson. "Editors' Introduction." *Critical Inquiry* 40, no. 4 (Summer 2014): 285–297.

Ganti, Tejaswini. *Bollywood: A Guidebook to Contemporary Cinema.* New York: Routledge, 2013.

Ghosh, Arundhati, and Appupen. "Water Stories." In *This Side, That Side: Restorying Partition*, edited by Vishwajyoti Ghosh, 129–135. New Delhi: Yoda Press, 2013.

Ghosh, Palash. "'Reunion': Google's Ad Evoking Partition Separation a Big Hit in India and Pakistan." *International Business Times*, November 19, 2013. Available at https://www.ibtimes.com/reunion-googles-nasdaq-goog-ad-evoking-partition-separation-big-hit-india-pakistan-video-1477042.

Ghosh, Vishwajyoti. "Inverted Calm: An Interview with Vishwajyoti Ghosh." By Ryan Holmberg. *The Comics Journal*, October 23, 2013. Available at http://www.tcj.com/inverted-calm-an-interview-with-vishwajyoti-ghosh/.

———, ed. *This Side, That Side: Restorying Partition.* Delhi: Yoda Press, 2013.

Gilroy, Paul. *Postcolonial Melancholia.* New York: Columbia University Press, 2004.

Green-Lewis, Jennifer. *Framing the Victorians: Photography and the Culture of Realism.* Ithaca, NY: Cornell University Press, 1996.

———. *Victorian Photography, Literature, and the Invention of Modern Memory: Already the Past.* New York: Bloomsbury, 2017.

Gulzar. *Footprints on Zero Line: Writings on the Partition of India.* Translated by Rakhshanda Jalil. Noida: Harper Perennial, 2018.

Gulzar, Govind Nihalani, and Saibal Chatterjee, ed. *Encyclopaedia of Hindi Cinema.* Mumbai: Prakashan, 2003.

Gupta, Aditi, and Rajat Mittal. "The Taboo." In *This Side, That Side: Restorying Partition*, edited by Vishwajyoti Ghosh, 235–247. New Delhi: Yoda Press, 2013.

Hajari, Nisid. *Midnight's Furies: The Deadly Legacy of India's Partition.* New York: Houghton Mifflin Harcourt, 2015.
Hall, Stuart. "Cultural Identity and Diaspora." In *Colonial Discourse and Political Theory,* edited by Patrick Williams and Laura Chrisman, 392–403. New York: Harvester Wheatsheaf, 1993.
Harikrishnan, Charmi. "Fiction Not Being Real Undermines Fiction: Arundhati Roy." *Economic Times,* June 2, 2017.
Hasan, M., and Sukanya Ghosh. "Making of a Poet." In *This Side, That Side: Restorying Partition,* edited by Vishwajyoti Ghosh, 137–147. New Delhi: Yoda Press, 2013.
Hasan, Mushirul. *Moderate or Militant: Images of India's Muslims.* Delhi: Oxford University Press, 2008.
Immel, Andrea. "Frederick Lock's Scrapbook: Patterns in the Pictures and Writings in the Margins." *The Lion and the Unicorn* 29, no. 1 (2005): 65–85.
Iqbal, Sheikh Zaffar. "Race to Take Credit as Refugees in Jammu and Kashmir Get Settlement Funds." NDTV, November 11, 2017. Available at https://www.ndtv.com/india-news/race-to-take-credit-as-refugees-in-jammu-and-kashmir-get-settlement-funds-1774257.
Jain, Anupama. *How to Be South Asian in America: Narratives of Ambivalence and Belonging.* Philadelphia: Temple University Press, 2011.
Jain, Kajri. *Gods in the Bazaar: The Economies of Indian Calendar Art.* Durham, NC: Duke University Press, 2007.
Jalal, Ayesha. *The Pity of Partition: Manto's Life, Times, and Work across the India-Pakistan Divide.* Princeton, NJ: Princeton University Press, 2013.
James, Jennifer. "Ecomelancholia: Slavery, War, and the Black Ecological Imaginings." *Environmental Criticism for the Twenty-First Century,* edited by Stephanie LeMenager, Teresa Shrewry, and Ken Hiltner, 163–178. New York: Routledge, 2011.
Jayawardena, Kumari, and Malathi de Alwis, eds. *Embodied Violence: Communalising Women's Sexuality in South Asia.* London: Zed Books, 1996.
Joshi, Priya. *Bollywood's India: A Public Fantasy.* New York: Columbia University Press, 2015.
Kamra, Sukeshi. *Bearing Witness: Partition, Independence, End of the Raj.* Calgary: University of Calgary Press, 2002.
Karampelas, Gabriella. "70 Years Later, Tales from the World's Largest Refugee Crisis Find a Home at Stanford Libraries." Stanford University Libraries, August 11, 2017. http://library.stanford.edu/node/122490.
"Kartarpur Corridor: India Pilgrims in Historic Visit to Pakistan Temple." *BBC,* November 9, 2019. Available at https://www.bbc.com/news/world-asia-india-50342319.
Kaul, Suvir. *Of Gardens and Graves: Kashmir, Poetry, Politics.* Durham, NC: Duke University Press, 2017.
Khaleeli, Homa. "Sharmeen Obaid-Chinoy: 'I Know There Will Be an Attempt to Silence Me.'" *Guardian,* June 27, 2017.
Khan, Kabir, dir., *Bajrangi Bhaijaan.* DVD. Mumbai: Eros, 2015.
Khan, Yasmin. *The Great Partition: The Making of India and Pakistan.* New Haven, CT: Yale University Press, 2008.
Khandelwal, Peeyush. 2013. "Muzaffarnagar Riots: News of Death Shadows Fleeing Refugees." *Hindustan Times,* September 13, 2013. Available at https://www.hindustantimes.com/india/muzaffarnagar-riots-news-of-death-shadows-fleeing-refugees/story-aWg7Twze3eRqkHHFh5sRQM.html.

Khanna, Ranjana. "Ethical Ambiguities and Specters of Colonialism." In *Feminist Consequences: Theory for the New Century*, edited by Elisabeth Bronfen and Misha Kavka, 111–125. New York: Columbia University Press, 2001.
Kothari, Rita. *The Burden of Refuge: The Sindhi Hindus of Gujarat*. New Delhi: Orient Longman, 2007.
Kothari, Smitu, and Zia Mian, eds. *Bridging Partition: People's Initiatives for Peace between India and Pakistan*. New Delhi: Orient Black Swan, 2010.
Kumar, Priya. *Limiting Secularism: The Ethics of Coexistence in Indian Literature and Film*. Minneapolis: University of Minnesota Press, 2008.
Kumar, Radha. *The History of Doing: An Illustrated Account of Movements for Women's Rights and Feminism in India 1800–1990*. New Delhi: Zubaan Books, 1997.
Kumar, Ravish, Ikroop Sandhu, and Shveta Sarda. "Which Side?" In *This Side, That Side: Restorying Partition*, edited by Vishwajyoti Ghosh, 51–57. New Delhi: Yoda Press, 2013.
Litwa, Maria M. "Welcome to Geneva Camp." In *This Side, That Side: Restorying Partition*, edited by Vishwajyoti Ghosh, 249–257. New Delhi: Yoda Press, 2013.
Lokhande, Sanjeevini Badigar. *Communal Violence, Forced Migration, and the State: Gujarat since 2002*. Cambridge: Cambridge University Press, 2016.
Loomba, Ania and Ritty A. Lukose, eds. *South Asian Feminisms: Contemporary Interventions*. Durham, NC: Duke University Press, 2012.
Lowe, Lisa. *The Intimacies of Four Continents*. Durham, NC: Duke University Press, 2015.
Mahajan, Karan. *The Association of Small Bombs*. New York: Penguin Books, 2016.
Mahmood, Saba. *Religious Difference in a Secular Age: A Minority Report*. Princeton, NJ: Princeton University Press, 2015.
———. "Secularism, Sovereignty, and Religious Difference: A Global Genealogy?" *Society and Space* 35, no. 2 (2017): 197–209.
Malhotra, Aanchal. *Remnants of a Separation: A History of the Partition through Material Memory*. New York: HarperCollins, 2017.
Malkki, Liisa. *Purity and Exile: Violence, Memory, and National Cosmology among Hutu Refugees in Tanzania*. Chicago: Chicago University Press, 1995.
Mankekar, Purnima. *Unsettling India: Affect, Temporality, Transnationality*. Durham, NC: Duke University Press, 2015.
Masand, Rajeev. "*Delhi-6*, a Film with Heart." *news18.com*, February 21, 2009. Available at https://www.news18.com/videos/india/now-showing-54-309381.html.
Masoodi, Ashwaq. "Partition through the Eyes of Women." *Livemint*, August 15, 2017. Available at http://www.livemint.com/Politics/OobQ0j4Sj7eBjsLopbemHM/Partition-through-the-eyes-of-women.html/.
Mathew, Biju, and Vijay Prashad. "The Protean Forms of Yankee Hindutva." *Ethnic and Racial Studies* 23, no. 3 (2000): 516–534.
Matthew, Annu Palakunnathu. Official website and online gallery available at: http://www.annumatthew.com/.
McLain, Karline. *India's Immortal Comic Books: Gods, Kings, and Other Heroes*. Bloomington: Indiana University Press, 2009.
Mehra, Rakeysh Omprakash, dir. *Delhi-6*. DVD. Mumbai: Eros Entertainment, 2009.
Mehta, Deepa, dir. *Earth*. DVD. Mumbai: Eros Entertainment, 1998.
Menon, Jisha. *The Performance of Nationalism: India, Pakistan, and the Memory of Partition*. New York: Cambridge University Press, 2012.

Menon, Ritu, and Kamla Bhasin. *Borders and Boundaries: Women in India's Partition.* New Brunswick: Rutgers University Press, 1998.
Menozzi, Filippo. "'Too Much Blood for Good Literature': Arundhati Roy's *The Ministry of Utmost Happiness* and the Question of Realism." *Journal of Postcolonial Writing* 55, no. 1 (2018): 20–33.
Mishra, Vijay. *Bollywood Cinema: Temples of Desire.* New York: Routledge, 2002.
Misri, Deepti. *Beyond Partition: Gender, Violence, and Representation in Postcolonial India.* Urbana: University of Illinois Press, 2014.
Mondal, Anshuman. "The Limits of Secularism and the Construction of Composite National Identity in India." *Alternative Indias: Writing, Nation, and Communalism,* edited by Peter Morey and Alex Tickell, 1–24. Amsterdam: Editions Rodopi, 2005.
Mowtushi, Mahruba. "The Urban Experience of Displacement: Re-viewing Dhaka through Street Art and Graphic Narrative." In *Graphic Narratives about South Asia and South Asian America: Aesthetics and Politics,* edited by Kavita Daiya, 227–238. London: Routledge, 2019.
Mukherjee, Ankhi. *What Is a Classic? Postcolonial Rewriting and Invention of the Canon.* Palo Alto, CA: Stanford University Press, 2014.
Mukherjee, Upamanyu Pablo. *Postcolonial Environments: Nature, Culture, and the Contemporary Indian Novel in English.* New York: Palgrave MacMillan, 2010.
Murthy, Bharath. "An Art without a Tradition: A Survey of Indian Comics." *Marg Magazine* 61, no. 2 (December 2009): 38–53.
Muthukumar, K. "Godrej Group—Enterprise, Ethics: The Two Pillars of an Empire." *Hindu Business Line,* August 17, 2016. Updated March 10, 2018. Available at https://www.thehindubusinessline.com/specials/godrej-group-enterprise-ethics-the-two-pillars-of-an-empire/article21689683.ece1.
Nadkarni, Asha. *Eugenic Feminism: Reproductive Nationalism in the United States and India.* Minneapolis: University of Minnesota Press, 2014.
Naeem, Asma. "Partition and the Mobilities of Margaret Bourke-White and Zarina." *American Art* 31, no. 2 (Summer 2017): 81–88.
Naficy, Hamid. *An Accented Cinema: Exilic and Diasporic Filmmaking.* Princeton, NJ: Princeton University Press, 2001.
Naim, C. M. *Ambiguities of Heritage: Fictions and Polemics.* Karachi: City Press, 1999.
Nair, Neeti. *Changing Homelands: Hindu Politics and the Partition of India.* Cambridge, MA: Harvard University Press, 2011.
Nandy, Ashis. *The Intimate Enemy: Loss and Recovery of Self under Colonialism.* Oxford: Oxford University Press, 2010.
Nasrin, Taslima. *Lajja: Shame.* New Delhi: Penguin India, 2014.
Nayar, Pramod K. *The Indian Graphic Novel: Nation, History, and Critique.* New York: Routledge, 2016.
Needham, Anuradha Dinwaney. *New Indian Cinema in Post-independence India: The Cultural Work of Shyam Benegal's Films.* New York: Routledge, 2013.
Needham, Anuradha Dingwaney, and Rajeswari Sunder Rajan, eds. *The Crisis of Secularism in India.* Durham, NC: Duke University Press, 2007.
Negt, Oskar, and Alexander Kluge. *The Public Sphere and Experience: Toward an Analysis of the Bourgeois and Proletarian Public Sphere.* Translated by Peter Labanyi. London: Verso, 2016.

Nguyen, Mimi Thi. *The Gift of Freedom: War, Debt, and Other Refugee Passages*. Durham, NC: Duke University Press, 2012.
Nguyen, Viet Thanh. *Nothing Ever Dies: Vietnam and the Memory of War*. Cambridge, MA: Harvard University Press, 2016.
Nixon, Rob. *Slow Violence and the Environmentalism of the Poor*. Cambridge, MA: Harvard University Press, 2011.
Norland, Rod. "A Mass Migration Crisis, and It May Yet Get Worse." *New York Times*, October 31, 2015. Available at https://www.nytimes.com/2015/11/01/world/europe/a-mass-migration-crisis-and-it-may-yet-get-worse.html.
Oh, Stella. "Movement and Mobility: Representing Trauma through Graphic Narratives." *Asian American Literature: Discourses and Pedagogies* 7 (2016): 66–67.
Ollapally, Deepa Mary. *The Politics of Extremism in South Asia*. New York: Cambridge University Press, 2008.
"Over 30,000 Refugee Families Struggling in Jammu." *Governance Now*, September 26, 2011. Available at http://www.governancenow.com/news/regular-story/over-30000-refugee-families-struggling-jammu.
"Pakistani Hindu Refugees Get Respite, MEA Extends Their Visa." *India Today Online*, April 9, 2013. Available at http://indiatoday.intoday.in/story/pakistani-hindu-refugees-get-respite-mea-extends-their-visa/1/261429.html.
Pal, Chandrima. "Colaba's Sindhi Connection." *Mumbai Mirror*, November 19, 2017. https://mumbaimirror.indiatimes.com/others/leisure/colabas-sindhi-connection/articleshow/61706962.cms.
Panayi, Panikos, and Pippa Virdee. *Refugees and the End of Empire: Imperial Collapse and Forced Migration in the Twentieth Century*. New York: Palgrave Macmillan, 2011.
Pandey, Gyanendra. *Remembering Partition: Violence, Nationalism, and History in India*. Cambridge: Cambridge University Press, 2001.
Parikh, Crystal. *Writing Human Rights: The Political Imaginaries of Writers of Color*. Minneapolis: University of Minnesota Press, 2017.
Park, Josephine Nock-Hee. *Cold War Friendships: Korea, Vietnam, and Asian American Literature*. New York: Oxford University Press, 2016.
Peer, Basharat "Epilogue." *Curfewed Night*. New Delhi: Random House, 2008.
Pinney, Christopher. "Introduction: How the Other Half. . . ." In *Photography's Other Histories*, edited by Christopher Pinney and Nicholas Peterson, 1–14. Durham, NC: Duke University Press, 2003.
———. *"Photos of the Gods": The Printed Image and Political Struggle in India*. London: Reaktion, 2004.
Prashad, Vijay. *The Karma of Brown Folk*. Minneapolis: University of Minnesota Press, 2000.
Puar, Jasbir K. *Right to Maim: Debility, Capacity, and Disability*. Durham, NC: Duke University Press, 2017.
Pundir, Pallavi. "Stories from the Other Side." *India Express*, August 30, 2013. Available at http://indianexpress.com/article/cities/chandigarh/stories-from-the-other-side-2/#sthash.YXYTMm1H.dpuf.
Quayson, Ato, ed. "Introduction." In *The Cambridge History of Postcolonial Literature*, 1–29. Cambridge: Cambridge University Press, 2011.
Rai, Satya M. *Partition of the Punjab: A Study of Its Effects on the Politics and Administration of the Punjab (I) 1947–56*. New York: Asia Publishing House, 1965.
Rajan, Gita, and Jigna Desai. *Transnational Feminism and Global Advocacy in South Asia*. New York: Routledge, 2013.

Ramaswamy, Sumathi. "Artful Mapping in Bazaar India." Tasveer Ghar. Available at http://www.tasveergharindia.net/cmsdesk/essay/116/index_3.html.
———. *The Goddess and the Nation: Mapping Mother India*. Durham: Duke University Press, 2010.
Ramaswamy, Sumathi, and Martin Jay, eds. *Empires of Vision: A Reader*. Durham, NC: Duke University Press, 2014.
Ramdas, Lalita. "Dismantling Prejudice: The Challenges for Education." In *Bridging Partition: People's Initiatives for Peace between India and Pakistan*, edited by Smitu Kothari and Zia Mian, 191–218. New Delhi: Orient Black Swan, 2010.
Ratti, Manav. *The Postsecular Imagination: Postcolonialism, Religion, and Literature*. Abingdon, UK: Routledge, 2013.
Ray, Sangeeta. *En-Gendering India: Woman and Nation in Colonial and Postcolonial Narratives*. Durham, NC: Duke University Press, 2000.
"Refugee and Migrant Health." World Health Organization. Available at https://www.who.int/migrants/en/.
Richter, Gerhard. "Between Translation and Invention: The Photograph in Deconstruction." In *Copy, Archive, Signature: A Conversation on Photography*, edited by Jacques Derrida, ix–xxxviii.
Roy, Arundhati. *The Ministry of Utmost Happiness*. New York: Knopf, 2017.
———. *Power Politics*. Cambridge, MA: South End Press, 2001.
Roy, Arundhati, Pankaj Mishra, Hilal Bhatt, Angana P. Chatterji, and Tariq Ali. *Kashmir: The Case for Freedom*. New York: Verso, 2011.
Rudolph, Lloyd I., and Susanne Hoeber Rudolph. *In Pursuit of Lakshmi: The Political Economy of the Indian State*. Chicago: University of Chicago Press, 1987.
Sabnani, Nina. "Know Directions Home?" In *This Side, That Side: Restorying Partition*, edited by Vishwajyoti Ghosh, 99–111. New Delhi: Yoda Press, 2013.
Saif, Lubna. *Authoritarianism and Underdevelopment in Pakistan 1947–1958: The Role of Punjab*. Oxford: Oxford University Press, 2010.
Saikia, Yasmin. "Interview." The Free Library, 2014. Available at https://www.thefreelibrary.com/INTERVIEW.-a0286561779.
———. *Women, War, and the Making of Bangladesh*. Durham, NC: Duke University Press, 2011.
Saltz, Rachel. "Indian Soul." Review of *Delhi-6*, directed by Rakeysh Omprakash Mehra. *New York Times*, February 9, 2007.
Samaddar, Ranabir. *The Marginal Nation: Transborder Migration from Bangladesh to West Bengal*. New Delhi: Sage Publications, 1999.
———, ed. *Refugees and the State: Practices of Asylum and Care in India, 1947–2000*. Thousand Oaks, CA: Sage Publications, 2003.
Sangari, Kumkum, and Sudesh Vaid, eds. *Recasting Women: Essays in Colonial History*. New Delhi: Kali for Women, 1989.
Sarkar, Bhaskar. "The Melodramas of Globalization." *Cultural Dynamics* 20, no. 1 (2008): 31–51.
———. *Mourning the Nation: Indian Cinema in the Wake of Partition*. Durham, NC: Duke University Press, 2009.
Sarkar, Jayita. "Rohingyas and the Unfinished Business of Partition." *Diplomat*, January 16, 2018. Available at https://thediplomat.com/2018/01/rohingyas-and-the-unfinished-business-of-partition/.
Sarkar, Sreyoshi. "The Art of Postcolonial Resistance and Multispecies Storytelling in Malik Sajad's Graphic Novel *Munnu: A Boy from Kashmir*." In *Graphic Narratives*

about South Asia and South Asian America: Aesthetics and Politics, edited by Kavita Daiya, 104–124. London: Routledge, 2019.

———. "Conflict Ecologies: Gender, Genre, and Environment in Narratives of Violent Conflict in Postcolonial India." Ph.D. dissertation, George Washington University, 2017.

Sarwar, Beena. "Google's Tearjerker 'Reunion' Ad, and the 'Milne Do' Campaign." Journeys to Democracy, November 14, 2013. Available at https://beenasarwar.com/2013/11/14/googles-tearjerker-reunion-ad-and-the-milne-do-campaign/.

———. "Women's Role in Building Peace." In *Bridging Partition: People's Initiatives for Peace between India and Pakistan*, edited by Smithu Kotari and Zia Mian, 169–190. New Delhi: Orient Black Swan, 2010.

Sarwar, Beena, and Prasanna Dhandharphale. "Milne Do." In *This Side, That Side: Restorying Partition*, edited by Vishwajyoti Ghosh, 311–315. New Delhi: Yoda Press, 2013.

Sassen, Saskia. *Expulsions: Brutality and Complexity in the Global Economy*. Cambridge, MA: Belknap-Harvard University Press, 2014.

———. *Territory, Rights, Assemblages: From Medieval to Global Assemblages*. Princeton, NJ: Princeton University Press, 2008.

Schlund-Vials, Cathy J. *War, Genocide, and Justice: Cambodian American Memory Work*. Minneapolis: University of Minnesota Press, 2012.

Sengupta, Debjani. "From Dandakaranya to Marichjhapi: Rehabilitation, Representation and the Partition of Bengal (1947)." *Social Semiotics* 21, no. 1 (2011): 101–123.

Sethi, Srishtee. "Tribes at the Borderland: Locating 'Pakistani Hindu Bhils' in Jodhpur." *Journal of Adivasi and Indigenous Studies* 8, no. 2 (August 2018): 51–62.

Shire, Warsan. "Home." *Facing History and Ourselves*. Available at https://www.facinghistory.org/standing-up-hatred-intolerance/warsan-shire-home.

Sidhwa, Bapsi. *Cracking India: A Novel*. Milwaukee: Milkweed Editions, 1991.

———. "Grief and Survival in *Ice-Candy Man*: In Conversation with Bapsi Sidhwa." In *Partition Dialogues: Memories of a Lost Home*, edited by Alok Bhalla, 221–240. New York: Oxford University Press, 2006.

Singh, Rashna B. "Traversing Diacritical Space: Negotiating and Narrating Parsi Nationness." *Journal of Commonwealth Literature* 43, no. 2 (June 2008): 29–47.

Sinha, Suvadip, and Amit R. Baishya, eds. "Introduction: Postcolonial Animalities." In *Postcolonial Animalities*, 1–25. New York: Routledge, 2019.

Sontag, Susan. *Regarding the Pain of Others*. New York: Picador, 2003.

Soon, Andrew Hock. "Nationalism and the Intangible Effects of Violence in Malik Sajad's 'Munnu: A Boy from Kashmir.'" In *Graphic Narratives about South Asia and South Asian America: Aesthetics and Politics*, edited by Kavita Daiya, 159–174. London: Routledge, 2019.

Spivak, Gayatri Chakravorty. "Can the Subaltern Speak?" In *Marxism and the Interpretation of Culture*, edited by Cary Nelson and Lawrence Grossberg, 271–314. Urbana-Champaign: University of Illinois Press, 1988.

Sprinker, Michael. *Edward W. Said: A Critical Reader*. London: Blackwell, 1992.

Spurr, David. *The Rhetoric of Empire: Colonial Discourse in Journalism, Travel Writing, and Imperial Administration*. Durham, NC: Duke University Press, 1993.

Srikanth, Rajini. *Constructing the Enemy: Empathy/Antipathy in U.S. Literature and Law*. Philadelphia: Temple University Press, 2012.

"State of Fear from Kashmir to Kanyakumari." *Outlook Web Bureau*, November 6, 2019. Available at https://www.outlookindia.com/website/story/india-news-state-of

-fear-from-kashmir-to-kanyakumari-jamiat-ulama-i-hind-demands-law-against-lynching/341820.
Sumar, Sabiha. "Interview with Sabiha Sumar." By Nermeen Shaikh. *Asia Society*, April 8, 2005. Available at https://asiasociety.org/interview-sabiha-sumar.
———, dir. *Khamosh Pani/Silent Water*. DVD. Delhi: Excel Home Videos, 2003.
Sundar, Pavitra. "Silence and the Uncanny: Partition in the Soundtrack of *Khamosh Pani*." *South Asian Popular Culture* 8, no. 3 (2010): 277–290.
Sunder Rajan, Rajeswari. *Real and Imagined Women: Gender, Culture, and Postcolonialism*. New York: Routledge, 1993.
———. *The Scandal of the State: Women, Law, Citizenship in Postcolonial India*. Durham, NC: Duke University Press, 2003.
Tang, Eric. *Unsettled: Cambodian Refugees in the New York City Hyperghetto*. Philadelphia: Temple University Press, 2015.
Tejani, Shabnum. *Indian Secularism: A Social and Intellectual History, 1890–1950*. Bloomington: Indiana University Press, 2008.
"This Collection." The 1947 Partition Archive, Stanford University Libraries. Available at https://exhibits.stanford.edu/1947-partition/about/this-collection.
Vanaik, Achin. "Hindutva's Forward March." *Jacobin*, September 19, 2017. Available at https://www.jacobinmag.com/2017/09/india-modi-bjp-cow-vigilantism-judiciary-corruption.
———. *The Rise of Hindu Authoritarianism: Secular Claims, Communal Realities*. London: Verso, 2017.
Vargas, Jennifer Harford. *Forms of Dictatorship: Power, Narrative, and Authoritarianism in the Latina/o Novel*. New York: Oxford University Press, 2017.
Vasudevan, Ravi. *The Melodramatic Public: Film Form and Spectatorship in India*. New York: Palgrave Macmillan, 2011.
Vinson, Ben, III. *Before Mestizaje: The Frontiers of Race and Caste in Colonial Mexico*. New York: Cambridge University Press, 2017.
Virdee, Pippa. *From the Ashes of 1947: Reimagining Punjab*. New York: Cambridge University Press, 2017.
Vora, Neha. *Impossible Citizens: Dubai's Indian Diaspora*. Durham, NC: Duke University Press, 2013.
Wennman, Magnus. "Where the Children Sleep." *UNHCR*. Available at https://www.unhcr.org/news/stories/2016/6/5702c1594/where-the-children-sleep.html.
Williams, Linda. "Melodrama Revised." In *Refiguring American Film Genres: Theory and History*, edited by Nick Browne, 42–88. Berkeley: University of California Press, 1998.
Williams, Randall. *The Divided World: Human Rights and Its Violence*. Minneapolis: University of Minnesota Press, 2010.
Woodward, Paul. "Google's Bold and Deceptive Partition Ad Campaign." *War in Context*, November 17, 2013. Available at http://warincontext.org/2013/11/17/googles-bold-and-deceptive-partition-ad-campaign/.
Wright, Christopher. "Supple Bodies: The Papua New Guinea Photographs of Captain Francis R. Barton, 1899–1907." In *Photography's Other Histories*, edited by Christopher Pinney and Nicholas Peterson, 146–169. Durham, NC: Duke University Press, 2003.
Yoneyama, Lisa. *Cold War Ruins: Transpacific Critique of American Justice and Japanese War Crimes*. Durham, NC: Duke University Press, 2016.

Young, Robert J. *Postcolonialism: A Very Short Introduction.* Oxford: Oxford University Press, 2003.

———. "Postcolonial Remains." *New Literary History* 43, no. 1 (2012): 19–42.

Zakaria, Anam. *The Footprints of Partition: Narratives of Four Generations of Pakistanis and Indians.* New Delhi: HarperCollins, 2015.

Zamindar, Vazira Fazila-Yacoobali. *The Long Partition and the Making of Modern South Asia.* New York: Columbia University Press, 2007.

Zia, Ather. *Resisting Disappearance: Military Occupation and Women's Activism in Kashmir.* Seattle: University of Washington Press, 2019.

Zitzewitz, Karin. *The Art of Secularism: The Cultural Politics of Modernist Art in Contemporary India.* New York: Oxford University Press, 2014.

Index

1947 Partition Archive (1947PartitionArchive.org), 7, 17, 29–30, 35, 84–85, 148, 151, 161–162, 164, 168–173; as memory work, 173
1947Partition.org, 148, 161, 203n62, 203n63

Abduction, 3, 7, 16, 65, 91, 93–94, 101, 139, 151
Abidi, Bani, 50, 78–79
Able-bodiedness, 32, 90, 92, 96, 135, 201n40
Accented cinema, 32–33, 111–112, 138–145
Adorno, Theodor, 43, 157
Advertising: border crossing in, 34, 137, 149–150, 156–159, 178; secularism in, 149–150, 152; technology and, 34–35, 150, 157
Aesthetics, 21, 38, 49–50; as critical praxis, 5, 28–29, 39–40, 74, 80, 105, 111, 145, 152, 158
Affect, 82–83, 150–151, 152, 157–158
African American literature, 75
Agamben, Giorgio, 22
Ahuja, Ankur, "The Red Ledger," 57
Amar Chitra Katha, 30, 45, 52–56
Anderson, Benedict, 45, 85. *See also* Imagined community
Anjaria, Ulka, 31, 89, 98, 105
Anti-colonialism, 10, 27, 40–42, 53, 82, 138
Arendt, Hannah, 22–26, 58, 62, 69, 104, 110, 114, 128; *The Origins of Totalitarianism*, 25–26
Art: digital, 15, 171, 174; post-Partition, 4–9. *See also* Art exhibits

Art exhibits: 1947 Partition Archive, 30; Bikaner House, 174; Indian Memory Project, 175–177; *Lines of Control*, 5; multimedia, 171; *Open Wound*, 35; photo, 174; *Refugees of the British Empire*, 84; Voices of Partition event, 27–29
Asad, Talal, 5, 9, 13–15, 37, 42–43, 118
Asian American: Asian American studies, 6–7, 21–22, 26, 115–117; identity and culture, 11, 14, 33, 56, 63, 86, 88, 122, 173; history and Asia 179–182. *See also* South Asian America
Assimilation, 26, 35, 69, 77, 92, 122, 134, 162–163, 165
Asylum (right to), 25, 70, 101
Auden, W. H., "Partition," 2
Avril, Ellen, 5

Bahri, Deepika, 5
Baishya, Amit, 70–71
Bajrangi Bhaijaan (Khan), 32–33, 111, 113, 134–138, 157, 160; critical reception of, 135, 137
Baldwin, Shauna Singh, 14, 31–32, 166; *What the Body Remembers*, 32, 62, 86–89, 95–100, 105, 127, 140, 144
Banerjee, Sarnath, *Corridor*, 53
Bangladesh: 1971 War of Independence, 3, 31, 33, 50, 56–58, 67, 71, 73, 77, 79, 101, 129, 168, 199n54
Bascara, Victor, 22
Basu, Lopamudra, 11

Beitz, Charles, *The Idea of Human Rights*, 14
Benegal, Shyam, 33, 112, 125, 127, 144, 166
Benjamin, Walter, 17, 38, 40, 80
Berlant, Lauren, 34, 95, 127, 157–158
Bhabha, Homi, 123, 145, 182
Bhalla, Guneeta Singh, 28, 35, 148, 161–162, 169–172
Bhasin, Kamla, 18, 19, 96, 99, 127, 155, 161, 166
Bollywood, 33, 112–117, 129, 132–135, 138, 145, 152, 154–156
Bombay (Mumbai), 20, 34, 126, 128, 151, 160–161, 163–164, 166, 175
Bombay (film, dir. Mani Ratnam), 119, 137
Border crossings, 9–10, 78, 96, 114, 147–149; as cultural metaphor, 18, 106, 115, 158; in film, 32–33, 112–113, 132, 134–135, 139–140, 145; in media, 34, 50, 58, 78, 151, 155, 158, 178; and peace, 124, 134–135, 156, 162; restrictions of, 24, 26, 152–154, 200n15; violence and, 75, 91, 98, 107, 131, 166, 167. *See also* Advertising: border crossing in
Bourke-White, Margaret, 31, 79–85, 175, 192n94
Boym, Svetlana, 19, 128, 156
British colonialism: responsibility of, for Partition and violence, 2, 21, 39, 57, 82, 102, 199n54
Brown, Wendy, 10, 76, 112
Buck-Morss, Susan, 38
Butalia, Urvashi, 3, 19, 79, 147, 161, 166
Butler, Judith, 9, 14–15, 26, 37, 80–82, 97–98, 128, 143–144, 155, 175

Calling Sehmat (Sikha), 33–34, 129
Capitalism, 28–29, 32, 53, 87, 96, 99, 100–101, 157–158; as factor in statelessness, 26, 87, 100
Cartier-Bresson, Henri, 84
Caruth, Cathy, 18
Caste, 10, 16, 21, 30, 32, 45, 48, 53, 56, 63–64, 69, 85, 87, 91–93, 100–101, 105, 109, 116–117, 122, 136–137
Chakrabarty, Dipesh, 165; "provincializing the nation," 6, 35, 50, 173, 181
Chandra, Nandini, 45, 53
Chandra, Vikram, 95
Charts, 30, 38–49, 85, 111, 189n12. *See also* Educational charts; Prints
Chatterjee, Partha, 92
Cheah, Pheng, 86
"Children of India" (chart), 45, 46f
Chiu, Monica, 56

Chopra, B. R., 21
Chopra, Yash, 21, 120, 134
Chute, Hillary, 56, 67
Cinema, 21, 32–33, 111–112, 125, 197n5; fantasies of nation in, 33, 113, 133, 136, 145, 157; gendered citizenship in, 125–128; history of in India, 113, 115, 125; and melodrama, 111, 115; and peace, 144–146; as public culture, 113, 117, 137; and the secular, 117–119, 124, 144–146; violence, 138–144. *See also* Bollywood; Accented cinema
Citizen historians, 35, 170, 172, 203n62, 203n63. *See also* 1947 Partition Archive; Oral history
Citizenship, 5–6, 8, 24, 37–38, 102, 109, 114, 134, 137, 153–154, 163, 165–166; cultural ambivalence and, 97, 108, 128; ethnic, 7; gender and, 8, 45, 62, 64, 87, 89, 96, 114, 140, 142; gendered citizenship, 125–128; minority experience of, 45, 89, 105, 108, 125, 128, 140, 158, 162, 175; normative, 43, 89, 156; race and, 119; as related to rights endowed by nation-states, 24–25, 108, 156; and secularism, 39–40, 49
Cohabitation, planetary, 14–15, 182
Cold War (1945–1991), 1, 6, 19, 35, 61, 179
Comics, 30, 45, 49, 50, 53, 56, 59, 67, 111. *See also* Graphic narratives
Corpothetics, 43
Cosmopolitanism, 14, 45, 118
Counterdiscourse, 30, 38, 49, 63, 78, 85, 89, 131, 178–179, 182; counterhistory, 13, 62, 155, 168; counternarrative, 12, 36, 39, 49, 63, 168–169
Cracking India (Sidhwa), 86–89, 137, 140; disability, 92–93; displacement, 86, 90; intimacy, 93–94 mass migrations, 86, 90; patriarchal violence, 91–95
Critical Refugee Studies, 4, 6, 18, 22, 26, 35. *See also* Espiritu, Yen Le
Cutter, Martha J., 56, 69–70

Dadi, Iftikhar, 5
Dandakaranya Project, 60, 190n41
Debt, 87, 92, 95, 99–100, 109
Decolonization, 2, 4–8, 16, 23, 26, 31–32, 35–36, 39, 57, 89, 112; migration and, 13–14, 32, 39, 49–50, 61, 80, 83, 86, 155, 162, 170–171, 179; religious and ethnic violence and, 13–14, 32, 39, 49, 67, 93, 140, 199n54; trauma of, 58, 144
Delhi-6 (Mehra), 32–33, 106, 111, 113, 115–124, 135, 138; critical reception of, 117, 135, 197n25

Deportation, 25, 77, 126, 145. *See also* Expulsion
Diaspora, 6, 86, 100, 156, 161, 169, 172; cultural identity and, 3, 11, 31, 76, 115, 120; diaspora studies, 87; ethno-nationalism and, 121–122, 185n30; homeland and, 33, 65, 121, 123–124, 127, 156, 176; storytelling as mode of exilic intimacy, 17–18, 75–76, 95, 116, 118, 127, 149, 159, 172
Digital humanities, 40, 148–149, 161, 170–174, 203n63
Digital media, 7, 15, 17, 34–35, 40, 138, 148–153, 155, 157, 160–161, 169–175, 203n63
Disability, 16, 32, 90, 92–93, 134–135
Discrimination, 10–11, 56, 64, 87, 102, 108, 112, 119, 121, 124, 141, 158, 164, 166, 181–182, 196n79; in news media narratives, 19–20, 122, 165
Displacement, 21–22, 25, 27, 39, 53, 64, 67, 90, 93, 96, 101, 134, 141–142, 145, 158, 172, 175, 181; in *Mammo* (Benegal), 33, 112, 126–127
Dubnov, Arie, 5

Eco-criticism, 30, 50, 57, 70, 79, 190n62
Ecomelancholia (James), 31, 73, 75–76, 202n47
Educational charts, 30, 38–40, 43, 47–48
Eisner, Will, 57
Eng, David, 1, 3, 168
Embodiment, 16, 31, 48, 57–58, 65, 73, 92, 94–95, 97, 128, 135, 168
Empathy, 18, 21, 33, 35, 80–81, 83, 107, 131, 136, 157, 173, 182
Erasure, 14, 22, 30, 48, 70, 80, 125–128, 142, 154, 164
Espiritu, Yen Le, 4; *Body Counts: The Vietnam War and Militarized Refugees*, 6, 26
Ethno-nationalism, 5–6, 9–10, 12–16, 27, 62–63, 106, 113–114, 119, 122, 125–126, 140, 165, 172; as root of violence, 85, 89–92, 101, 116, 137, 141–144
Exile, 19, 24–25, 120–123, 128, 143–145
Expulsion, 4–5, 26, 31, 49, 70, 100, 103–104, 106–107, 145–146, 173, 182
Extremism, 10, 30, 67, 106, 116, 119, 124, 143

Family, 31, 33–34, 95, 105, 114–115, 129, 137, 173, 175; heteronormative, 91, 98; nonnormative, 95, 115, 126; as symbol for nation, 115, 125, 128, 131–132, 136, 138. *See also* Kinship
Family separation, 61–62, 70, 126–127, 132–133, 159, 165, 176, 180

Farhana, Syeda, 50, 62, 71
Farooqui, Mahmood, "A Letter from India," 57
Fatah, Sonya, 64
Felman, Shoshana, 19, 147
Feminist, 6–8, 16, 19, 26, 29, 30–31, 39, 56–57, 62–63, 67, 86, 88, 90, 92, 95–98, 100, 114, 124–125, 166, 177, 179; cinema, 125–145; postcolonial, 26, 92, 114, 144; South Asian studies and, 56
Film. *See* Cinema
Fragmentation (narrative device): in graphic narratives, 57–58, 69–70, 77; in literary fiction, 31–32, 89, 98, 104–105; in refugee oral testimonies, 169; in visual arts, film, 83, 139–140, 150

Gandhi, Leela, 35, 180
Gandhi, Mahatma, 40–42, 53, 80
Gender, 6–7, 16–17, 37, 40, 56, 78, 87, 99, 105–108, 124, 139, 171, 175; experiences of migration and, 35, 61–63, 69–70, 86, 125–128; masculinity, 16, 130; media representations of, 31, 114, 121, 151; precarity, 67, 128, 136, 140–145; refugee experience and, 4, 29, 31, 33, 39, 62–63, 77, 84, 92, 96, 138–140, 151, 165–166. *See also* Feminist; Masculinity; Heteronormativity
Genocide, 16, 38, 75, 86, 102, 199n54
Geopolitical, 3–5, 8–9, 15–16, 21–22, 27, 33, 35, 39, 52, 56, 58, 78–79, 112, 129, 136, 138, 144–146, 179, 181–182
Ghosh, Vishwajyoti, 30–31, 49–50, 53, 56, 58–59, 99, 109; *Delhi Calm*, 49–50, 53; *This Side, That Side: Restorying Partition*, 30–31, 33, 49, 50–52, 56, 58–72, 99, 106, 114, 152–154, 158
Gilroy, Paul, *Postcolonial Melancholia*, 1
Globalization, 7, 13, 22, 88, 116, 119, 149, 154, 157, 161, 179–182, 203n62, 203n63, 204n76
Global South, formations of secularism in, 12
Godrej India Culture Lab, 27–30, 175–177, 188n92. *See also* "Remembering Partition"
Google *Reunion* (commercial), 7, 112, 34–35, 138, 149–150, 153, 156–157; and intergenerational memories, 149, 152, 155–156; transnational sentimentality, 151–154, 158. *See also* Advertising: border crossing in
Graphic narratives, 30–31, 38, 50, 52, 56, 104; composition of, 52; displacement depicted in, 50, 53, 56; gender in, 30, 49, 50, 56, 65–72; history of (India), 56–57; photography and, 42–43, 45, 57, 67, 71, 85; war depicted in, 58, 79, 106–107

Green Cardamom (arts organization), 5
Green-Lewis, Jennifer, 30, 81, 83
Grievability (Butler), 81–82, 85, 97, 132, 155, 175, 182
Guha, Ranajit, 8
Gulzar, Meghna, *Raazi*, 32–33, 111, 129–134
Gupta, Malini, 62–63

Haider (Bhardwaj), 132
Harud (Bashir), 132
Hasan, Mushirul, 12–13
Hashmi, Salima, 28
Heteronormativity, 7, 16, 30, 48–49, 85, 87, 96, 107, 115, 131, 136, 156, 158
Hindi cinema. *See* Accented cinema; Bollywood; Cinema
Hong Kong, 160–169
Hussain, Intizar, 57

Identity, national belonging and, 14, 20, 31, 48, 76, 84, 99, 109, 113, 115, 121, 128, 172, 175
Imagined community, 9, 13, 42–43, 53, 88, 105, 121, 167
Immel, Andrea, 43
Imperialism, 4, 24, 26, 88–89, 106, 179; American imperialism, 22
India Book House, 52–53
Indian Book Depot (Map House), 45–46
Indian Memory Project, 175–177
Inside Geneva Camp (Litwa), 67
Installations, art. *See* Art exhibits
Intergenerational memories, 98, 147, 149, 152, 155–156, 160–169
Internment camps. *See* Statelessness: internment camps; Refugees: refugee camps
Intimacy, 6, 89, 95, 115, 118, 154, 158–159, 176, 181, 191n62; exilic intimacy, 19, 97, 156; as interethnic coupledom, 115, 120, 125, 129–130, 133, 156, 160, 198n27; and interethnic solidarity and, 34, 65, 67, 91, 93, 97, 112, 122, 135, 149, 157–158
Islamophobia, 10–11, 103, 167

Jain, Kajri, 30, 39–40
James, Jennifer, 31, 75
Journalism. *See* News media
Judicial system: citizenship and, 26, 127; justice and, 88; reparations and, 37, 109
Justice, 19, 22, 26, 84, 87–88, 106, 114, 134, 147, 149, 181; and redress, 37, 63, 70, 100, 109, 150, 155, 169, 172. *See also* Nguyen, Viet Thanh: just memory

Kalpa Taru: Independence Is Our Birth Right: Galaxy of Congress Leaders Who Wrought for Independence for Sixty Years, 40–42
"Karachi Delhi Katha" (Fatah and Sreenivasan), 64–67
Kartarpur Corridor, 9–10
Kashmir, 3, 9–10; 1965 India-Pakistan war, 50, 108–109, 153
Kazanjian, David, 1, 3, 168
Khamosh Pani (Sumar), 14, 34, 112–114, 138–144; critical reception of, 138
Khan, Aisha, 18
Khan, Kabir, 32–33, 111, 129, 134–138
Khanna, Ranjana, 86–87
Kinship, 16, 95, 114, 127, 137. *See also* Family
Komagata Maru incident, 20
Kumar, Priya, 11, 15
Kumar, Ravish, 72
Kurian, Priya, 57

Labor, 4, 35, 38, 70, 96, 130–131, 134, 161–162, 166, 168–169, 173; domestic, 65, 129–130; in refugee and internment camps, 58–59, 67–68
Liberal democracy, 13, 141
LIFE (magazine), 2, 31, 80
"Lines of Control" (exhibition), 4–5
"Little Women" (Farhana and Mohanty), 71–75
Litwa, Maria M., 62, 67
Lost-and-found (film genre), 80, 132–133, 135, 137. *See also* Kinship
Lowe, Lisa, *The Intimacies of Four Continents*, 6, 181

Mahmood, Saba, 9, 12
Malhotra, Aanchal, 29
Malkki, Liisa, 20, 22, 126
Mammo (Benegal), 14, 32–33, 111–112, 125–128, 140, 144
Mankekar, Purnima, 147, 152
Masculinity, 76–77, 101, 116, 154; Asian American, 117–124; ethno-nationalism and, 114, 119, 139; patriarchal violence and, 87, 91, 93, 95, 98–99, 126, 140; and religion, 125–126, 134–135, 137–138, 140, 157. *See also* Heteronormativity
Matthew, Annu Palakunnathu, 35, 173; *Open Wound* (photo animation series), 35, 173–175, 204n76
McLain, Karline, 30, 53
Media. *See* Digital media; News media; Print culture

Mehra, Rakeysh Omprakash, *Delhi-6*, 32–33, 111, 113, 115–124
Melodrama, 32–33, 111, 113–115, 134, 156, 201n24; as performance of secularism and religion, 118–119, 123, 135, 154; as political critique, 117, 122, 124, 135–136, 145
Memorialize, 16, 19–20, 29, 35, 88, 149, 151–152, 170, 172
Memory: collective remembering and, 4, 17–18, 70, 147, 150, 175–176; refugee memory, 8, 38, 58, 73, 76, 82, 85, 103, 140, 154, 164, 167–169, 174; storytelling and, 18, 74, 83, 98, 152, 168. *See also* Intergenerational memories; Nguyen, Viet Thanh: ethics of memory, just memory
Memory work (Schlund-Vials), 7, 17, 28, 30–31, 34, 50, 76, 83–85, 88, 99–100, 106, 152, 169, 173, 180
Menon, Ritu, 16, 19, 96, 99, 127, 161, 166
Migrants, 8; definition of (Arendt), 24; gendered representations of, 15, 23, 62–63, 85, 88, 112, 114, 152, 155, 161–164; national belonging and, 75, 109, 120, 137; public discourse concerning, 84, 149; storytelling and collective experiences of, 70, 150, 166–167, 170, 174–175, 180–181. *See also* Refugee
Migration: archives of, 3, 7, 15–16, 21, 30, 80, 86, 96, 160, 170; forced, 20, 49–50, 77, 82, 163, 169, 199n54, 201n41; geopolitics and, 4, 8, 24–25, 61, 114, 149, 179–180, 187n79, 199n54; imperialism and, 82
"Milne Do" (Let Us Meet), 152–153
The Ministry of Utmost Happiness (Roy), 87–88, 100, 132; citizenship, 102–103; expulsions, 101–102, 104–107; violence, historical, 101–106
Minorities: citizens, 7, 70, 107–109, 114, 145; precariousness, 24, 112–114; precarity, 24, 145. *See also* Discrimination
Misri, Deepti, 96, 108
Mittal, Dyuti, 62–63
Modernism (aesthetic), 31–32, 89, 96, 194n39. *See also* Novel
Modernity, 5, 9, 12, 25–26, 37, 53, 80–81, 92, 116, 118–119, 122–123, 126, 128, 145; vernacular modernity, 43, 45
Mohanty, Nitesh, 62, 71
Mokammel, Tanvir, 28
Mondal, Anshuman, 11–12
Motherhood, 61–62, 96, 132; as a metaphor for nation, 40, 42–43. *See also* Women: reproductive and nonreproductive femininity

Mukherjee, Ankhi, 88
Mukherjee, Upamanyu Pablo, 26, 37
Mumbai, 160–169
Munnu: A Boy from Kashmir (Sajad), 53, 79

Naeem, Asma, 80–82
Naficy, Hamid, 32, 112, 142
Nandy, Ashis, 14
Narrative: as memory work, 30–31, 35, 39, 75–76, 78, 88, 100, 166
Nasar, Hammad, 5
Nasrin, Taslima (*Lajja: Shame*), 105
Nationalism, 40–42, 53, 72, 102, 105, 129, 133, 167, 179; aesthetic practices and, 53, 92, 148, 188n9. *See also* Ethno-nationalism
Nation formation, 39, 42, 91–92, 99, 173, 177, 202n49
Nation-states, 10, 22, 24, 39, 57, 71, 103–104, 112, 130, 132, 136, 156
Nayar, Pramod, 58
Needham, Anuradha Dingwaney, 10, 127
Nelson, Deborah, 35, 180
Neocolonialism, 19, 21, 48, 187n89
Neoliberalism, 7, 109–110, 151, 158
New India (print), 43–45
News media: broadcast journalism, 78–79, 122–123, 138, 144, 149; print journalism, 19–20, 23, 31, 103, 107–108, 138, 149, 162, 165, 202n53; rhetorical violence in *Delhi-6* (Mehra), 116, 120–121, 123
Nguyen, Mimi Thi, 22
Nguyen, Viet Thanh, *Nothing Ever Dies*, 7; ethics of memory, 4, 18, 157; just memory, 4, 6–7, 18, 105, 144, 149, 163–164, 168, 181
Nixon, Rob, *Show Violence and the Environmentalism of the Poor*, 26
Nonprofit organizations, 5, 170–172; collaboration between, 172, 174; higher education and, 5, 172–173; public education and outreach, 30, 170–171
Nostalgia, 52, 117, 120, 123, 127, 150, 156, 176; ethno-nationalism and, 64, 116, 122
Novel: Asian American, 90–100; decolonization in, 86–90; graphic, 32, 58; Indian, 100–107

Obaid-Chinoy, Sharmeen, 28, 161, 177
Oh, Stella, 74
Ollapally, Deepa, 13, 128
Open Wound (Matthew), 35, 173–175
Oral history, 7, 34–35, 148, 151–152, 160, 163–165, 167–170, 178, 203n62, 203n63
Orientalism. *See* Said, Edward

Pakistan-India Peoples' Forum for Peace and Democracy (PIPFPD), 148
Pakistan Peace Coalition, 148
Pao Collective, 56
Parikh, Crystal, 87–88
Park, Josephine Nock-Hee, *Cold War Friendships: Korea, Vietnam, and Asian American Literature*, 6, 22
Partition (1947), 14, 49, 57, 69, 101–102; archives of, 5, 7, 28, 43, 112, 114, 144–145, 148, 170–171, 196n79, 203n63; forced migration and, 75–77, 128–130; historiography of, 39, 56, 63, 102, 161; memories and legacies of, 1–2, 49–50, 76–77, 79, 88, 101, 110, 113, 141, 147, 151, 154, 161, 165–166, 178; photographic representations of, 79–81, 84, 171–172; prominent refugees of, 21, 166; "restorying" of, 4–6, 49, 70; scholarly discourses around, 14. *See also* Art exhibits; Oral history
Partition (geopolitical), 5, 56, 72, 91, 153–154, 172, 179
Partition Studies, 6–7, 16, 34, 149, 162
Patil, Amruta, *Kari*, 53
Patriotism, 131–134; in Indian cinema, history of, 145
Patwardhan, Anand, 126
Peace, 21, 28, 34, 178, 182; cross-border, 124, 134–135, 156, 162; geopolitical, 3, 15, 18, 27, 35, 112, 136, 138, 144–146; initiatives, 148, 153, 169; studies, 148; through oral history, 169–178
Persepolis (Satrapi), 56
Photography, 31, 38, 37–42, 67–69, 79, 171, 174–176, 192n96, 204n76; Bourke-White, Margaret, 79–85; Cartier-Bresson, Henri, 84; culture of realism, 81; digital photo animation (Matthew, Palakunnathu Annu), 173–175; nationalism, 82–84; Victorian, 83; Vyarawalla, Homai, 84–85; *Where the Children Sleep* (Magnus Wennman), 83. *See also* Yadav, Anusha
Photojournalism, 31, 70, 80, 84, 192n94
Pinney, Christopher, 38–39, 42, 80
Planetary cohabitation, 14–15, 182
Political secularism, 3, 7, 9–17, 26, 30, 32, 48, 70–71, 78
Poole, Deborah, 38
Post-47, 3, 6, 11, 16, 35, 73, 86, 87, 99, 101, 111, 146, 168, 180
Postcolonial critique, 5, 26, 49, 114, 197n25
Postcolonial public sphere, 7, 38, 87, 145–146, 148–149, 171, 176

Post-partition public culture, 4–9, 14
Poverty, 31, 50, 59, 69, 101, 158, 201n40
Precariousness, 97–98; of citizens, 143; and ethnicity, 156–157; of minorities, 24, 112–114; under nationalism, 120, 126, 134, 141, 156–157, 163; refugees and, 32, 57, 72, 82–83, 85, 108, 110, 173–174; and the secular, 124, 137; of the subaltern secular, 32, 96, 181
Precarity, 32, 109, 143–144, 181–182; gender and, 32, 62, 66–70, 97–98, 140, 143, 164; of migrants, 62, 82–83, 98, 108, 134, 156–157, 165, 168, 181; statelessness and, 26, 69, 83, 104, 181; visibility of, 82, 135, 143, 157, 172
Print culture, 3, 8, 16, 30, 37, 38–49, 85–86, 111, 189n12
Prints: nationalist, 40, 47–48; gender in, 39–40, 42, 189n12
Priya Paul Collection, 40, 43
Public culture: audiovisual exhibit, 84; cinema and, 113, 117, 137; diasporas, 36; melodrama, 32; post-Partition, 4–9, 14; representations, 9, 23; "Reunion" commercial, 152; secular, 42; transnational, 147
Pune, 160–169

Raazi (Gulzar), 32–33, 106, 111, 113, 129–134; critical reception of, 131–132
Rajan, Rajeswari Sunder, 10, 15–16
Ramaswamy, Sumathi, 30, 42
Ramdas, Lalita, 28, 171
Rape, 7, 91, 93–94, 98–99, 106, 132, 139, 143–144, 151
Ratti, Manav, 15
Ray, Sangeeta, 62, 91–92
Realism (aesthetic), 31–32, 57, 67, 81, 89, 98, 104–105, 111, 126, 144. *See also* Novel
Redress, injustice, 19, 37, 63, 70, 100, 109, 150, 155, 169, 172
Rehman, Fariha, 57
"Remembering Partition" (event), 27–30, 177–178
Refugees: abjection of, 57, 126, 164, 167; as agents of history, 8, 58, 148; as constitutive of the nation, 8, 59, 60, 99; cultural identity and status as, 18, 21, 50, 57, 61, 98, 127, 130, 153; Critical Refugee Studies, 22, 26; definition of (Arendt), 24–25; dehumanization of, 23, 67–69, 71–73, 75, 155; descendants of, 29–30, 35, 169, 174; justice and redress for, 19, 62, 88, 100, 109, 155, 161, 169; oral histories from, 163–166; poverty, 59, 61, 65, 201n40; public

discourse concerning, 17–23, 83–84, 155; refugee camps, 25, 62–64, 67–68, 77, 91–92, 164–166, 169, 175; suppression of, 20, 48, 80, 102, 199n54, 201n41; Syrian, 23; United States acceptance, 22–24; U.S. international aid, 61; vantage point, 79; Western attitudes towards, 22–23, 81. *See also* Migrants; Migration; Precariousness; Precarity

Refugees of the British Empire (1947 Partition Archive), 84

"Remembering Partition," 27–36, 177

Resettlement, 7, 21, 35, 77, 87, 109, 153, 162, 173, 201n41

Reunion. See Google *Reunion* (commercial); critical reception of, 151–153; in comparison to other ads, 158–159. *See also* Advertising

Robson, Laura, 5

Roy, Arundhati, 14, 100–107; *The Ministry of Utmost Happiness*, 62, 87–88, 100–107, 132

Rudolph, Lloyd and Susanne, 11

Sabnani, Nina, "Know Directions Home?" 28, 77

Sacco, Joe, 52–53

Said, Edward, 14

Saikia, Yasmin, 8, 161, 166, 168

Sandhu, Ikroop, 72

Sarda, Shveta, 72,

Sarwar, Beena, 50, 152–153

Sassen, Saskia, 4, 24, 26, 49, 106, 157, 168

Schlund-Vials, Cathy J., 16, 18, 26, 31–32, 56, 69–70, 83. *See also* Memory work

Secular: intimacy, 90, 97, 136, 150–151, 155–156, 160; as performative, 40–45, 111, 115–119; as political and ethical practice, 14, 19, 34, 76, 95, 101, 105, 111, 124, 128, 164, 172–173, 181. *See also* Subaltern secular

Secularism, 5–6, 8, 37, 42, 85, 112, 155–156, 183n11, 184n28; as constitutional principle (India), 10–11; citizenship and, 6, 8, 43, 45, 105, 108, 111, 114, 137–138, 141, 156, 165–166; crisis of, 3, 9–15, 30, 32, 56, 64–65, 89, 100; embodied, 8, 14, 39, 42, 45, 48, 71, 87, 141; graphic representations of, 39, 48–49; in film and film industry, 113, 123–124; of refugees, 39, 151, 167; resistance and, 26, 42, 87, 128, 143; scholarly discourses around, 12–17

Sen, Orijit, *River of Stories*, 53

Sen, Priya, 50

Sensationalism, 116, 122–123

Sentimentality, 144, 155, 157–159; national sentimentality, 34; transnational sentimentality, 151, 154

September 11, 2001, 10–11, 13

Sequential art. *See* Graphic narratives

Shahani, Parmesh, 27–28

Sharma, Amit, 152. *See also* Google *Reunion*

Sidhwa, Bapsi, 2–3, 14, 31–32, 93–94, 166; *Cracking India*, 32, 62, 86, 88–89, 90–95, 97, 105–106, 140, 144

Sikka, Harinder, *Calling Sehmat*, 129

Singh, Khushwant, *Train to Pakistan*, 80, 84, 130

Sontag, Susan, *Regarding the Pain of Others*, 79

South Asian America, 4, 6, 8, 15–16, 21–22, 26, 32, 37, 56–57, 86, 115, 173, 179, 181

South Asian Free Media Association, 149

Spectrum (chart publisher), 45, 47

Spiegelman, Art, 53

Sreenivasan, Archana, 64

Srikanth, Rajini, 21–22

Statelessness: in comics, 50, 58, 67–71, 78; cultural narratives and, 38, 71, 87, 89, 102–104, 176, 181; gender and, 26, 39, 62, 84, 125; internment camps and, 58, 62–63, 69; as invention of system of nation-states, 9, 22, 24, 50, 104, 128, 176; loss of nationality, loss of rights, and, 58, 84, 109, 163; in photography, 81. *See also* Bourke-White, Margaret

Storytelling, 18–20, 74, 96, 98, 161, 182

Subaltern secular, 6, 8–9, 15, 19, 32, 39, 58, 62–63, 73, 87, 89, 94–98, 107, 114–115, 118, 135, 137, 148, 166, 172, 181

Subaltern Studies Collective, 8, 9, 15

Subjectivity, 15, 48

Sumar, Sabiha, 112, 138, 141, 166

"The Taboo" (Gupta and Mittal), 62–63

Tang, Eric, 31

Tasveer Ghar (archive), 40, 43

Tauro, Dianne, 27

Technology, 34, 43, 138, 149, 155–157, 162, 174–175; transnational discourse and, 27–28, 174, 177

Tejani, Shabnum, 10, 13

Testimony, 18–19, 34, 59–60, 67–68, 147, 163–166, 168–169, 172

This Side, That Side: Restorying Partition (Ghosh), 30–31, 33, 49–79, 154; anthropomorphism, 71–72, 76; ecomelancholia, 75; gender, 61–63; "A Good Education,"

This Side, That Side (continued)
(Ghosh) 58–62; human and nonhuman worlds, restorying, 70–71; "Karachi Delhi Katha" (Fatah and Sreenivasan), 64–67; "Know Directions Home?" (Sabnani), 77–78; "Little Women" (Farhana and Mohanty), 71–75; "Making a Poet," 75–76; "Milne Do" (Sarwar and Dhandharphale), 76; nationalism, 78–79; "90 Upper Mall or 1 Bawa Park" (Alam and Khosla), 76–77; "Profit and Loss," (Rehman and De) 68; "Welcome to Geneva Camp," (Litwa) 68–70
Transnational, 4–5, 7, 17, 22, 29, 34, 49–50, 61, 88, 103, 114, 147, 149, 151, 153, 169, 173; public culture, 147; sentimentality, 151–154, 158
Trauma, 7, 18, 34, 56–58, 71–73, 75, 103, 129–130, 132, 163, 174, 176, 198n47, 204n76
Twelve Gates Arts, 17–19

Vasudevan, Ravi, 113, 115, 137, 154
Vinson, Ben, 45
Visual culture, 5, 38, 77–78, 152, 175, 177
Visual economy, 38, 43, 48, 69–70, 78, 80, 155
Violence: against women, 6–7, 62, 65, 87, 93, 94, 98, 124, 127, 139–140, 143, 166; ethno-nationalism and, 22, 52, 65, 101, 168; interethnic, 94, 107–108, 116; of the modern state, 39, 41, 57, 59, 61–62, 74, 102, 104, 106, 130, 132, 163, 179–180, 196n79; sectarian, 12; "slow violence" (Nixon), 104
"Voices of Partition" (event), 17–19, 27, 171
Vora, Neha, 15, 87
Vyam, Durgabai, *Bhimayana*, 53

Vyarawalla, Homai, 84–85

War of Bangladesh (1971), 50, 58
Washington, D.C., 160–169
"Well of Remembrance" (art installation), 29
Wennman, Magnus (*Where the Children Sleep*), 83
What the Body Remembers (Baldwin), 86–89, 140; citizenship, 99–100; femininity, 95–98; migration, 96–98; violence, 96, 99
Williams, Linda, 111
Witnessing, 16–17, 31–32, 49, 57, 77, 79, 105–106, 155
Women: as agents, 94, 99, 129, 132, 137, 139, 142, 157; citizenship and, 98–99, 125–126, 128, 142; as migrants and refugees, 94, 106, 114, 125–126, 164–165; as symbol of nation, 126, 131–132, 189n11; reproductive and nonreproductive femininity, 95–96, 126, 131; as witnesses to 1947 Partition, 86, 89–90, 96, 138, 151, 164–166, 171. *See also* Gender

Yadav, Anusha (The Indian Memory Project), 28, 84, 175–177
Yang, Chi-ming, 179
Yang, Dr. Ho-chin, 179–180
Yoda Press, 49, 53
Yoneyama, Lisa, *Cold War Ruins: Transpacific Critique of American Justice and Japanese War Crimes*, 6, 19, 22
Young, Robert J., 12

Zamindar, Vazira Fazila-Yacoobali, 36

Additional titles in this series:

Elda E. Tsou, *Unquiet Tropes: Form, Race, and Asian American Literature*
Tarry Hum, *Making a Global Immigrant Neighborhood: Brooklyn's Sunset Park*
Ruth Mayer, *Serial Fu Manchu: The Chinese Supervillain and the Spread of Yellow Peril Ideology*
Karen Kuo, *East Is West and West Is East: Gender, Culture, and Interwar Encounters between Asia and America*
Kieu-Linh Caroline Valverde, *Transnationalizing Viet Nam: Community, Culture, and Politics in the Diaspora*
Lan P. Duong, *Treacherous Subjects: Gender, Culture, and Trans-Vietnamese Feminism*
Kristi Brian, *Reframing Transracial Adoption: Adopted Koreans, White Parents, and the Politics of Kinship*
Belinda Kong, *Tiananmen Fictions outside the Square: The Chinese Literary Diaspora and the Politics of Global Culture*
Bindi V. Shah, *Laotian Daughters: Working toward Community, Belonging, and Environmental Justice*
Cherstin M. Lyon, *Prisons and Patriots: Japanese American Wartime Citizenship, Civil Disobedience, and Historical Memory*
Shelley Sang-Hee Lee, *Claiming the Oriental Gateway: Prewar Seattle and Japanese America*
Isabelle Thuy Pelaud, *This Is All I Choose to Tell: History and Hybridity in Vietnamese American Literature*
Christian Collet and Pei-te Lien, eds., *The Transnational Politics of Asian Americans*
Min Zhou, *Contemporary Chinese America: Immigration, Ethnicity, and Community Transformation*
Kathleen S. Yep, *Outside the Paint: When Basketball Ruled at the Chinese Playground*
Benito M. Vergara Jr., *Pinoy Capital: The Filipino Nation in Daly City*
Jonathan Y. Okamura, *Ethnicity and Inequality in Hawai'i*
Sucheng Chan and Madeline Y. Hsu, eds., *Chinese Americans and the Politics of Race and Culture*
K. Scott Wong, *Americans First: Chinese Americans and the Second World War*
Lisa Yun, *The Coolie Speaks: Chinese Indentured Laborers and African Slaves in Cuba*
Estella Habal, *San Francisco's International Hotel: Mobilizing the Filipino American Community in the Anti-eviction Movement*
Thomas P. Kim, *The Racial Logic of Politics: Asian Americans and Party Competition*
Sucheng Chan, ed., *The Vietnamese American 1.5 Generation: Stories of War, Revolution, Flight, and New Beginnings*
Antonio T. Tiongson Jr., Edgardo V. Gutierrez, and Ricardo V. Gutierrez, eds., *Positively No Filipinos Allowed: Building Communities and Discourse*
Sucheng Chan, ed., *Chinese American Transnationalism: The Flow of People, Resources, and Ideas between China and America during the Exclusion Era*
Rajini Srikanth, *The World Next Door: South Asian American Literature and the Idea of America*
Keith Lawrence and Floyd Cheung, eds., *Recovered Legacies: Authority and Identity in Early Asian American Literature*

Linda Trinh Võ, *Mobilizing an Asian American Community*
Franklin S. Odo, *No Sword to Bury: Japanese Americans in Hawai'i during World War II*
Josephine Lee, Imogene L. Lim, and Yuko Matsukawa, eds., *Re/collecting Early Asian America: Essays in Cultural History*
Linda Trinh Võ and Rick Bonus, eds., *Contemporary Asian American Communities: Intersections and Divergences*
Sunaina Marr Maira, *Desis in the House: Indian American Youth Culture in New York City*
Teresa Williams-León and Cynthia Nakashima, eds., *The Sum of Our Parts: Mixed-Heritage Asian Americans*
Tung Pok Chin with Winifred C. Chin, *Paper Son: One Man's Story*
Amy Ling, ed., *Yellow Light: The Flowering of Asian American Arts*
Rick Bonus, *Locating Filipino Americans: Ethnicity and the Cultural Politics of Space*
Darrell Y. Hamamoto and Sandra Liu, eds., *Countervisions: Asian American Film Criticism*
Martin F. Manalansan IV, ed., *Cultural Compass: Ethnographic Explorations of Asian America*
Ko-lin Chin, *Smuggled Chinese: Clandestine Immigration to the United States*
Evelyn Hu-DeHart, ed., *Across the Pacific: Asian Americans and Globalization*
Soo-Young Chin, *Doing What Had to Be Done: The Life Narrative of Dora Yum Kim*
Robert G. Lee, *Orientals: Asian Americans in Popular Culture*
David L. Eng and Alice Y. Hom, eds., *Q & A: Queer in Asian America*
K. Scott Wong and Sucheng Chan, eds., *Claiming America: Constructing Chinese American Identities during the Exclusion Era*
Lavina Dhingra Shankar and Rajini Srikanth, eds., *A Part, Yet Apart: South Asians in Asian America*
Jere Takahashi, *Nisei/Sansei: Shifting Japanese American Identities and Politics*
Velina Hasu Houston, ed., *But Still, Like Air, I'll Rise: New Asian American Plays*
Josephine Lee, *Performing Asian America: Race and Ethnicity on the Contemporary Stage*
Deepika Bahri and Mary Vasudeva, eds., *Between the Lines: South Asians and Postcoloniality*
E. San Juan Jr., *The Philippine Temptation: Dialectics of Philippines–U.S. Literary Relations*
Carlos Bulosan and E. San Juan Jr., eds., *The Cry and the Dedication*
Carlos Bulosan and E. San Juan Jr., eds., *On Becoming Filipino: Selected Writings of Carlos Bulosan*
Vicente L. Rafael, ed., *Discrepant Histories: Translocal Essays on Filipino Cultures*
Yen Le Espiritu, *Filipino American Lives*
Paul Ong, Edna Bonacich, and Lucie Cheng, eds., *The New Asian Immigration in Los Angeles and Global Restructuring*
Chris Friday, *Organizing Asian American Labor: The Pacific Coast Canned-Salmon Industry, 1870–1942*
Sucheng Chan, ed., *Hmong Means Free: Life in Laos and America*
Timothy P. Fong, *The First Suburban Chinatown: The Remaking of Monterey Park, California*

William Wei, *The Asian American Movement*
Yen Le Espiritu, *Asian American Panethnicity*
Velina Hasu Houston, ed., *The Politics of Life*
Renqiu Yu, *To Save China, To Save Ourselves: The Chinese Hand Laundry Alliance of New York*
Shirley Geok-lin Lim and Amy Ling, eds., *Reading the Literatures of Asian America*
Karen Isaksen Leonard, *Making Ethnic Choices: California's Punjabi Mexican Americans*
Gary Y. Okihiro, *Cane Fires: The Anti-Japanese Movement in Hawaii, 1865–1945*
Sucheng Chan, *Entry Denied: Exclusion and the Chinese Community in America, 1882–1943*

Kavita Daiya is Director of the Women's, Gender, and Sexuality Studies Program, and Associate Professor of English at George Washington University. She is the author of *Violent Belongings: Partition, Gender, and National Culture in Postcolonial India* (Temple).